Praise for *Ma Lineal*

"Faith Holsaert's beautiful storytelling speaks to me as a daughter of the Student Nonviolent Coordinating Committee who is Black, a feminist, queer, and a survivor of childhood sexual abuse. Her authentic words create a sacred container that breaks silences, draws profound connections between the intimate and the political, and traverses the complexities that life offers with accountability and love."

—Aishah Shahidah Simmons, editor of *Love WITH Accountability* and producer and director of *NO! The Rape Documentary*

"*Ma Lineal: A Memoir of Race, Activism, and Queer Family* is a beautifully written exploration of highly complex and critically important subjects. Faith Holsaert reflects the importance of truth-telling and the power of loved experience."

—Jaki Shelton Green, North Carolina Poet Laureate

"This is a book of daughtering. Faith Holsaert shows us intimately what it means to be a daughter of multiple movements, mothers, monsters, and systems of harm. She shows us how mothering brings daughtering back into its queerest, most transformative potential. She shows us how to never take for granted who we are, how we got here, and the stakes of how we tell the tale. Read this book to learn important submerged histories, but also to unlearn whose story you can live inside and with what consequences."

—Alexis Pauline Gumbs, PhD, coeditor of *Revolutionary Mothering: Love on the Front Lines*

"*Ma Lineal* is a compelling account of one anti-racist woman's journey through activism, parenting, and queer family over more than seven decades. Especially gripping is Holsaert's time working in the early 1960s South with the Student Nonviolent Coordinating Committee as a dedicated white participant in a Black-led movement. This is an important book that weaves seemingly disparate threads into a powerful whole that raises questions for us all. Highly recommend."

—Catherine Fosl, PhD, professor

MA LINEAL

MA LINEAL

A Memoir of Race, Activism, and Queer Family

Faith S. Holsaert

WAYNE STATE UNIVERSITY PRESS
DETROIT

© 2024 by Faith S. Holsaert. All rights reserved. No part of this book may be reproduced without formal permission.

ISBN 9780814350799 (paperback)
ISBN 9780814350805 (e-book)

Library of Congress Control Number: 2023941181

Cover image © Queek / istockphoto.com. Cover design by Ashley Muehlbauer.

Published with the assistance of a fund established by Thelma Gray James of Wayne State University for the publication of folklore and English studies.

Wayne State University Press rests on Waawiyaataanong, also referred to as Detroit, the ancestral and contemporary homeland of the Three Fires Confederacy. These sovereign lands were granted by the Ojibwe, Odawa, Potawatomi, and Wyandot Nations, in 1807, through the Treaty of Detroit. Wayne State University Press affirms Indigenous sovereignty and honors all tribes with a connection to Detroit. With our Native neighbors, the press works to advance educational equity and promote a better future for the earth and all people.

Wayne State University Press
Leonard N. Simons Building
4809 Woodward Avenue
Detroit, Michigan 48201-1309

Visit us online at wsupress.wayne.edu.

To my loves: ancestral family and the community that nurtured me; Vicki and our children by birth and family by affection. With special thanks to the children who required I learn to love myself, so I could mother them. And with gratitude for the daughter who returned.

Contents

Acknowledgments	ix
Tell	1
1. Bedrock: Dreaming My Self	3
How I Was Mothered	3
Mother Ground	31
Life with Fox	40
Transition	44
2. Outcrop	49
Harlem	50
SNCC: Been Down into the South	75
SNCC: New York Office	98
New Mexico and Detroit	112
West Virginia	126
3. Find a Home Place	155
Sundered	155
Layered, 1991–2009	155
Nevertheless, We Mothered, 2009–2014	171
Find a Home Place	179
4. The Practice of Mothers	199
Showing Up, Autumn 2014	199
Incised Lines	223

Full Circumference, 2015	234
Dissociations	248
Sing	267
Living With	273
Coda: White Woman Reading Audre Lorde	281
I.	281
II.	285
III.	288
IV.	301

Acknowledgments

Sections of the essay "Matrilineal" won the 2019 Alex Albright Creative Nonfiction Prize competition and were published by *North Carolina Literary Review* in the spring of 2020.

An earlier version of "Find a Home Place" was published at *Red Earth Review* in July 2017.

Tell

You go through the stuff tangled at your feet. It turns out to be a single, strong rope. There is a beginning and an end and a middle, and the rope drapes over the pine needles and pavers, sometimes seeming to veer off course but overwhelmingly going from the front steps to the spot at the curb where your Subaru is parked and ready to go.

One could think the rope runs from the street to the front door. Another might ask, but did you see the barn owl perched on your neighbors' hammock slung between two pine trees?

You find that you do not have one strong rope, but heaps of filaments, some apricot, some steely, some walnut, with bits of cat hair and pollen thrown in. Separate the filaments into three clumps, as when braiding challah. When you are done, the strands will rise side by side in chronological order.

What's chronology got to do with it, and, besides, your apricot is my conflagration or sunset.

Write many miniatures and collage them, seemingly unlike with seemingly unlike here, seemingly like with seemingly like or unlike over there. When laid out on the uneven ground, their mottled (I want to say pied) gray brown black ivory colors may form a strand from one to the next across the dirt. When you pour water over them, some of the stones may surprise you because they are cerulean and that changes everything. Everything.

Did you not see the ogre?

1
Bedrock
Dreaming My Self

How I Was Mothered

My father James wants his mother's attention, but she is behind a door and they say, *Shh*. The house is cold, the wood wainscoting dark. He plays with his toy trains. There is a photo of him as a one-year-old, angry black eyes, head a long boulder; he sits amid his baby skirts. He has four names: James Manning Burton Hulsart.

His mother is an *invalid*; he looks it up in the dictionary on its stand—*inauthentic* or *sick*.

His sister's hair flames like an apricot, bushy *like a heathen's*, their Episcopal father says. His wife has absented herself from family life, so the father judges their appearances before church. The boy, with his neat skull, wears gray pants like his father, a white shirt, and a tie. His father says, *Where is that jacket? Damn it, James.*

His father was the minister at the church, but left the ministry because, the boy has heard him say, it was wrong to expect the parish to provide for a man with an invalid wife. Now his father is a banker. James has no idea what this means, except the bank is as cold as their Manasquan, New Jersey, house.

The boy dreams—because it will never happen and he can't bear to think of it not happening—of going outdoors, dreams the sun turns his hair apricot, dreams he can feel the smile in his mouth, dreams his father is beside him. They are running round and round a driveway. The boy begins to sweat into his fine white shirt and his shoes are scuffed. He is talking while he is running.

Dad, look. Dad. Look at me. I am a horse. Dad. Look. His father in sober gray is running and sweating and tipping his head, which is wreathed in light, to gaze down and sideways. If it wouldn't topple them, he would stretch out his gentleman's hand and lay it briefly upon the boy's neat hair.

My mother Eunice says her mother wouldn't feed her eggs, or butter, or chocolate, because Grandma did not want my mother to be *sallow*, code for *dark* and *not American enough*, also *too Jewish*. My mother scours her dusky skin with Dr. Palmer's Almomeal, which comes in a dark blue tin. Her skin looks peeled and glassy when she is done, but not paler. My mother favors my younger sister, but she watches my sister, darker than me, for signs of *sallowness*. In that late elementary school time when we don't always wash scrupulously, my mother takes a rough cloth to my sister's neck and scrubs as if that darkness is a pestilence.

My mother says, the photographer tossed the tulle at her at the last moment because she would not lie smiling and naked on her belly on the sheepskin. She was to be in one of a set of framed cameos: her brother Howard, who would molest my mother; her sister Toni, who would commit suicide; her brother Bob, who would give her a massive collie dog. In the sepia photo, my mother's lip has only just stopped trembling, and the tears would still be on her cheek if someone had not wiped them away.

My mother says, her father drank because of her mother. In how many stories is there a bad mother? My mother says every morning there was an empty bottle in his trash in the bedroom. Did she, the youngest of the bad mother's four children, find those bottles, youngest and alone, roaming the empty apartment? Dead set against the mother who couldn't nourish her, the mother who would have believed the older, blue-eyed brother?

My mother says, her brother Howard, the Yalie in the days when Yale had such a strict Jewish quota that my grandfather applied for Howard's enrollment on the day of Howard's birth, this Howard who did the un-Jewish but very American thing of fighting in World War I, the Navy, forever on my grandparents' armoire in black and white under glass in his pale uniform, that Howard—I see my mother trying to remember who she is, now after the before and the when of it—that Howard *tried* to molest her. She says.

Something about his trying to catch her in a corridor in the apartment. She says, he *tried*, as if he didn't succeed, but I know if I juxtapose her lifelong diffuse terrors, her lifelong valor of a little dog throwing itself at the churning tires of a moving coal truck, know from her anxiety, know from her marvelous and imprisoning marginality—that if I place *tried* against those eruptions, *tried* is a lie. There are unexplained breaks between *before*, *when*, and *after*, those breaks with her the rest of her life. I know that he, ten years older than the dark and fierce five-year-old, succeeded. That break is in every story she tells. And the merciful brother, Bob, saw or guessed, or she told him, and Bobby won the massive cream-and-mahogany collie in a card game and brought it home to his little sister and said, "Buddy sleeps in your room. Every night. Every single night."

Recently seized from the womb, I am ready. My eyes are big with astonishment at this place in which I have found myself. My mother, to whom I'd been tethered, drifted in ether. My mother's dark hands are bone and sinew. Because of her cough, my mother wears a paper mask. Nearby, a tiny glass bottle with a rubber nipple. In 1943 they thought this was best for a newborn. Maybe the ether, the mask, the glass bottle, and my mother's startled near-black eyes were the only way she knew to breathe the same air as me and protect herself against her love for me, a being from another place.

The folds in my white organdy dress, a crisp grid from my neck to my feet, are from the box. I am less than a week old. My dark eyes open to this world and the fingers of one hand pluck at the organdy, the dress bought by my redheaded aunt, my father's older sister, who calls my mother *the Jewess*.

I gaze upon a world that I have no reason to fear. Not quite the case, as I have made the birth journey in a 1940s hospital named Misericordia in the Bronx, territory unknown to my parents—Misericordia, a Catholic hospital, where my parents fear if a choice must be made, the baby would be saved at the expense of the mother's life.

The ether straightened my mother's wavy black hair for the rest of her life. It severed the breathing connection between myself in her dark insides and her, who had carried me. I was yanked down the birth canal. Five pounds, three ounces, the baby of a cigarette-smoking mother.

Resting on my silken pillow, resplendent in white, I am perfect, my parents' jewel in an organdy dress with department-store folds, little feet peeking from under the hem. I am perfect.

I am perfectly alone. My mother holds me, her shoulders high. We cannot see her mouth, as she wears a pleated mask. Is she smiling? Is she tight-lipped? She feeds me from a small bottle, her dark hand large, almost the length of myself. She rests me in a receiving blanket on my father's lap. The red-and-cream cocker spaniel watches with dark eyes. My cloth diaper, which my mother still struggles to pin into place, is wet. My mouth is a rosebud. My parents will panic when it crumples into a cry.

My father touches my two-year-old shoulder. "The baby was born last night." Still dopey with sleep, I hold his hand and he guides me to their bedroom. The bedsheets are heaped here and there. The rocking chair has been moved from the living room to their bedside. The window shades have not been drawn open. There are garments on the floor. I don't know a story for this disorder.

My mother, in her nightgown, which smells like *bed*, bends over the low portable crib. For all my life, it has been the three of us. For all my life, it has been lonely and frightening. I peer through the crib slats. My sister. My mother is oiling the baby's back. My sister's backbone a universe. Her head, no larger than my dolly Elizabeth's. Never only three of us again.

My mother pours oil into my hand. My hand is so small its entirety rests in her warm palm. She places my hand upon my sister's back. My sister sends heat up my arm. I like smoothing oil on the squirming beadwork of her spine, and down to the feet, each smaller than my father's thumb.

I am touching a universe.

My mother with her vein-roped hands picks up the baby, the baby's head in one of my mother's hands and the skinny bottom in the other. "Deborah," my mother says, presenting her to me. The baby frowns, which makes me smile, unlike when my parents frown, which makes me go still. The baby thrusts out one arm, a twig, the fingers stiff and going in all directions. She makes a kitten noise.

"Hi," I say and reach for her hand. I want to tickle her, imagining she will play like a kitten.

"Faith, be careful," my father warns. I ignore him. I have fallen into the enormity of my sister, slipped through those quivering navy-blue eyes to her heart. I understand that my parents think *Deborah* is fragile, but after that swift fall into her eyes, I know my sister is the toughest person I have ever known. They think my sister is theirs, but I know she is mine and I am hers.

It is the autumn of 1947 when my mother takes my four-year-old hand in hers and walks me three blocks to my first day at the Little Red School House, a brick building in New York City's Greenwich Village.

Every day at school, I go up flights of stairs to the very top. I have a cubby and a pad for nap time and we finger paint and play with blocks. I place a bean seed in a paper cup of soil and eventually watch it emerge in science. I run and shout in the autumn air of the rooftop playground with its brick lattice walls, where only we, the youngest students, are allowed.

I have loved the promise of September mornings ever since.

There is a special thing that happens on some days, when our teacher, Sarah, says, *Children, take off your shoes and socks and put your chairs in a circle*. We are very quiet because we *can't wait* until Charity arrives and we love the cool silky floor under our baby-plump feet. We will sing and dance and play the tambourine and the Chinese gong and the rattles and we will feel happy the way Charity makes us feel. We will roll around on the floor like little brass wagons; in the sedate 1940s, even in Greenwich Village, this is wildly fun and somewhat naughty. We all love Charity because she is Charity and because we are four.

She arrives, wheeling a cart a-jangle with instruments. The cart doesn't make noise, but the effect on me, a small and timid child, is as if the Autoharp is playing, as if the guitar and the red Chinese gongs in the shape of grimacing dragons with bared teeth and the finger cymbals and the tambourines are all making music. We sing and dance to songs about country gardens in a world where none of us has lived; we sing cowboy songs because cowboys are workers; we sing about shrimp boats and we dance in Louisiana: *Put your little foot. Put your little foot. Put your little foot right here.* We wrestle with the storm-tossed oceans from ship decks in sea chanteys. We children wear dungarees and turtlenecks because our school is a Progressive school, but Charity—her wide skirt swirls like in a storybook, and she laughs and we sing.

I learn my first Yiddish when I sing, *Schluf mein fagele*. Charity teaches us the Yiddish words, one sound at a time, like my mother feeding the kitten with an eyedropper. I don't understand about the little bird in the song, but. *I gave my love a cherry that had no stone.* Charity strums the Autoharp. *I gave my love a chicken that had no bone. I gave my love a baby that had no cry in.* And Charity, who opens her mouth to sing like she is laughing, looks sad when she sings this, and so we children in our dungarees and turtlenecks fall still. The contiguous but not necessarily related songs are unexplained pieces of a world we do not yet know. A crazy quilt.

I stand beside the piano, my ear level with the keys and Charity plays a note. The only way I can describe the note is that it is soft and shaped like a teardrop. She asks me to sing it. I imagine the note rising inside my chest, climbing my throat, and soaring out of me into the air, but no sound comes. She bends her head so that her hair touches mine. She whispers into my ear, "Darling, you can." I fall in love with her, as four-year-olds do. I open my mouth and the note floats out, entire and perfectly shaped. I sing another note and she laughs as she always laughs, because she somehow knows I, the child of her affection, can do anything.

When I go home, it is *Charity this*, and *Charity that*.

At the first PTA meeting, my parents tell her, "Faith is so infatuated, she wants you to come live with us."

She said, "Do you have a room?"

And they said, "Yes."

They said yes. The effortlessness of this: did it initiate me, a small white female child, into a larger universe than the one into which I'd been born? I acted on my love for Charity and it interrupted who I had been slated to become. Did it tell me, despite their crotchets, that my parents listened to me?

Home, two floors in a house on Sullivan Street a few blocks from Washington Square, a place of my mother/mothers, my father gone to work during the day. His office at Simon and Schuster. My sense of who he was included the Rockefeller Plaza esplanade from Fifth Avenue with ice skaters on the rink at its base and desks and lots of office-dressed people, all of whom knew my father, and typewriters and pages of words and the hush in my parents' voices when they said *editor*.

My father sang me to sleep as a toddler. Other times, with me on his lap, he leafed through the *Fireside Book of Folk Songs*, voicing words like *Ah, poor bird, take your flight, high above this sad night*. He could have been speaking another language, except I could feel that the song was sad and that he liked it. There was the song: *In Dublin's fair city, where girls are so pretty, I first set my eyes on sweet Molly Malone as she wheeled her wheelbarrow through streets broad and narrow, crying cockles and mussels, alive, alive, oh*. I had no idea what this was about, though I liked the picture of a pretty working-class girl, hands on her wheelbarrow, mouth open in song. And *My bonny lies over the ocean* made no sense; to me the word *bonny* was actually *bonnet*, despite my father's assertion that bonny meant beloved. Who cared about a bonnet across the ocean and what was a bonnet doing across the ocean and wasn't it pretty stupid to call your beloved *bonny*? I kept this to myself, as I was learning to do.

In another book, the story of "The Fox and the Grapes." My father explained that the fox was like a person, but Aesop, the storyteller, had made him into a fox. Why, my father did not say, but it struck me as peculiar. Foxes were cunning, my father said. I knew foxes in picture books were beautiful. I didn't know what "cunning" meant, but I could tell he thought it was bad. I looked at the pictured fox with his neat black paws, his gleaming red fur, and his pretty white bib, and I could not see cunning there at all. My father said stories like this were called "fables," but I didn't care about fables versus the stories of my playmates and me. I didn't say this though, because my father, who could be prickly, clearly thought calling something a fable was important. I still thought foxes were beautiful. I hated that the fox only got a mouthful of sour grapes and some blah blah blah about beyond his reach. Why couldn't he have had too few grapes but sweet ones?

And then my father was living elsewhere, three flights up on East Tenth Street. I was the six-year-old child of a *broken home*.

My mother told me later that when she became pregnant with my sister, he told her having a second child was "too much like having a family." He was impatient with my sister, who was physically competent, strong-willed, and emotional (read: *Semitic*). Also, a sin in an editor's eyes: my sister did not learn to read until she was ten. On our weekends in his austere apartment, my father often lost his temper with her; to me, those mean-spirited outbursts felt dangerous. I was not only in the middle of but also mediating the teeter-totter of how my father treated my little sister. I might have quarreled with her—that's what sisters did. Fathers, on the other hand, should not. I loved her, and my mother expected me to take care of her.

In spite of this, I liked our weekends with him on East Tenth Street. I loved some of the things he cooked, including *Hawaiian* chicken with canned pineapple chunks. I loved the cans of French-fried onions he always had on hand and how they smelled when he heated them in the oven. I loved the children's books he brought home to us, including Margaret Wise Brown's *Golden Egg Book* and Ludwig Bemelmans's *Madeline* and the bound books with blank pages in which Debbie and I could write and draw. The blank pages invited anything we could imagine. I loved how he looked in *The New Yorker* and found things for us to do, like go to Gilbert and Sullivan operettas at the Jan Hus Playhouse. I loved my father's two parakeets, Daphnis and Chloe, who would not speak to us people but tweeted to one another and exchanged beaky kisses. I felt the birds had made a choice not to speak with us and I loved that. When one of the two birds died, we discovered that the still-living bird had been blind, perhaps for a long time, and the seeing bird had helped its mate live. I don't remember what happened to the survivor, perhaps because I don't want to.

It was, I think, when my sister and I spent a weekend with our father in the country that I first saw how vulnerable he was. We were climbing up a rocky creek bed and he fell. He said in a temperate voice that he had hurt himself. He was taken off to a doctor and returned with his left arm in a sling. My father, left-handed, now couldn't even feed himself; the sling itself seemed like a badge of brokenness. He would not say how much it hurt him, but his lips were thin from biting back the unspoken.

I think about my eight- or nine-year-old self, who had learned to watch him carefully.

The summer I was five, we walked out on the tarmac and I saw Charity climb the stairs to disappear into a plane bound for Haiti. How bright the relief when she returned a month later.

But then my mother said she, my sister, and I would go to Haiti with Charity. Two women, taking two girls. No man. A Jewish mother and her Jewish daughters. An African American woman, a music teacher with a degree from Juilliard.

Our mother wanted my sister and me to listen to her read from a gray book about speaking French. There were stick figures that did not look like people, which is exactly what I told my mother. Learning French from a *pocketbook* with stick figures outraged me; it was work; it was unimaginable: *Go someplace and speak French.* I had no Little Golden Book about a girl going to Haiti.

My mother said, "Our plane will stop in Miami on the way." My sister and I stared back at her. We knew there was more. "Miami is in the south," she said. "In the South, Negroes are treated differently."

We knew about this word. Some Italian people had egged our stoop and slashed the hood of our convertible car because of Ethiopia. My sister and I knew about these things.

"In Miami," my mother said, "when a Negro is walking down the street and a white person comes walking in the opposite direction, the Negro has to step into the street."

"Will Charity have to do that?" we asked.

"Yes. It's wrong, but."

"Couldn't she just . . ." we wondered.

"No."

"And what would we do?"

"We would walk in the street with her," my mother said.

A directive neither my sister nor I would have dreamed of violating. Template for my life. *We would walk in the street with her.*

Charity went on ahead to rent a house. My mother, sister and I flew to join her, my sister and I in matching navy-blue dresses with full skirts and white trim, going out to the nighttime plane across the dark airfield. Flying above the East Coast of the continental United States, we slept. When I awoke, my sister and mother still slept. Deeply. Unreachably. I was alone, a child in an adult-size seat with bristly upholstery. We were flying above a snowy layer of clouds. I thought we were flying above the sky. I stared and stared out the window while the others slept; it was just me, looking down upon the other side of the sky.

I see her, my mother Eunice, embarking on a life without her husband, with her two small daughters, and Charity, a miracle who had come into our life. I see Eunice, the youngest and most disobedient daughter of a self-taught lawyer and his imperious wife, flying toward her new life, for which nothing except her heart had prepared her. She had rushed into the romance of it, sweeping us up with her to meet Charity in Haiti. Where we would speak French. They would wear wide skirts with pockets, short-sleeve shirts or *peasant* blouses, and sandals that laced from their toes to their ankles. Eunice, who loved cars, would drive the Jeep Charity had bought, taking us into the green hills, to the aquamarine ocean, to the outdoor market where we bought mackerel. My mother would be the boss of herself, and that is how I would see her. There must have been questions from her parents; she was leaving Manhattan with a *colored woman* and taking her children to a country run by Black people. There would have been our father to deal with, his questioning her autonomy, and if he had been more forceful, he would have taken us from her.

The boundlessness of it: taking her children to be with Charity on a Caribbean island in 1949. Flying in from the white-laced Caribbean, flying into the deeply green island, we flew so close and low, I felt I could touch this place where I was going to live the year I turned seven. Within minutes, the plane door was flung open to warm air and we were clanking down the metal steps and running to Charity, who called us *Darling* and *Lovey* as she always had. And my mother would have been so happy.

For our meals in Haiti, we sat around a table on the veranda, we two little girls in the light of the kerosene lamp, listening to grown-up talk, listening to the drumming from the hill facing our house. Charity might sit in the lamp's light and transcribe the rhythms of those drums onto sheet music in her optimistic turquoise ink. Late, our mother extinguished the lamp's flame and we were enveloped in night.

Debbie and I slept in the only room on the second floor, a dark space where we never played or went during the day, but slept deeply to be awakened by the crowing of roosters springing out of the dark when the sky began to lighten and the outside world was restored.

Next to our room, an enclosed sunporch, on which Eunice and Charity slept. My bed next to the window; their bed on the window's other side. The women slept in one bed parallel to my own. Or: were there two beds?

One night, a moan. Eunice on her back, Charity bent over her. My sister had crept into bed beside me. Our mother cried out. Charity rubbed her forehead. My sister drew in her breath. Our mother tossed her head side to side. Deep shadows. My sister and I were silent. Our schooling in silence was deep. Long after the two women had stilled, my sister went back to her bed and we all fell asleep.

We must have asked in the morning. We must have. Maybe not when all four of us were together, maybe I asked our mother Eunice, or my sister and I asked. We must have.

Here is what I imagine: our mother rubbed the bridge of her nose, her temple. "The neuralgia," she said, "was awful."

We may have asked why she didn't go to the doctor. Maybe not.

She would have said, "The doctor won't help." We didn't know *neuralgia*. How big was it? The place between her eyes, which our mother touched as she said *neuralgia*, how could that make her moan in the night? Thinking: *Would she die?*

Knowing: *neuralgia* was not the entire story. We never got the entire story, which as we grew older opened the door to guesses upon guesses.

Daytimes, I sat at the table on the silky concrete veranda and did the homework my mother had assigned. Dick and Jane and their blond selves. See Dick. See Jane. A teenage boy sat too close beside me, with just my sister and me, she across from us. He touched my thigh. My scalp went cold. And I went steadily on, tracing letters in the workbook. I burst through the cold and away. Extinguished. Run Dick. Run Jane. And his finger inched knowingly under the elastic of my little girl panties. Restored to my sister across the table, the unchanged table, from me. Concrete silky under my feet.

• • •

We jumped rope with Fifine Marie and Marie Denise. Our shirts were striped in blues and reds. We wore sandals. We had a dog named 'Ti L'homme who ate cornmeal mush and whatever he caught behind our stucco house with the corrugated roof that sang when it rained.

He also did it to me on the ground on the hillside. The cold began in my scalp. I was returned to the dusty earth, the tiny dry flowers speaking in my ear. And above our house beside a tree when a door slammed in the yard a century below us, over and over again.

Hairy tarantulas could drop from the wall and run after us on their hind legs. There was a Haitian dance, impersonating the tarantula upright, arms crooked and menacing. *Gedezanya*. My sister and I ran and jumped onto our beds and my mother would kill the tarantula with the stiff broom.

I can see New York City from here, my sister would say at night on the veranda. Extinguished. Restored.

Returned to Manhattan from Haiti, my sister and I were sent to New Hampshire to be with our father's sister, Pat, the redhead, who lived with the woman we called Aunt Marg. We liked Aunt Marg because she told us stories about long-ago times like the death of Queen Victoria; she took us into the white-birch-and-pine woods to find mushrooms. Debbie and I rode on top of the jostling hay wagon pulled by horses; we loved the lake in town, cool, dark, a world where we were competent and swift. In my aunt's gift shop, we ate sandwiches with the crusts cut off. We two sisters talked in the dark, far from home, and where was home if it wasn't Haiti and it wasn't the old apartment on Sullivan Street, and what were our mother and Charity doing right now in New York City? Our mother sent us postcards with tinted drawings of cats eating dinner at a table, playing violins, and dancing with one another in frocks and jackets.

The best room in the new apartment was Charity's. A Marc Chagall print of a rabbi hung there. The rabbi, shawled and somber, held a scroll as big as his torso. I knew nothing about rabbis or scrolls or the oddity that my Black loved one had chosen this image to hang in her room, but it had been Charity, after all, who'd taught me my first Yiddish words: *Schluf mein fagele*.

Charity's was the only room where my sister and I, and probably our mother Eunice, knocked to enter. There was a bubbling tank of fish, neon tetras, and guppies, and angelfish, and whiskery catfish. There were Haitian statues, wood that looked like it would be silky, but I didn't touch them. On one wall, a brilliant Haitian oil painting in blacks and greens and pinks and blues, a tired woman, holding her twin babies to her breasts. Charity slept among all this.

I sat in Charity's room and did my homework, while she worked at the table desk at the foot of her bed, her form lit by a gooseneck lamp; she wrote lesson plans or read the *Guardian* newspaper, or with her Parker fountain pen in her turquoise ink wrote the melodies of folk songs onto blank sheet music. I loved lying on the floor with my work, at the edge of the light from her lamp. I remember the balanced perfection of her clefs. I do not know if she sent her bedsheets to the laundry with ours, and I do not remember if all of our dirty clothes went into the cotton drawstring bag that my mother hauled in a cart to the laundromat. At the same time as Charity's separateness within our togetherness, there was the intimacy of living together, of eating dinner together nightly, of eating Charity's fragrant crullers, of eating my mother's spaghetti with meat sauce, of walking dogs, of hearing the name *Emmett Till*, of hearing the word *lynching*, of family outings when my mother drove us to Harlem so Charity could buy hair products.

    I do not know what was irrevocably intertwined in my two mothers' lives and what was not.

Weekly, my mother Eunice sank bodily into the tub to wash her hair. Short and blue black, her hair licked through the water. Her toes, crowded by bunions, stuck out at the foot of the tub. Two fingers held her cigarette. She set the cigarette in her blue enamel ashtray and soaped and rinsed her hair.

. . .

Charity washed her hair with Castile soap cut from a long ivory bar she bought uptown. Charity toweled her hair dry until it fluffed. Then she sat with a towel about her shoulders and my mother Eunice unfurled the cord of the straightening comb. Two of my mother's fingertips dipped in pomade. Those fingertips touched Charity's scalp at the roots of her fine hair, and then the comb was drawn section by section from the scalp out to the end of the hair, and again, from the scalp to the ends.

My mother and Charity passed a cigarette back and forth, just as their talk lazed back and forth. The smell of cigarette smoke mingled with the creamsicle scent of the cream. They didn't mind that I was there, though I knew enough to stay quiet if I wished to stay.

They opened the pine-smell nail polish remover. With cotton balls, each swabbed old polish off the other's nails, until there was a mound of cotton with gobs of polish in Charity's trash can. Charity shook the dusty pink by its white cap. My mother smoked and painted Charity's nails. Charity puffed her cigarette and painted my mother's nails. They waved their hands in the air to speed the drying. This, the intimacy of living together, the years of a long time of every single day.

Autumn 1953, following the June executions of Julius and Ethel Rosenberg, my classmates and I entered the tens, taught by Mimi Cooper Levy, a small-boned woman with a blazing smile and a dry wit. We studied electricity, human physiology, art, music, and Jewish history. We sat in a circle, with Mimi, like us, sitting on a child's chair, while she told us what she knew. Studying spelling, we moved to sprawl on the floor, to play word games Mimi had invented, transcribed to graph paper, and pasted onto five-by-seven-inch cards: crosswords, fill in the blanks, and rebuses. Compositions in our childish scripts covered the bulletin boards. We left our classroom to visit the Egyptians at the Metropolitan Museum of Art and afterward scuffed our shoes in acrid autumn leaves.

My classmates and I were ten. Some of us had been to vigils for the Rosenbergs. My mother, like many parents at the school, had stood vigil in Union Square before their executions, the executions a marker of the red-baiting and Cold War finger-pointing that threatened many among the families at my school. Though we no longer played on the cloistered rooftop, with Mimi we felt happy and safe and adventurous, the offspring of a righteous struggle as we made our way through Jewish history as a history of fighting oppression. I felt strength in where I had come from and attached to my community. With Mimi and Charity, we wrote a December play based on Yiddish folktales of the Wise Men of Chelm and performed it to school-wide acclaim.

We returned from winter break primed for the spring of 1954. Rather than the autumn teachings of the alimentary canal and the nervous system, we would study human reproduction. We giggled. In social science we would move from Jewish history to what Mimi called Negro history. We didn't know what Negro history was and perhaps neither did she that January in 1954.

She opened with Crispus Attucks, a free Black man, the first person to fall in the Revolutionary War. In our circle, on breathless February mornings, the classroom hot and radiator dry, we learned about Benjamin Banneker, the Black man who completed the wheel-spoke design of Washington, DC. Afternoons, Mimi told us about the vagina and the penis. Mornings: slave ships and auction blocks. With Charity, we danced—mournful Isadora Duncan—to "Sometimes I Feel Like a Motherless Child." Erections, wet dreams, budding breasts. Sojourner Truth. We went by subway to the Schomburg library in Harlem. I checked out biographies of Harriet Tubman and John "Osawatomie" Brown—figures whose intransigence fired my well-mannered girl soul. Our improvised dance became "Go Down Moses." Sitting in our circle, we said *Dred Scott*—in 1857 the U.S. Supreme Court declared that he, as a Black man, was not a citizen and had no right to sue for his freedom. With the brave and bleeding hearts of ten-year-olds, we railed against the injustice. We opened our mouths and James Weldon Johnson's "Lift Every Voice and Sing" poured forth, but the next day we might be snaking through the classroom singing *Naa naa naa* and doing the bunny hop, that 1950s line dance.

Coincidentally, some girls were reading Nancy Drew (even little girls in a liberal enclave read racist shit), while others devoured horse books with that hunger of concrete-locked girls. My best friend received a pair of knee-high nylons at Easter; there were playground murmurs of *training bras* and *camisoles*. Like other children, we walked our dogs, did our homework, borrowed books from the public library, but unlike other children, we had at least one classmate whose unemployed father raged at the Army-McCarthy hearings on the family television.

We followed Harriet Tubman and Frederick Douglass into the Civil War. Scorchingly, we asked, "How could our government call people *contraband*?" In Reconstruction glee, we danced syncopated to "Free at Last," though some grumbled they preferred the Lindy Hop. In 1898, *Plessy v. Ferguson* was decided by the U.S. Supreme Court. "Separate but equal?" We were dumbstruck by the hypocrisy of this judicial setback, which reminded us: the father unemployed; Charity unable to rent an apartment; the Rosenbergs.

Mimi, teacher of spelling cards and talking circles and stories on walls, proposed we create a time line of Negro history. In our final weeks, as it became warm enough to open classroom windows, warm enough to shed our unisex turtlenecks for shorter sleeves, we assembled a pastiche of our own history reports (*Dred Scott*, *Plessy*) on lined paper, with occasional newsprint photos like one of Mary McLeod Bethune shaking the hand of my mother's hero, FDR, and newspaper articles, rising up and along the bulletin boards like latticed bricks, threaded into sequence by a heart line of crimson rickrack. Seated in the room, we were embraced by these names and dates; we brimmed within them, inhabited them. With Langston Hughes, Jesse Owens, Marian Anderson, Jackie Robinson, Wilma Rudolph, Paul Robeson, Daisy Bates, and Ralph Bunche, our time line reached the 1950s. Our work was almost complete.

On May 18, 1954, Mimi handed coins to one of us. "Go get the *Times*. I think the desegregation case has been decided." One of us, perhaps a girl with thin braids down her back, ran into the May sunshine and around the corner to the newsstand. Within minutes, the metal fire door in the stairwell slammed open. Pounding up the stairs, she screamed, "We won." *Brown v. Board of Education* had been decided. *Plessy* had been struck down. We spread the newspaper on the floor. We cut apart the columns of newsprint and glued them onto construction paper before tacking them onto the bulletin board, completing the history that encircled us, *Brown* in its place, at the end of the feathery red line. We rose. There was no sound in the tens' room, just the external grate of the Italian coffee grinder three buildings down, a bus accelerating up Sixth Avenue.

Mimi bumped her hip against one of ours. A girl hummed, *Naa naa naa naa na na*. A boy grabbed me from behind. *Naa naa naa naa na na*. We held one another, hands to still childish hips, flinging out one leg and then the other. Pen in hand, Phylliss Wheatley spun past as we jumped and panted below her. Feet out, feet in. *Contraband*. The bunny hop is a silly dance, jerking forward and back. *Naa naa naa naa na na*. Langston Hughes and Marian Anderson. *Lift Every Voice and Sing*. Together jerking forward, together jumping back, over the floor where we had sprawled, dancing, our teacher in the lead, her laugh fierce and her smile brilliant.

When she had a car, my mother drove us north on the Taconic Parkway, to Hawthorne Circle and out a smaller road. It may not have been legal when she drove up a rutted road and pulled over where there was no parking space. I may be imagining this, but I think we had to climb under barbed wire to reach the path beside a rocky river with sun-dried boulders. I remember the woods around us as not being leafed out, so we must have gone there in the spring and autumn; I do not remember swimming, though I remember walking the riverbed, making our way from rock to rock. My mother gave the impression of never being happier than when she was in the woods, telling us about *Indians* (stereotypes we took in as gospel) walking soundlessly without stepping on twigs. We kids, in our Keds, would try to do the same as we followed her.

Charity came with us in her midcalf flared skirt and her clodhopper Murray Space Shoes. Even down a not quite legal path, Charity wore jackets she had quilted with wool scraps. These were worked like *crazy quilts*, irregular shapes sewn to a sturdy underlying foundation fabric. Within the dappled sun and shadow of those woods, the quilted pieces mapped distinct adjoining entities, each outlined in a unifying strand of handworked red or gold featherstitching.

We let our dogs run loose in the rustling leaves. With her often proclaimed disregard for the law, this was allowed under my mother's code. We must have stopped going there when I was in elementary school, because the friends I remember in this spot are eager little girls in jeans and cardigans. We searched for kindling for the fire. We found straight sticks for roasting hot dogs. My mother didn't truck with the niceties of s'mores, but we roasted marshmallows, some of us gently heating them to honey brown, others going for conflagration, letting the flames lick until the outside had turned to carbon, plucking the treat off the stick, burning fingers and tongue. This, too, an intimacy, Charity Bailey of Providence, Rhode Island, and of the Juilliard School, in the woods with my mother and us little girls.

My mother would tramp further back into the woods, where the path shrank to a trace. Where water welled up between rocks. She would brush the leaves aside. "Ahh." She would pull loose a few green stems. "Watercress." She would hand Charity a stem and Charity might say, "Very nice, Darling." And then we kids could taste. Pepper. Green. Wet. My mother would smile her wolfish smile, settle back on the ground and light a Pall Mall. This is how I remember my mother happy, in this woodsy, perhaps not legal, haven. There, she let us as close to who she was as she could stand.

The used Studebaker was the color of a battleship. It had headlamps that jutted out and, on its front, a rocket-like protrusion. Very modern. I don't remember my mother liking the Studebaker, but she tended it, carrying buckets of water from our second-floor apartment down to Jane Street to wash it, waxing it from the tin of Johnson's paste wax she kept in the trunk. In winter, she wore the ratty raccoon coat she had acquired somewhere, her embarrassingly clunky shoe boots. Like most of our cars, it was high maintenance: old hoses splitting; batteries spending their energy into copper-green deposits; tires collapsing upon themselves, but it took us everywhere from trips to procure hair supplies in Harlem, to the beach, to the secluded picnics in the woods.

Debbie and I woke to the scrape of snow shovels on sidewalks. Our mother would shovel the car out from the snow. She needed her escape in place. Maybe my mother had what she called *the Tail End of a Cold*; maybe it was her teeth, which poisoned until they were all pulled; maybe it was what she called *La Grippe*. Maybe it was melancholy and inertia. The snow fell. My mother stayed in bed. While our school resumed and Charity went back to work, the dogs had to be walked. My mother said she would move the car but stayed in bed, smoking, eating Wheat Thins, smoking, sleeping. A neighbor said the city had ticketed the cars. He offered to move the Studebaker but trudged back up our stairs to say the battery was dead. My mother wanted to move the car *if it killed her*, but she let it be hauled off by the city. She did not muster the money to retrieve it.

Red Scare.

We were a family whose sidewalk was chalked by neighbors; we were a Jewish and Black family. In 1955 Eunice produced *Sing a Song with Charity Bailey*, an NBC TV children's show. My sister and I and a half dozen children appeared on the show: a half-hour music lesson taught through folk songs. It rang with the sounds of guitar and Autoharp, the Chinese gongs, the Haitian drum with its paintings on the side and stray hairs on its skin surface, and tambourines. It was the first interracial children's TV show, a win for everything our family believed, in opposition to the dominant culture, there on the screen our family and our friends, fleeting in black and gray, but there on the screens of New York. Sunday morning, our family was up early to go to the studio. Sunday night, dinner over, we sat around the dining room table and answered fan mail.

The network *expressed concern* that before World War II Eunice and Charity had been *prematurely antifascist*. Eunice thought it was those petitions she'd signed: *Lift the Embargo on Loyalist Spain*. Charity had *friends*. Talks in Charity's room from which my sister and I were excluded. Phone calls. A lawyer met with the network. The threat of losing the show went away. What I learned as a junior-high-school child: the terror in my mother Eunice's eyes, her fury that *they* were threatening our existence. Learned in a new way, there is a *they* and there is an *us*. Learned that our family might have been small and isolated, that NBC could, if it wanted, cancel the show, but that we, not only our family of four, but those who were with us and like us, were true. We were the real reality.

Charity's people in Rhode Island were descended of people who bought their freedom. *Manumission papers*: I liked to say these words as if they were beads or a silk scarf I used to secure my ponytail. A green-and-white scarf I chose with Charity from a sparkling glass counter at B. Altman's on Fifth Avenue. No one I knew, except for Charity, shopped there. *Manumission papers*.

But I, Charity's daughter who chose her, knew nothing of Rhode Island, would not see Rhode Island until after Charity's death. Rhode Island and Greenwich Village were not contiguous. Pinny, Charity's sister, lived in New Jersey for a while, working at a girls' school, maybe. Maybe Pinny was there for decades. At least, once Eunice and Charity and my sister and I spent a week, visiting Pinny in New Jersey. My sister and I entertained ourselves during days when nothing seemed to happen by roller-skating up and down the sidewalk out front.

Rhode Island and Greenwich Village never touched.

When Pinny died, Charity traveled alone, leaving our family vacation, to the funeral. I remember Eunice wanted to go. Schooling us, Charity insisted she would bury her sister without us.

She was the granddaughter of enslaved people who bought their freedom and moved to Rhode Island, and when she was a little girl, when her father took her to the farmers market, he would sort through the white farmers' corn, discarding cob after cob, saying, *For the horses.* He knew corn and he wasn't going to feed his family produce best suited to barnyard animals.

She lived with us in our apartment in Greenwich Village.

She came from Rhode Island.

She had lived in Harlem. When we caroled family and friends on Christmas Eve, we would visit her friend Bobbi and a couple—I think the man was a judge—in Harlem.

Once, some of Charity's family visited us on Jane Street. I remember commotion. I think she was harsh with a brother who *drank*.

When I was learning to read, she and I were looking through a *Look Magazine*. There was a picture of a Black man in a military uniform, with medals. She said, "He used to be my husband," and turned the page. I put my hand on the page. "What do you mean, your husband?" But she brushed my hand aside. "Nothing, Darling." Schooling.

In our apartment, including her bedroom, there were no photos of Charity as a child or of her family, except maybe one photo of Pinny, which I imagine but don't actually remember.

In the 1990s, at a conference on working class studies, I met a man who had learned guitar from Charity's brother who had lived in Brooklyn in the 1950s. "Are you sure?" I asked. He was sure. This brother of Charity's had been important to the man. She had excluded the brother from our life. So conflicted, because this man had known more about Charity than I did, but years after her death, in my middle-of-the-heartland, middle-aged life, here was a man who knew who Charity had been. *Before. After. When.* This was not subtle, ruinous revelation, was not my mother's brother or the teenager in Haiti, but the incremental distances and unknowing of domestic life.

I had known so little and yet within this little was the universe as I knew it, and within the unknowing, the gift of daily love—the sound of Charity in her room playing the Autoharp, the barking of our two dogs when neighbors entered their apartment downstairs, the rat-a-tat of my mother's brown-and-black Corona typewriter, the scratch of my pencil on a page, the energetic noise of my sister when she was silent.

There had been gifts.

Charity bought the pearl ring for my mother, because. With Yankee frugality Charity had saved to do so. My mother thought the ring *too extravagant*. I think she felt unworthy of its beauty, that slowly accreted beauty that Charity had wanted her to have. I can imagine Charity saying, *Darling, you deserve it.*

My mother gave me a ring of four Bohemian garnets, because: my future, her future in me—college, a life free from debt, a *regular* life such as had eluded her. My mother would have paid for the ring over time. One of the stones was higher by a small increment, a difference I could stroke with my fingertip. The maker had honored this difference, had not cut the stone down to match the other three. From when I was sixteen until I gave the ring to one of our daughters, I ran the pad of my finger over that too-high stone, assuring myself that the remarkable imperfection was there. The ring disappeared in the next few years, but. I feel that higher stone, that good difference.

As for the pearl ring, both women gone, the pearl ring persists on my sister's hand, the slim aging hand of a woman older than either mother had been at her death.

. . .

My mother called me *hard* and *unloving*. A bad Faith. I said in my clenched-fist heart, *I am not hard*. And yet, my father had read to me, *"There was a little girl who had a little curl right in the middle of her forehead. When she was good, she was very, very good, and when she was bad, she was horrid."* I hated that word, *horrid*. I was the only member of my family with curly hair. My mother kept my hair short so it wouldn't be *unruly*. I now hear that behind unruly lurked the unspoken words, *Semitic* and *foreign*. Before I went to sleep, I'd mutter, *Am not*. Jewish child mothered by a mother who feared her own difference. No one said it, but behind *Semite* lurked *untrustworthy*. You know. Iago. *Am not*.

Within years, I would happen. Me, the girl on the front lines. Neither *hard* nor *unloving*.

Thirteen-year-old child and her mother, my mother smoking in the rocking chair with the scrolled arms. There are photos of my mother in that chair holding infant me, she masked because of her cough, but to my mind's eye now, her nervous, wolfish grin is visible behind the mask, her eyes startled. My mother always afraid. I must have felt this in my infant backbone resting against her. Hers the body that harbored me for nine months, hers the body that supported me in this new world of gravity and intransigent surfaces. The air I breathed suffused with the smoke of her Pall Malls. This is who she was. This is the person who nurtured me despite her terrors, her large-veined hand holding a nippled glass bottle to my lips, my eyes fastened upward upon her. How easy, now, to feel sad and grateful for her physical harbor and to name her terrified, reluctant spirit.

My mind was full of my transgression into the world: I was reading the novel *The Borrowers*, where minuscule Arrietty had betrayed her family by yearning for the larger world. I feared my mother might find me guilty of questioning our self-contained world. Our family had had enough of fending off changes to the fragile *normal* we had constructed: my eleven-year-old sister had announced that she was changing her name. She was tired of being one of several *Debbies* in her class and no one would pronounce the more formal

Deborah properly, with the stress on the middle syllable, so my sister threw the burden and expected pronunciation aside.

One afternoon, the sun made me woozy, a soft feeling to be inside the warmth with my mother, despite my moves out and away, moves unknown to her, or so I thought. She was planning errands, a walk to the fruit and vegetable store on Twelfth Street, the dry cleaners on Eighth Avenue, Nicky the butcher on Hudson. We would take the dogs.

She lit another cigarette, sucking in hard, and said, "You know my sister committed suicide." I did know. She knew I knew. For crap's sake, I had known the word *defenestration* before I left elementary school.

"Can Katie come over?" I asked.

Eunice had been ten years younger than her sister Toni, an adoring baby sister dressed in white flounces when Toni was wearing silks and damasks and a wide-brimmed hat with a ribbon.

"Don't you have to. . . ." She was coughing. She struggled to catch her breath, but as she came out of it, she was striking a match and lighting up.

"I want to go to the library with Katie."

"I thought you were running errands with me," she said.

"Have you read *The Borrowers*?" I didn't really want to share the book, but I felt a terrible need to distract her.

"It sounds charming," she said. *Charming* turned me from her. The borrowers were me, hiding in plain sight, clever, brave in the face of a wide and dangerous world populated by enormous feet that could crush me in an instant. The borrowers saw things.

My mother said, "I worry about your sister. I worry that she, too, will. You know. Like Toni."

"Ma." I did not say, *You can't have her. My sister is mine.*

I despised her for imagining that what had seized Toni could take my sister.

When I was barely into my teens, my best friend Katie and I went to a French movie, *White Mane*, about gray-white horses in the French Camargue. As elementary-school girls, we had spent hours drawing and painting horses, talk-dreaming horses, and riding horses when we could. The Camargue is half water and half land, an overarching sky, and fugitive horses moving like spirits across the marsh. Local men subdued the horses they could capture. One stallion, White Mane, would not be captured. How I loved that. A dark-haired boy man with burning eyes gentled the elusive stallion, gentled him, rather than breaking him. Katie and I were learning French in school, though I had learned to speak French in Haiti, so we experienced the movie through a second language, which deepened its mysteriousness.

As we left the theater, I said, "That horse."

Katie answered, "The garçon was yummy."

We had both been wild for horses, but Katie had noticed the boy, a mere part of the scenery to me. It's funny to think how betrayed I felt. Two girls on the edge of leaving childhood and horses; one fixating on boys, the other thinking that particular fixation would come to her in due time; I had a fuddled sense of my unfolding self as foreign and fugitive, beautiful like the horse and at the same time felt I was wooden, plump, and clueless about this game called *boys*.

In a few years, Katie was officially boy crazy and I was learning to be quiet about my crushes on teachers and other magnetic women. The landscape of the Camargue accepted me. It sheltered my fugitive crushing-on-women self, offered shelter in my precarious adolescence, in a canoe, down close to the water, sheltered by branches. Though I had never canoed, that sound of an oar being pulled from the water and the droplets of water falling. Always something good was about to happen, something bad averted. The horse present deep within the trees.

When I was finishing high school, Charity moved to an apartment on Manhattan's west side. Just: bam. Charity is moving. There was *Before*. There was *When*. There was *After*. Why, really, did Charity leave my mother, my sister, and me? Why did she move to Park West Village, across from Central Park? I knew the answer I'd been given: more convenient to her job in Westchester, but. How could she leave me, her chosen child? Before her move, I went to the empty apartment to wait with her for the utilities to be turned on. Blond floors, clean windows, a kitchen no bigger than a closet—so different from the Jane Street kitchen in which we cooked and ate and the pets milled around and somebody might stand and kibbitz while another cooked or ironed or washed dishes. Charity and I sat on the floor in afternoon sun. No furniture, no electricity, no food. I was seventeen and felt a surge of love for her, an older woman, between homes. I brimmed with tenderness for the smallness of her. I looked at her hands and was a four-year-old again. I didn't remember when she and my mother had stopped doing one another's nails. I wanted to say, *Don't leave me*, but that was babyish. I loved her. I loved our life. Charity's homemade crullers and my mother Eunice's hearty spaghetti and Charity's klutzy Murray Space Shoes.

Ten years later, Charity phoned me in West Virginia on New Year's Day to say she had taken my mother to Lenox Hill Hospital. The teacher-principal of the two-room school up Prenter Holler granted me leave to be with my mother, whose hips were moth-eaten with cancer. My sister and I as irreverent teenagers had called cigarettes *cancer sticks*, voicing a fear we could not explicitly name, fear we hoped, in this naming, to forestall.

Three-year-old Carmela would stay with her father and her brother Jonah, who was six. I packed the black-and-brown mohair scarf knitted by my lover. I arrived in nighttime New York, ungreeted, and took a cab to my mother's apartment. I slept in her neatly made bed, with the black-and-brown mohair scarf wrapped around me. The next morning, I scavenged: the heavy cream was curdling and the bread stale, the fruit wrinkled. The steak in the tiny freezer was freezer burned, discolored, and dried out. I don't know whether I spent January 8, my thirty-first birthday, in New York or West Virginia. For five months, I was both places at all times. Mornings, I caught an Eighth Avenue bus in front of my mother's building at 101st Street. At Sixty-Sixth, I took a crosstown bus through Central Park to the hospital. In West Virginia, my housemate Susan gave birth to her baby, Josh. At Lenox Hill, my mother told the social worker through a rictus of pain, *Lots of people who smoke don't get cancer.* I ate crackers and dull cafeteria food. I brought in Chinese food and she picked at it. I'd kiss her good night and go back to the apartment. I spoke to Carmela and Jonah by phone.

My mother said, *Maybe I can have a device with wheels. I can get to the ocean's edge on my stomach and roll into the ocean.*

February 1974. Above on repeat. Or maybe this was the month my mother's molesting brother took me out to lunch. My mother sent us off with a wave. We ate in a luncheonette. He talked dirty to me about "going down" on a boy in college. I sat extinguished, waiting for him to finish.

March 1974. Ice cream and crackers and coffee, that's pretty much what I ate. When I tried to cash one of my mother's checks at the store near her apartment, the manager claimed he didn't know who she was, as if *Holsaerts* were a dime a dozen. The refrigerator remained empty, but I had cleaned it and the shelves above the stove. Dinner with our family doctor at 1 Christopher Street in the Village. *Darling*, our family doctor Fritz and his wife Inga phoned. They served me fresh asparagus, so I realized it was spring. I said I planned to take the teacher certification exam. *I need to stay certified to teach in the autumn.* He said, *She may not still be here by then.* In those days, they, all the theys, never said *cancer*. Never said *death*, though someone—maybe that social worker—suggested I read Elisabeth Kübler-Ross's book on grief and dying. Kübler-Ross recommended pounding pillows with a baseball bat. I could not imagine myself doing any such thing. There were no baseball bats in my life. That asparagus night, Fritz and Inga sat with me while I phoned my sister in Paris—she would have to come. Soon. Phoned through transatlantic cables buried below the ocean running from me to Debbie, who now went by the name "Shai."

We have to consult someone, Charity raged. *We have to do something.* I could not tell her, *It's too late.*

April 1974. The social worker talked about my mother coming home. This seemed as improbable as the idea that pounding pillows would help with the private harm of every moment. I went home to West Virginia to take the certification exam. Up Joe's Creek, sunny green washed over the hill, a canopy over the path to our tall-shouldered house. My son was off school that week, so my children were with me and my woman lover. I have a photo of Carmela in Kanawha State Forest, in her puffy blue coat, hair wispy in the brisk air, smiling toward the camera, open and expectant and still. At four, she is small; the picnic table is the same height as her delicate ear.

Back in New York, I'd forgotten the Cancer Society had delivered a hospital bed to the apartment, but there it was when I snapped on the light. I went to the hospital every day. I went to my first lesbian bar. I went to the Oscar Wilde Bookstore on Christopher Street, down the street from Fritz and Inga. My mother could not come home. Did not want to. The social worker arranged for her to move to a hospice, a place called Calvary. Mind fuck. I wanted it to be "cavalry," where she could ride into battle on a gray-white horse, not die on the hill with Jesus and two thieves.

May 1974. My sister came. Our mother knew when Shai walked through the door. *They won't let me smoke*, she said, *not unless I call them to wheel my bed into the corridor*. She who had smoked casually and at will since her early teens. A woman in the business office saw our name and came to my mother's room. Her son had once been my sister's boyfriend. This woman brought an earlier time when this had been our city and we had been our mother's girls and she had been our mother; the woman brought teenage love and hope into the room with its two hospital beds and its quietude. The staff brought my mother a meal of things I had said she liked: two spears of asparagus, a small dinner roll with a pat of butter, and a single scallop. She brushed it aside and closed her eyes. My sister stood vigilant at the foot of the bed, holding our mother by the toe—*Mommy*—fending off rupture. My sister was 29 years old. We went home to bed. They phoned past midnight, to say our mother had died. May 9, 1974, three days before Mother's Day.

I have a photo of Carmela, half-naked in the early May heat, in Charity's lap. Carmela's small hand holds Charity's arm and she stares upward with delight at Charity, who smiles down at the child with equal delight, despite the haze of sorrow in Charity's eyes.

My kids were entranced with their French auntie Shai—"auntie" said in a haughty accent—entranced with the frock she had brought Carmela and the handsome shirt for Jonah. Friends came to our mother's flower-filled apartment, the mahogany table shining, the windows open, voices both hushed and merry. My New Jersey cousins carried away the Norfolk pine that had stood in the bedroom. My sister took the silver and our mother's brown-and-black Corona typewriter. My lover rented a U-Haul in East Harlem and we carried off the teal Naugahyde couch and the rocking chair with the scrolled arms. We drove Shai to the airport. She wouldn't let us go in with her. She walked away from us and into the vast building, toward the plane that would take her to Paris. Both children wept passionately—*Auntie Shai!*—and I cried, too, as my lover drove us toward the tunnel and the trip home, New York no longer home without my mother, without my sister.

Faith, toddler Jonah, and baby Carmela in 1971.

Baby Faith in box pleats, 1943.

Faith, Eunice, and Shai passport photo going to Haiti in the late 1940s.

Shai, Faith, and Charity, Christmas card, mid-1950s.

Mother Ground

With gratitude to the women of Revolutionary
Mothering: Love on the Front Lines.

The radical potential of the word "mother" comes
after the "m." It is the space that "other" takes in our
mouths when we say it. We are something else.[1]

I grew up, unknowing, on the site of a Lenape village. Where I placed my feet when I walked to school or when I walked my dog or roller-skated was land that people before me had walked and not the cardboard cutout props that appeared in parades and on the TV show *Howdy Doody* as Princess Summerfall Winterspring. To me, indigenous history was *ancient history, nothing-to-do-with-me history*, the degraded history of a people who, I was told, had sold the island of Manhattan for twenty-four dollars' worth of beads. I did not learn that the paths I followed in Central Park, the vista I saw across the Hudson from Manhattan, the briny scent of the Hudson had all—all!—been experienced for fully lived eons by women, men, and children who were indigenous. That some of my high school classmates, some of the people with whom I brushed shoulders on the subway, were indigenous. In 2019, there were 100,000 people living in New York City who were enrolled members of indigenous tribes.[2] I have lived in six states and one other country, coming to Durham, North Carolina, at the age of 65, settling with impunity in former Occoneechee lands. Growing up, everyone was a renter. Almost no one I knew owned their home. In the mid-70s I bought my first home, up Middle White Oak Holler in Boone County, West Virginia. We paid $19,000 for a coal miner's hand-built, asbestos-sided, five-room house. We financed it with a bank loan, the kind of loan people take out to finance their cars.

    • • •

---

1. *Revolutionary Mothering: Love on the Front Lines*, Alexis Pauline Gumbs, China Martens, and Mai'a Williams, eds. PM Press, 2016, page 21.
2. https://barnard.edu/news/tour-native-new-york.

As young children, during New Hampshire summers, my sister and I roamed. We roamed the open hayfield behind my father's sister Pat's house and one winter skated on our city girl shoes on the frozen brook beyond that field. We knew our aunt owned the house. We knew everyone we met in town knew her. We knew our aunt's companion, Aunt Marg, owned the woods and fields above my aunt Pat's house and a Guernsey farm from which in the morning a man brought a glass jug of cream for my aunts' coffee. We followed Aunt Marg into the woods, where she gathered mushrooms and put them in the basket she carried over her arm. She taught us to walk unafraid into a pasture of cows, walk unafraid until we could touch their wet black noses, could see ourselves reflected in their muddy brown eyes. And once, once, Aunt Marg, who was not really our aunt but also really was, found a translucent teacup in the duff in the hollow at the foot of a tree.

I floated above my mother's back in the ocean, my hands on her shoulders. I trusted the restless salt water because I trusted her. She drove me and other schoolgirls to the beach for a spring birthday. We ate outdoors from baskets, and while our mothers sat in the sand, we ran in our dungarees, fully clothed because we hadn't intended to go in and our mothers hadn't intended it either, but we couldn't resist the ocean's surge and wet roar. In Saint Croix, my sister and I tumbled in and out of the daylight, the water tinkling inside our eardrums, as we somersaulted in cycles of air and ocean. In the water, my sister and I were golden. I can feel my mother's shoulders below my hands, tethering me. Not only her shoulders below my hands but the pressure of the ocean floor rising into me.

In Haiti, the drums on the hill opposite arose from land that in the night we could not see.

My mother said her family had been pearl button merchants in Europe. They would not have their sons drafted into the military of the anti-Semitic nations where they lived. Their trade allowed them to move across borders and evade the draft. True? I don't know.

Before we left New York City, my husband-to-be and I had dinner with his parents in Bensonhurst in Brooklyn. After dinner, at the table in the kitchen, my future mother-in-law recreated the story of her emigration as a youngster from Russia to the United States. My future husband recorded her words. She located the story in time by naming the yahrzeits—the dates of family deaths memorialized with the burning of candles, so she began parts of the story, saying something like, *the year after Uncle so-and-so's yahrzeit*, or, *the same year as . . .* She had been born in a village near Odessa, I think. Her mother fled with her two children, walking out of Russia. At the border into Poland, mother and daughter crossed successfully, but soldiers stopped the school-age boy. Mother and daughter stayed for a year in the village on the Polish side, until the boy, who had been taken in on the far side, could cross. They made their way on foot, probably with help from farmers in carts, all the way to Marseille, France. With nothing more than a dream, they boarded a ship bound for the United States. Memory, strung along the flames of yahrzeits, told her story. She was granted US citizenship on the basis of her telling and her son's recording that night.

We did not sing "The Star-Spangled Banner" at the Little Red School House. Was it in this context that I first heard my mother use the word *jingoism*?

In the midst of McCarthyism, we sang Woody Guthrie's "This Land Is My Land," *this land is your land—from the Gulf Stream waters to the New York island,* but I had no idea where the Gulf Stream waters were. We sang "America the Beautiful." I loved the words *amber waves of grain*, which played like one word in my mind: *amberwavesofgrain*. I loved the purple mountains' majesty, though I didn't have a sense of those mountains or where they were in the place, the continent, where my home was an island at the mouth of an *estuary* that flowed inward from the sea.

• • •

In a West Virginia coalfields school, I taught Louisa, not her name, who lived with her parents and her siblings in a nearby holler. Louisa worked very hard on her lessons, though she was often distracted and disorganized, as third graders can be—moving at speed into their eight-year-old selves. In that classroom, hard as it is to believe of myself, I led the children in the song "My Country, 'Tis of Thee." Daily. That school had a public address system, so maybe we sang along to a recording piped in from the principal's office as we stood at our desks. For sure, the singing was mandated. Louisa and the rest of us would glide through *our father's god to thee, author of liberty* . . . As we sang the words *land where our fathers died*, Louisa's face would brim with glee and relish as we all sang, *land where my father died*.

In Greenwich Village, the grown-ups said their coffee was *the only real choice*. Dark! Strong! In Greenwich Village, the parents and uncles and grown-up friends had jobs like editor, or teacher, freelance this or freelance that, painter, or music teacher and performer, or dance teacher, or film editor, and they called themselves *outside the mainstream*. In Greenwich Village, dinner tables were for amiable quarreling; things were thought out and overthought out; words were put on the dinner table in one conversation and the grown-ups were back the next morning with the same ideas with a nuance discovered overnight. In Greenwich Village, I knew which families read the *New York Times*, the *New York Post*, the *Herald Tribune*, the *New Yorker*, and I knew that *we* did not read the *New York Journal-American*. The one time the vender was out of the *Times* and I bought *Journal-American* for my mother, the man in the newsstand, whom I thought was somehow against us and our household, warned me that I did not want to buy that paper. I felt exposed, but grateful. My mother would have made me return the *Journal-American*. In Greenwich Village, during the Suez Canal crisis, my mother said it was *a rattling of sabers*. In Greenwich Village, we nine-year-olds passed out campaign material for Adlai Stevenson, because we knew—knew!—that if Eisenhower were elected it would be World War III. In my Greenwich Village, the abhorrence of war was universal.

. . .

My mother said we were not white people. My father's sister, Aunt Pat, called my mother, *the Jewess*. I knew if I had lived in Germany, I would have been killed, but people said *Faith is not a Jewish name*, so I was not Jewish enough and I lived with a chosen mother who was Black, and that was not very Jewish, either. And our neighbors chalked our sidewalk *because Ethiopia*, my mother said. And my mother did not know Yiddish and she stopped us from speaking with our hands or too loud. But Jewish was our dark, dark coffee. It was knowing the people in the Bible and I were connected. I was ten or eleven and a few of my boy classmates left school early to go to Hebrew school, and it had nothing to do with me, except the Chagall rabbi in Charity's bedroom, and I knew I was Jewish, and that was a good thing. One High Holy Day, our family walked out West Fourth Street to Charles Street and entered the imposing door of a synagogue. Everyone, all men, turned around to stare at us. We sat in the very last row in the back and escaped as soon as we could. And yet. I knew I was Jewish, something more than Greenwich Village. Something ancient.

When I was a white nineteen-year-old registering Black voters in Southwest Georgia, a congregant in mass meeting asked me who I was. Without a pause, I answered "Jewish." She said with a smile, "Oh, you are one of the Hebrew children." I liked that identity, one of the dusky Hebrew children, but by the time my children were born, it was becoming clear that I was, in fact, white, no matter how many times I applied for a driver's license and marked my race as *other*. Estranged as I might feel from *white*, I was white; I benefited from the white theft of a continent, benefited from the destruction of ancestral relationships to the land and the attempted obliteration of indigenous people. Though not personally responsible, having been born white though Jewish in a nation founded on slavery, I benefited from how the trade in African peoples and the practice of slavery in the United States had built the nation's wealth. Many of these things, I had not grasped when I was raising my children, but all of these things are part of what my children inherited from me.

We'll be eaten alive: my mother's words for our family's financial peril. Waiting for my father's weekly fifty-dollar check to arrive before going to the market. A few times a year, my mother had to get money from Household Finance

Corporation and add it to the tally in her wallet as she paid them back monthly. We were OK, but I felt as a child that the next check might not come, and then Household Finance would come for us up the narrow stairway into our apartment. *Making ends meet*, my emotion as a mother. My first teaching job in West Virginia in the early 1970s paid $5,700 for ten months of work; I have never made more than $25,000 in a year. Unimpressive compared to many Barnard graduates of 1966. Because of my whiteness, struggling to make ends meet, frightening as it has been, I have had the privilege of attending an elite college; the privilege of giving birth in relatively safe hospitals; the privilege of geographically locating and relocating about the United States; the privilege of receiving some money at my father's death, though my mother died in her sixties with less than $200 in savings, eaten alive by cancer.

I was to steel myself against catcalls in the street; to ignore gropes in high school classrooms and in restaurants. I learned the word *plump*. For Christmas, my best friend Katie received a camisole, a sort of pre-bra, though neither of us had breasts. And she received stockings, silken and subject to snags, so fragile they were folded back into their box and never worn. Being female was practically a dread disease. My mother Eunice's name for menstruation was *the Curse*. Girls were girls. Boys were boys. I was not to wear clothing that I could feel against my body. I was female. I learned the word *vulgar*.

At seven, I had no language for the *BeforeWhenAfter* of sexual abuse, no words for what had happened, just the queasy memory of an extinguishing cold, the bursting out and up and away before restoration. Without the language, it was as if the experience had never happened; in the enormity of silence, in the labyrinth of barriers that held me inside silence, the shadow of the experience was present. My mother told me she had been *almost* sexually abused. My mother taught me to surreptitiously decode *almost*. My mother told stories, some of which were true because she wanted or needed them to be. The untold stories shaped the relationship between her truth and herself. The same for me.

In Haiti, Charity did ask me if I had been touched in a way that was wrong. I stridently said, *No*. End of conversation. What had happened to Charity, that she knew to ask this question? What stopped her from pressing me further?

And how much of what happened did I *know*, having lived briefly within the cold that began in my scalp.

My mother Eunice and I wrongly accepted culpability for the misuse of our bodies. It must have been our fault, right? Therefore, neither of us believed it could happen to our children, whom we knew to be innocent.

I am the child of two lesbian mothers and a father who was a tortured version of gay, but I was schooled to discount the emotional evidence for this. It is the story my mothers told in omissions and silences. In my teens and well into my forties, I didn't have language for who I was. Most of the language I heard in the 1950s, or, more accurately *overheard*, when I became still and invisible while grown-ups talked, was pejorative, so I knew they couldn't be about me or my mothers. Because they were my mothers and I was their daughter, they would have told me, right? If being queer was such a damning secret, how could I disclose that I was their own worst nightmare?

For most of my mothering years until my children were in their teens, I was living with the woman I loved and thought I would live with forever. Secretly, we might use the word *lesbian*; sometimes we might obfuscate with *woman who loves women*. We lived a social pact resembling *Don't ask, don't tell*. Friends or family who articulated our relationship or asked became those in the know. Another category of friends, particularly in our rural West Virginia county, never asked, never said, but acted as if this woman and I were a couple. Until they were in their teens, we did not explicitly tell the children; an impulsive word of theirs to outsiders could have brought down our world. Each year I signed a contract as a public schoolteacher; the contract included a pledge that I was not guilty of *moral turpitude*, but if the board had known, they most certainly would have considered me guilty. We could have lost our jobs. I did not use the word *queer* to describe myself until I moved to Durham in the summer of 2008, almost forty years into my queer life. Ironically, when, on the eve of my son's bar mitzvah, I finally told my children that my *roommate* and I were lovers, my fourteen-year-old daughter said, "You mean like when my friends say, '*Oh, you're queer?*'"

What did it mean for each of my parents, as parents, probably to be gay and closeted? To be fair, my sister did not think our mother was a lesbian and we never discussed our father's sexuality. Do I have the right to out them on the basis of my believed history? If I glide over it, the old narrative holds: homes without both birth parents are "broken"; gay people are unfit to raise children; being queer is a curse and not an inheritance. Could my father, especially, have been a happier and kinder person if he had felt safe to claim a gay identity? Could I, as his child and my mothers', have had an earlier and different sense of my value and lineage?

I carried an other, my unborn child. When I labored to bring him into the world, I entered a new relationship to my present, my future, and my past. What happened to me and what happened to this new one was generated from my own tissue, not just until birth, but for the rest of our time on this earth. Everything from the quality of the air we breathed, to my family history of child sexual abuse, to my household income, to my class and privilege, to my activism, to the ever-present white supremacy of the United States—everything was ours.

Christmas 1967, the eyes of God graced our living room. Ojos de Dios, crossed toothpicks wound with turquoise and crimson yarn—spirit in our Santa Fe living room. My belly was round and hard. At sunset, below the Sangre de Cristo Mountains, the blood of Christ spilled across the snowy fields; the aspens rampaged golden. Preparing to leave behind our selves as we'd been before the baby, unable to imagine parenting, as if it were Egypt. Santa Fe light in January penetrates, is snow tinged. On the night of my twenty-fifth birthday, cough overlapping contraction overlapping the absence of my mother, night overlapped by morning before sunrise, moving into the final stages of labor, but contractions dying, the nurse midwife stepping aside, the doctor with his gloved hands pulling forth the baby; the baby blue with the waters of another world but his eyes wide open to this one. The baby nestled on the doctor's hand, a self-contained universe my body had made.

At his birth, Jonah and I separated and laid eyes on one another for the first time, I with my twenty-five-year-old eyes, he with his wandering newborn eyes of that navy blue from elsewhere. With his rose-petal ears, he heard my voice directly for the first time, though he had taken soundings of me for months. He took in my words without "having" my language. And though I loved him, though I had carried him and fed him from my own flesh, gazing down at his infant face, I felt that if I had once known it, I would never again know how he made sense of us. What did he know without words, looking at me; what did he see that I could not know? What did he know of where he had come from? We had become separate. And now would be always.

She took her sweet time arriving, lying inside me *sunny-side up*. For a baby to pass through the birth canal, she must face her mother's back, so she can crane her neck at the right angle to swan dive into the world. During transition, when she was almost in the world, Carmela didn't spin into place. The midwife reached inside me and turned her. Was that baby pissed to be out in the cold air, to be grasped by alien hands? And the light! How she fussed. Once she was out and weighed and swabbed off, once she'd been placed on my chest to stare at me, or maybe she was looking back to the place she'd come from, her tiny fingers twisted like stars, she settled down into a sleep from which the schedule-bound staff could not wake her. She knew she needed to rest as she knew many things, Carmela Sojourner.

My godmother, Betsy, had knitted a bunting for Carmela, who was a mid-December baby. Buntings are sleep sacks with no arms or legs. A garment for captured warmth and ease of slipping the baby inside, an envelope for a folded letter. Well, Miss Carmela at five days and six pounds, five ounces, did not like that bunting. She hated it so much she screamed until she turned beet red, her forehead pearled with sweat. "She doesn't know," the nurse told me. The next day at home, I slipped her into a discarded snowsuit of Jonah's, threaded her chicken-bone arms into the tops of the sleeves. With her arms unconstrained, she was content.

The night we brought her home was so cold, our Detroit neighbor brought his car battery indoors to keep it from going dead. Past midnight those winter nights, I'd hold my adamant child in my arms, a newborn who was amiably awake for hours at a time. Temperatures falling into the twenties, a working-class city, starlit. I had waited for Carmela for nine months. Had waited while she unfurled inside me from bulbous head and dangling appendages with finger and toe pads, not inside me but of my own fabric. Then she was born, the skin of my belly soft and folded like an old purse. In the Detroit apartment, her cry in the night seemed to originate from inside me. She did not immediately drowse off. My hands held her safe in the dark time between midnight and dawn. I felt her fall silent inside and outside. I bathed her skin, fine as the summer dew when my sister and I had walked straight outdoors from childhood beds; we had been hungry from the night, not yet fed by a mother or an aunt, but we knew, hunkering in the grass, that somebody would feed us so we could go swimming and dig grains of granite out of boulders at the quarry. My daughter had such a confidence in me.

My mother was overcome with excitement about our first baby. She, whose sewing skills included mending only, was helped by a friend to weave out of fine yarn blocks to create a yellow receiving blanket. To each corner, my mother affixed a small embroidered red strawberry that she had purchased, a finishing touch on this uncharacteristic project to mark an occasion that gave her more joy than she could express in words.

    Later, in Detroit, when we were expecting the birth of our second child, Charity helped her piece a baby quilt of disparate patches of bright cottons, rough and smooth side by side, striped and prim floral and African, outlined in small yellow featherstitches, with a lavender peace symbol at its center. She agonized over getting it right. Charity imagined my mother could do this, so a gift from both of them.

Life with Fox

There was that year or more I walked around in the world, a woman outside her own skin, a she rather than an I, looking down from a hilltop above a door that slammed for my ears alone, over and over again.

    That woman who was I was fed for years by the fox. This fox, not red-cliché-handsome but a dirty blond in a sheepskin coat, the off-white fur stained with mud, fingers the lapel, and the woman who was I finds this can't-sleep-at-night attractive. Dirty fingernails. Fox slips in from the car late, patchouli and the click of her dog companion's nails on the wood floor. So many nights have been fuckless, for Fox has been shrugging off and sliding past and turning her head, far from the woman who is I, who has followed Fox with her eyes. Foxes at the mouth of the holler, blasting their car horns across the field where the grackles gather; the grackles' feathers, compared to the dirty fox fur, gleam with purple stars embedded in black.

Fox, the one the woman who was once I follows with her eyes even when sound asleep.

The fields more dangerous than war.

At precisely the time we are to meet, the woman who was I waits outside Burger Chef in Marmet, West Virginia. *I am pissed.* And *I am pissed a lot of the time. I am becoming a shrew* (her father's word), *retrograde* (Fox's word). And the business with her own child, that woman who was I not enjoying being the Bad Mother. Although she'd done the grocery shopping. As for their time together. . . . Now twenty-three minutes past the time. And another thing. Anytime, she has to wait. Any one thing more and she can't. She protects her brain against heart grackles. She had given herself in love.

That gnawing winter afternoon time. The children are hungry, but it isn't yet time to eat. Fox walks into the empty field and her toe catches in her own contradictions. Back at the house, the woman who was I thinks, *I can make biscuits. Fox hates biscuits. My kids love them. Fox says they're too fattening, because she likes to force them open, soaking the soft white body with butter and honey. Fox must have both.*

My children run into the house, she in red sweater, he in no sweater. They smell like leaves crumbling into humus. My girl sees the dough in the marbled bowl. *Is that what we're having?* He says, *Oh, boy.* I say, *Who is feeding the dogs?* I need the narrow kitchen with the linoleum we have laid down, I need it to myself. *If you set the table,* I say to my girl, and she goes right into the pantry to get the plates. I pull a purple-brown oak leaf from the back of her sweater. In a few days, there will be leaves to rake into a pile large enough for the children and the dogs to jump into, and then we will stuff the leaves into an old pair of jeans and an old flannel shirt and prop them in a chair on the high front porch so everyone can see our Halloween dummy from the dirt road below.

Fox comes home. The woman who was I says, "You're late." Fox bites her own cheek in irritation. The children watch.

"Did I say I'd be home for dinner?" Fox asks. The gnawing dusk of winter when a shadow falls, cutting each one of them off from the others.

The woman who was I takes a breath; Fox growls, deep in her throat; the children watch. They have heard Fox say, "I can't take your emotionalism." Fox has done it. A shadow like a growl buried in a red chest with its pretty white bib.

Up Middle White Oak Holler, the front door is open to Sunday afternoon warmth. The bright nimbus of music from our stereo can fill the holler to the brim. Can reach Haredee and Betty's double-wide on the opposite hill, can reach our dogs messing around up in the woods. On the stereo, Bach, or is it Chris Williamson, or the hammered dulcimers of the West Virginia group named Trapezoid. My children are shouting from our porch into the holler. On the opposite hill, the cable wire Haredee ran comes down, unauthorized, from the top of the hill, into their living room, offering the sound and images of TV. The day's heat is in abeyance.

We have made this life.

The crow flying over Haredee and Betty's. The black snake under Haredee and Betty's porch sinking its fangs into the dog. The dogs treeing a raccoon and barking all night at the base of the tree. The raccoon high in the tree, eyes shining red. The feel of night when you are alone, a feeling that goes on and on like what her mother had called *the tail end of the cold*, that infection which took the mother's teeth and ruined her smile.

Then it is after dinner in the pink and gray and green asbestos-sided house perched on its point of land. The children are busy. She tells them, *To bed.* They say, *In a minute.* Tells them, *Now.* She thinks, *This is our little drama. To bed. Just the three of us in our house on the point.*

Tell me, the woman who was I had said that afternoon. But Fox had walked out.

The next holler over, Fox brushes her tail against desiccated Queen Anne's Lace; residue startles into the air and she sneezes from her black velvet snout. The dried plants of autumn make Fox want more, make her walk further into the holler. Somewhere there will be dying leaves that smell like Earl Grey tea. She might go home to the bed. Everyone asleep. Nothing expected of her; their disappointment in her glossed over. She likes them well enough, and then she doesn't. Then the very next day, or perhaps it will be a week, Fox needs them, needs the indoor-ness of them.

The cars won't start. The brakes freeze overnight and Haredee teaches the woman who was I to back up to unfreeze them. The flooded road, there in the bend before the paved road. No way through, except maybe with a truck, so they are going to the IGA in Haredee's pickup. When they come back from the store, the smell of Betty's pinto beans cooking. The woman who was I has brought coffee. Hunkering in my/her mind, just on the edge of visibility, *Where is Fox? Why hasn't she called.* While eating beans and drinking coffee with Haredee and Betty, hopeful that Fox has called the black rotary phone in her house across the road.

Back home, Fox comes blasting up the drive as is her habit. She is hungry, with a thorn deep between the pads of her paw. The woman thinks she should make the paw better. Isn't that her job? It might be her fault that Fox won't let her soak the paw in warm water and Epsom salts. Her fault she cannot fix it, even without knowing what *it* is. If only she had risen above the longing. Could she, the woman who was I, have spoken? Could her tongue have done that?

When winter quiet closes in, I remember the woman who was I. Sometimes I remember Fox until so many years have passed that I cannot, neither her thin lips nor her long nose.

The moon above Middle White Oak Holler, big enough to engulf her pillow. The evening when the lover collects the brown dog and walks out, firing up her car and driving off. An enemy. A lover. An enemy. Wet eyes at breakfast, lunch, and dinner. The other's car would never await her in the driveway. But there was macaroni and cheese to make, the roux first, her daughter grating the cheese, the son making the salad. Not that she didn't love them. Not that she didn't realize she was being *self-indulgent*. Not that she wanted to be this way. Next day. Next night. Not that her children disguised their unease, their impatience. None of their friends. A closet all their childhoods. Now this, a lesbian breakup. Nights they knew she was crying. Still crying. Maybe she could stop next month. She found another job and still she had to say *No* when her son needed new jeans. But everyone went to their lessons and their jobs. Every night they ate dinner together. They were the truth of the matter.

Transition

That place in the month that had always proclaimed, *Everything working down here*. No longer the paw of *the Curse*, as my mother had called it, the paw hot and hairy and muddy and vital. I walked by the river in Ravenswood and someone read me a poem. I remembered my long-legged kids with their Walkmans, carrying their music out of the house and down the road to the school bus. *I am the mother of a boy who smokes pot.* Itinerant teacher: classrooms in Charleston and up the Elk River. No one school where I belonged. Any time I started to feel at home at work, something happened and I guarded myself. Any time the other teachers asked about weekends, I was circumspect. Not like the earlier Boone County school when I had lived with my lover. Boone County, threaded with rivers and kinship, veined and sheeted with coal. The animals: the brown dog and the part shepherd, the orange cat. Springtime batting like moths against the window screens and bills overdue. A dance performance where Carmela enchanted an entire auditorium. A guitar concert with the electric guitar, a gift for Jonah's bar mitzvah. The spring the yellow jackets crawled out of holes in the grass in the sloping hill and stung him through his jeans. Another job. Another year. My daughter moved to Massachusetts to live with her father. Jonah and I ate dinner out once a week to catch up with one another. His graduation.

• • •

I brought the acceptance letter in from the mailbox and handed it to him on the couch. How did a schoolboy who lived up Middle White Oak Holler, the boy who loved his brown dog, played guitar, and had beautiful old-school cursive handwriting, how did he imagine himself at Berkeley? There was an end-ness to that August. Carmela and I drove Jonah the 2,500 miles to California. Before cell phones or the internet, it was just the three of us driving across the continent, encapsulated, stumbling out to the not-air-conditioned Dodge Colt in the dark, driving until midafternoon, stopping at motels no matter how cheesy, as long as they had swimming pools. As I drove, I watched the Colt's shadow running beside us and it looked very jolly, with Jonah's trunk on the roof and his bicycle strapped to the back. When the slant of the sun was just right, I might even see the shadow of one of us passengers skimming along. Nothing but me and my kids on the road.

That she at work.

I was pleased with the walls I had painted and the bedspread I had sewn. She in her outdoors denim jacket. She with the country ways. *Look how she sits in staff meeting. Sister*, I might have masqueraded. I was safe and solitary. In an office, but also in soft space where we did not *say* but we *knew*. We wrote back and forth. Soon we would speak. Maybe tomorrow. The waiting bedspread.

It is our first date, but she doesn't know that. It is the culmination of months of covert approaches within boundaries. She is married to a man. We don't say, but we do say, *Is this OK? Yes, that is OK*. Without ever saying what *this* might be. I am eternally subject to crushes. In the past have been infatuated with a straight married woman and survived. Friends have outed me to her, but I don't know this.

It is our first date. I stand in the audience beside her at a Holly Near concert. *We are a gentle loving people. And we are singing, singing for our lives.* An auditorium of people holding hands. Hot filament. Our first date and she doesn't know. I have fed her with homemade tacos. Forward through the winter months. Not saying. Noticing, oh her jacket is hanging in the corridor in the office: *She is here.* Summer letters and coded conversations. Winter coming on, I ride in the car beside her. Work related. She is driving. Our first night together, the car climbing into the night. Joan Baez on cassette. *Recently! Asimbonanga. Do*

Right Woman. Biko. I do not know what will happen in our room. Joan Baez sings. Vicki says, *I did not bring you all this way to have you sleep in that other bed.* The next morning, eating breakfast concealed in our booth while deer hunters talked and drank coffee. Going from the restaurant, stepping into November sun, walking through woods and over creeks. Letting her change the dimensions of the unsaid, stepping over a creek in the mountains.

October we offer bodies in conflagration. She had been four when her mother died. Rich in privation, but to discover the riches of the flesh, startling strata to her bedrock of two girls, the intrepid Chevy Wrangler that could cross the ridge whether there is a road or not.

Always, Vicki's girls. All her nights up Little Buffalo, when it rained she couldn't sleep, listening for the river to creep over its banks and cover the road, cutting her and her daughters off, but I lived on a ridge, the creek winding far below us. We could hear water running when I opened the windows on spring nights, letting in the calls of tree frogs. She was listening for the water to creep up and cut her off. She was always planning for disaster.

There was the business of the macaroni and cheese—I made the wrong kind. Ashes of the wood-burning stove in their old house, the house their father had built, ashes still scented their breath. All would be so easy, I had thought, because I knew how to mother, had done it before. We'd be driving the girls home to their father's and the younger needed hot chocolate there on the interstate in the speeding car. The older: we had to stop to buy her a curling iron for her hair. One child who loved boys. The other child who made gummy and inedible vanilla pudding and left it behind for us to eat when she went to her father's. Vicki calls her absent girls on the phone. Corkscrew of voices from my ridgetop to the holler an hour's drive away to her girls. One on the cusp, the other more of a cipher. They can't, not yet, not quite, have a status or name for me.

In the night, angry young spirit. She steals into every room in the dark house, smoking as she goes. Spirit is convinced if only her mother had not taken that wrong turn. In the morning, this will play out as toothpaste spattered all over the faucet and porcelain. It can show up in that can of tuna in the cupboard, pull tab slightly parted, maggots frothing. Spirit is intimately and profoundly angry. She no longer knows all the cheerleaders and will not become one. *I want my mother.*

. . .

Carmela and I sat in the Union Station rotunda. Nearby, four or five high school students were horsing around. We sat on a flat square of burnished wood, so large we could have lain down on it. The high schoolers were pushing one another and at the same time flirting in this public space where no one knew them. My daughter said, *I am disclosing to you. It is called disclose. I was sexually abused as a child.* Now I see the learned disconnect from my childhood, see it stopping me from spooling back to my own abuse. I had not protected her. Had not read her bursts of anger, her withdrawal, that time I'd turned a corner in the supermarket when she was twelve and she hadn't seen where I'd gone and she cried out, *Mom*—terrified I had disappeared. We talked until the sun had moved from one side of the rotunda to the other. I went to meet Vicki at her conference hotel. Vicki sat behind an information table and was busy, I didn't tell her, but went back out into the unfamiliar city to meet a friend. I didn't tell the friend either. The enormity. I could think of nothing. I was polite and attentive to my friend in the Middle Eastern restaurant. Finally, she rose to go. I went back to the hotel and told Vicki. I didn't doubt Carmela's word. I doubted myself. How could she have been hurt and I not know? All night, the city lights strafed the hotel ceiling. Vicki slept. My daughter had said, *The Courage to Heal.* I bought the book and began to read. While Vicki went to meetings, I read and I walked and walked, and read some more.

My girl in her teens, I wanted to know who had it been? She said, *I want to know why me.* I had stood in my children's room at night. Both so young they took stuffed animals to bed. I could not wrestle my love for them into submission. And the predator said to me, *Do you want to take a walk?* She said, *One day I will figure out what happened and I will tell you.* I said, *I don't care what. I know you are leaving us.*

She is by the ocean. Her bunion-knotted joints release themselves into the sand. Her smile is that of a woman whose teeth had all been pulled in one summer week, when her daughters were in New Hampshire. A woman whose denture gums were as pink as a polite lie. She walks straight ahead. She wants no one to stop her.

I know that face with its flinch of pain.

"Madre," I call, but she turns away. Although she had always been angular except for the pouch that marked her two pregnancies, no nonsense, and cheap in her clothes, this version of my mother, three decades dead, is filmy, more pastel than she would ever have tolerated in her denim blue and charcoal gray, but the woman walking in the sand keeps shifting, filmy by turns with seersucker.

"Madre," I call again, my voice swallowed by the gulls.

She keeps walking. She has a dog. Of course she has a dog. She and I had piled the two city dogs into her beater car, to run the dogs in the dawn, joyous and illicit on this very beach. "It's illegal, you know," she used to say with satisfaction.

My filmy mother is now further away from me.

There is another person, but she has no body. She says, "Go ahead, Faith Darling, call her back. Don't let her keep going."

A breath at my back, and then Charity is gone.

I am alone, my mother Eunice receding down the beach.

2
Outcrop

I wrote the first draft of this manuscript not long after my daughter, whose life is very hard, had come back into my life after an absence of 17 years. My early years had shaped who I was, and who my daughter and I together had been, so that is where my narrative began. I did not want the story of my life as an activist to overshadow the family story. This memoir took years of work, and early readers raised questions about the two different strands of my story during the uprisings over George Floyd's murder by the police. It was at this time that I realized the two strands formed a single story that I wanted to tell.

Glancing references to a mass meeting in Georgia and similar fragments, the sole references to my activism in that early draft, would not suffice. OK. But. Readers wanted *more about the Student Nonviolent Coordinating Committee* (SNCC), the militant Civil Rights group with which I had worked, but this created another dilemma. I am proud that SNCC is often seen as the youngest and *baddest* of the frontline groups fighting for racial justice, a reputation I believe is well-deserved, but I believe SNCC was not a singular phenomenon that burst, like Athena from the head of Zeus, onto the 1960s scene with the sit-ins. Decades later, with five other women, I would edit a collection of SNCC women's stories in their own words. One of the editors, Martha Prescod Noonan, pored through all of the typescripts (slightly more than fifty) and found that an astounding number of us had been involved in community work—through church, the NAACP, and similar groups—before joining SNCC. We were daughters of the 1940s and 1950s—McCarthyism and the death of Emmett Till (roughly our contemporary), to mention two influences. Following the pattern of consequential friendships I had learned at home, as an activist I formed similar lifelong connections. Many members of SNCC never stopped being activists, even into our sixties and seventies. In my case, my introduction to social justice began in my childhood, and my introduction to SNCC occurred through the National Council of Christians and Jews (NCCJ). I first met "Dr. Bob" Johnson, Charles McDew, Diane Nash, and other SNCC people through NCCJ, and my New York City work fed seamlessly into SNCC in Southwest Georgia and later in the New York SNCC office. If I were going to write about SNCC, I would have to talk about my work before SNCC as a teenager in Harlem, and the work that followed in Detroit, West Virginia, and Durham, North Carolina, the years during which I mothered my two children and lost my own mother.

Harlem

At the beginning of my last year of high school, bare arms still summer rosy, I was going somewhere I had never been, my first meeting of the Harlem Brotherhood Group, or HBG. I knew my New York City but not the streets of that afternoon. I had walked out Bleecker Street to elementary school; I had walked my dog for an hour each afternoon since I was eight; I had roller-skated from one end of West Fourth Street to the other. With my best friend Katie, I had taken the subway to the Donnell branch of the public library across from the Museum of Modern Art. And this past summer, with a hundred or more high school students, I had ridden the Hudson River Day Line to the Brotherhood Camp run by the National Conference of Christians and Jews, or NCCJ.

I walked toward a church on the edge of a park. Only a few blocks south, that same park spread below the different world of my high school perched on its outcrop over Harlem. That Sunday, though less than a mile from the school where I knew everyone and everyone knew me, I was going where I had never been and didn't know who would be there. The true fact is: that Sunday after Brotherhood Camp I was walking away from the bedrock of my mothers to a place they would never be, yet when I was in that place, they would always be with me.

In the street walking toward the church, I felt so white.

Anne Braden, Southern Conference Educational Fund and Southern Organizing Committee.

Amina Rachman, high school.

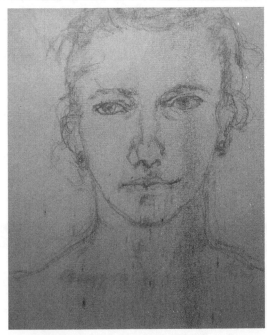

Faith Holsaert, pencil self-portrait.

Albany, Georgia (*left to right*): Agnew James, Penny Patch, Faith Holsaert, Larry Rubin, Charles Sherrod.

Candy Keeling Gordon, 1970s.

Madeline James, Welfare Rights Organization and women's health organizer, West Virginia, 1970s, *Mountain Life and Work* (Council of the Southern Mountains), June 1974.

Was it an Episcopal church with its distinctive red door . . . or? I don't remember. From the Village, I had taken the Abingdon Square bus, which originated around the corner from 48 Jane Street, where we lived. Did I realize how close I was to my high school, only ten blocks south, the walk through this same park up those steps?

What happened in the church that afternoon? I don't know. I greeted people from Brotherhood Camp; we probably heard presentations about what committees or projects we could join. I picked housing. Candy Keeling from camp did, too. Housing in New York City; in the old liberal *New York Post*, I had read stories of gulag-like housing projects where the corridors were dangerous; the *New York Post* had reported at least once that someone had been thrown to the ground from the roof of one such building. I knew some landlords were derelict and rented out apartments that could not be called safe shelter.

I knew the unfairness in housing had to do with the two-category dynamic of race: Black/white. Who was white, in a city with significant Irish, Italian, and Jewish residents, was malleable, a matter of political expedience. Though I had met my first Puerto Rican schoolmate when I was twelve, in high school I had been going to school with students from the Caribbean and Central and South America, some of whom were considered white and some not. What I knew was the unfairness in housing—we northerners did not say *segregation* about ourselves—was not only discriminatory but dangerous, that to my young eyes, the inequality represented endemic injustice. That inequity made me and the other young people on that Sunday indignant.

We were going to read and draw up questions to ask tenants. We were to read about housing conditions and about earlier projects that established racial discrimination in rentals (Black couple expresses interest in an apartment and is turned down; white couple with the same socioeconomic characteristics expresses interest in the same apartment and is accepted). I don't know if our work had any practical application.

After the meeting, I stood on the sidewalk, waiting for the Abingdon Square bus. Others came behind me, heading away from me up the hill toward 145th Street.

Candy came out of the church looking up at the boy beside her and laughing. He headed off, but she walked up to me, smiling.

"You take this bus?"

I nodded. "All the way down to Abingdon Square."

"Me too." She smiled. Like mine, her front teeth gapped.

"But." I stopped, embarrassed that I'd almost said, *I thought you lived uptown*, which is what people in the meeting had called Harlem.

She laughed hard. She was ridiculously small. She pulled out a cigarette and lit it. "Uptown. I live at the last stop." I laughed, not worrying about my gapped teeth. The gaps made room for the joy welling up in me.

"Makes us bookends," she said, laughing.

"Or something," I said, laughing back.

"Or something," she agreed.

The bus took me down to the north end of Central Park to cross out of Harlem. It continued down Central Park West, where my godparents lived, and where on weekday evenings Black women boarded after working in apartments up and down Central Park West; at Fifty-Ninth Street the bus veered west, passing through Hell's Kitchen, plunging south on trucking routes to Abingdon Square, where I disembarked and walked one block to Jane Street, an officially designated "play street." A blockaded street in which we could roller-skate, hopscotch, ride homemade wood-crate scooters, and gossip about the grown-ups walking by, the drunks and the mothers, the dog walkers, the office workers coming home in the evening, observing far more than I think those adults realized. "Drunk again," Betty Anne might say, when the man I thought of as White Hair slammed a brown paper bag into the trash can, causing a tinkle of broken glass bottles. An entire block for children playing. Walking home after the meeting in the church, I didn't know to wonder whether there were play streets in Harlem.

I take from the armoire a sketchbook from my senior year at New York City's public High School of Music and Art, the year I would spend all my between-sleep-and-waking hours in the world of HBG. At school, we must have been asked to draw a self-portrait. Looking out at me from the discolored page is an oval-faced girl with hazel eyes whose complexity I conveyed in penciled gray and black. I am amazed at my teenage skills; that penciled girl steps away from the elderly me to be herself. She is luminous but reticent, drawn into herself, a young woman who returned from Brotherhood Camp to pick up her old life, the life of the child who roller-skated on that play street, that girl who climbed the 139 steps through St. Nicholas Park to her high school, only blocks from the meeting at the church. That girl occupied her two worlds with aplomb but kept many details of her new life from her classmates as she negotiated the geographies of city and family and her new circle.

I wonder what my mother felt that year, her seventeen-year-old daughter, beautiful as the young are beautiful and vulnerable as city girls are, moving into a world the mother might never know, a world whose strangeness must at times have both exhilarated and frightened the girl in a racist way, and which must have frightened her mother, even that exemplary mother, in a racist way.

Yes, the girl in the sketchbook is soft, hair wispy tendrils, the earrings small and tasteful, but there is strength—I could say power—in her. The lips are set, more smiling than not. Those hazel eyes look beyond the viewer's ear. The brows dark and straight, chin firm. The neck long and muscular; below, collarbones and smooth shoulder, as if, perhaps, she is shirtless and doesn't care what the viewer might think. She could not have imagined sixty-five years later. She had thought that she would die at nineteen, in an electrical fire; she just thought that was how it would be.

At nineteen, I did walk into a conflagration, though not an electrical one. This girl's feet were on that path. The drawing portrays a muscle and strength I would never have associated with myself, but she will not let my timidity deter her.

Every morning she took the Eighth Avenue subway to 135th Street and climbed those steps through the outcrop of St. Nicholas Park. She was a good student, earning a State Regents Scholarship and a letter of commendation from the Merit Foundation. She applied to Barnard, the women's college at Columbia University. In the autumn of 1960, in a heather wool suit bought on sale at Macy's, she took the subway to Barnard, less than ten blocks north of her high school perched above the same outcrop of park overlooking the former farmland of Harlem. The director of admissions suggested the girl apply to an out-of-town school like Smith or Vassar, where she could cloister herself. Nicely, the girl told the woman, she wanted to stay in her city, where she was learning so much, where she was learning who she was—exactly what the director of admissions, also in a tweed suit, feared.

At my high school, it took many steps to go from the flatland at St. Nicholas Avenue to Convent Avenue above, the equivalent of almost ten residential staircases, a lot of work to breach that eruption, time for many conversations and laughter and arguments and whispered rumors as we walked, textbooks flung over our shoulders in book bags, our teen stuff permeating the air. Art teachers might take us into St. Nicholas Park to paint. I learned the hill might look like a unified whole, with those boulders over there, with the trees, including the one bent halfway to the ground: Easy, right? But so hard to pin down with a paint brush, the numerous particulars barely distinguishable even when I tackled them one by one, their proportions and relations elusive.

How to communicate a hillside? To get relationships and details, to convey the enormity of it: rock breaking free from the bedrock of Manhattan.

Three of us worked our way along the landings, from one apartment to the next. No one was home in a couple of apartments. A woman with children behind her slammed the door on us. It was me and Bruce McGee and Candy. One man answered our questions: his bathroom sink was pulling loose from the wall, rats of course, the young kids acting up in the hallway. At night, he stayed in his place, two rooms and a bath, but he liked to look out the window and watch the happenings out there. Jump rope. Stick ball. Old lady across the way coming up the block with her shopping cart.

On the top landing, a woman with a toddler in her arms answered our questions. Showed us the scar on her sleeping baby's cheek, a rat bite. "Would you sign a petition?" we asked, and she clammed up. Bruce said something and she turned on him in a rage.

• • •

She worked as a nurse, came home after midnight. Picked up her baby. Climbed three flights. "Nothing but a fifteen-watt light bulb in the hall. Do you know how much—actually, how little—light a fifteen-watt bulb sheds? And me carrying the baby and maybe some groceries and those kids running wild and sometimes men standing in the hall. They don't live here—they make those noises."

Candy and I exchanged looks. We knew those noises. The woman's brown skin flushed red with anger.

We thanked her and left. "What's up here?" Bruce asked. He always wanted to look around a corner, open a door, walk down a corridor. How little I know about Bruce, though he was always there, joking and questioning. We climbed a narrow staircase and shoved through a heavy door to burst into fresh air. On the cliffs above us: Barnard College, where I would start college in the autumn. Bruce shouted, "Whoopee." Candy smiled her closed-eyes smile as the sun played over her face.

"Fifteen damn watts," she said, leaning over the edge of the tarred roof. "That whole lady's life crammed into this space," and with her polio limp she paced it out on the black tar.

As an MFA student, mentors warned me away from ruptures, to spare readers feeling they were being dealt with arbitrarily. Everything must have a motivation and everything must be a shapely demonstration of my control. Control distinguished art from life, they said. I did not ask: whose art? Did not ask: What if abrupt breaks are the story? Unexplained and everlastingly abrupt? No adequate explanation, no satisfying explanation, just breakage everywhere? There are breaks of loss, but I've also had breaks of addition, like the outcrop that runs from Central Park North, escarpment making a space between Barnard College on its heights and Harlem, whose name means *Black* in Dutch. A different break—Harlem gentrified, Black people pushed out. Sometimes the break insinuates itself, as it did with me, arising imperceptibly between myself before I became an activist and myself after. The bedrock of St. Nicholas Park was formed millions of years ago, so it is not new, but it feels like an interloper disrupting Manhattan's crust, an indication of shifting plates below, floating on molten core.

· · ·

Carole Keeling, Candy—book ends, she'd said!—was born one day after me in 1943. She was small and dark-skinned and walked with a polio limp. She wrecked her shoes and so did I, though I'd never had polio. Candy's little brother Buzzy often tagged along with us when we canvassed. Buzzy might come to our apartment with Candy. Candy and I worked over sheets of paper and laughed and threw out lines from Carl Reiner and Mel Brooks's LP, *2000 Year Old Man*.

I'd rather eat a rotten nectarine than a fine plum, we quoted and cracked up. We had shared these words so often, they were ours, they were *us*. My mother sized up Buzzy's potential boredom and asked the nine-year-old if he wanted a ride in her red MG. Decades later, my mother gone, Candy gone, Buzzy remembered this moment, much as his sister and I had shared Carl Reiner and Mel Brooks.

Late nights, two or three of us might end up at Candy's family's apartment in the Dunbar Apartments. W. E. B. Du Bois and Countee Cullen had once lived in these buildings, under the roofs over which we flew, laughing girls, in the presence of a past we didn't know but which may have exerted its influence upon us. Some nights, we ran up the stairwell and across the roof to her sister Toni's building. How illicit, and at the same time, how safe it felt to burst into the city night and hurry over the roof and down the stairs to Toni's, where there was a baby. A baby! I often stayed in Candy's room on a trundle bed where Toni had once slept. In the morning, we'd slap our hair into shape, gather up our books, and run down the echoing stairwell to sprint to the subway, to go in opposite directions, she to Hunter College in the Bronx and I to Barnard on its heights.

With Candy, it was the excitement of thinking ideas we'd never thought before, ideas that made us laugh, but she was also close to a shadowed enormity out of which she had come and within which she could be. *Deep* we used to say, and nod, half making fun of ourselves. Carole Anne Keeling Gordon was *deep*. As in the photo in which the dark curtain behind her seems to erase the separation between the black crown of her head and the dark behind her. Did this stillness come from Harlem Hospital when she was a toddler, hospitalized in the 1940s with the polio that would shape how she walked for life, the polio that in the end would hasten her death? Her mother, Mommie T, worked downstairs in an office and would visit Candy on the ward. *That little baby. When I'd get ready to go, she'd hold up her little arms*: Take me. I imagine this three-year-old's hospital nights with other babies in cribs and women in white in charge and the high special railings to keep her from climbing out. After lights had been dimmed for the night, did Candy, with her smoldering eyes, settle in resignation? She would have taught herself not to cry and would have slipped back, as she sometimes did in her twenties, to seek counsel within herself. Was it cold there, where she went?

Janice Robinson was deliberate and kind and had a wonderful chuckle. Candy and Sherron and I stayed close until Candy and Sherron each passed, but we lost touch with Janice, who had gone off to nursing school in Connecticut. She and I tried to stay in touch, but in my life and possibly in hers, there were just too many other things demanding attention. Online in 2020, I learned that after a distinguished career in health care and health advocacy, Janice had become an Episcopal minister and furthered education and human rights within the church. I also learned that she had married a woman. And I learned that she had died eight years before, in 2012.

Sherron Jackson was in junior high, the junior high on 135th and St. Nicholas Avenue, at the foot of the hill on which the High School of Music and Art stood. Her school faced the avenue and the park, and along its side ran the broad expanse of 135th Street, which ended at the East River, where HBG members Hank and Peggy Dammond lived. On 135th was the YMCA memorialized in a Langston Hughes poem. Peggy and Hank's grandfather sat on the Y's board. With the Dunbar Apartments and the 135th Street corridor, I walked history I didn't yet know, was allowed into a past I ordinarily would not have been privy to.

At fourteen, Sherron could sit in a room where a few of us were also sitting. She'd clear her throat and sing: *This is a sermonette. Have you heard it yet? It tells you to love one another. Each man is your brother.* We would all stop what we were doing to listen. We didn't sing along. We never made a fuss. We let her be like that, among us, singing, her eyes explosive.

Walking to a meeting at St. Philip's Church, Sherron might say, "I went by the bookstore." Run by the Nation of Islam. "They want me to join. They say that is where I belong. They call me sister." She'd laugh in that same voice she used to sing. Muscular. Suave. Assured. And then we'd get to the church and we would pitch, passionate junior high school, high school, and college students, mostly Black, about half from outside Harlem, our idea for an organizing project. When the church people said they'd get back to us, Sherron might challenge them, or Peggy Dammond might speak up in her Dalton private school voice. When the church people shut us down, despite Sherron and Peg, Janice Robinson might speak up in her measured way. As we pleaded, probably overstating our case, and perhaps a touch arrogant, we shared the room with Peg's great-great-grandmother, Ellen Craft, an enslaved woman so white-skinned she could board a railroad train headed out of the south disguised as a white man and pass, and her dark-skinned husband William could pass as her personal servant. We were cocky. We were becoming tied to who we were when we were together.

We entered Sherron's apartment through a heavily locked door. The small square kitchen with its grated air shaft window was across from the front door. Sherron and I had shared so much at the table in that room: her home life with Sweetheart, the godmother who was raising her; my family in the Village. I never went beyond the kitchen, was never invited to, with most of the apartment, so much of Sherron's life, beyond my sight. Though in her early teens, Sherron performed adult tasks in the world for Sweetheart, so she and I might walk to a different Harlem neighborhood to the pork store. Pork store. At least one year, when things were rough at home, Sherron spent Thanksgiving with my mother, my sister, and me. I felt utterly at home with her; though I knew in my head from remarks passed at parties and in the streets, that white people were the enemy to many Black people. With good reason. Several of us had read C. Eric Lincoln's *The Black Muslims in America*, or read parts of it, as it was a long book and we were very young. I was confused about what racist violence meant for me. Emmett Till, just a few years older than I, and by now half a decade since his death. And Charity. Racism was a chasm. Looking back, the love—throwing around a word that should not be used lightly, but when it is there, it should be acknowledged, because acknowledging true love is rare, even among rambunctious teenagers. Our optimism about change, the confidence that we could understand and figure out how to fix things, was a break with the usual of the 1950s.

The autumn I went south with SNCC, Sherron was a freshman at the High School of Music and Art. She wrote me sarcastic and curiosity-filled letters, on paper in envelopes, sent through the US Postal Service and delivered to the three-room Freedom House at 504 South Madison Street. That autumn, without explanation, she told my former history teacher, Ira Marienhoff, that she was my younger sister—she brown-skinned African American and I ivory-skinned Jewish. She was the first student at Music and Art to have an Afro. That is now hard to imagine: *the first Afro in an entire high school*. What that must have meant as assertion to Sherron, and what it must have meant to her classmates. She had joined the Nation of Islam and in her teens was doing the research behind some of the speeches of Minister Malcolm X.

Not long before Minister Malcolm's death, she joined his party on a trip to Africa. Returned, she spent a night at our Brooklyn apartment, kneeling at sunrise to pray on my mother's rug. In a couple of years she would work with Harlem Youth Opportunities Unlimited (HARYOU), working on *Youth in the Ghetto: A Study of the Consequences of Powerlessness and a Blueprint for Change*, a document produced through participatory research; in her later working life, she worked with youth through the Urban League's Street Academy, then as a policy person in the David Dinkins administration, and last in the office of Randi Weingarten at the American Federation of Teachers. In the seventies, after the death of Minister Malcolm, she joined a traditional Muslim congregation, married, had a daughter, and changed her name to Amina Abdur Rahman, during the years when I was in New Mexico, Detroit, and West Virginia. Amina named her daughter Sabra. I knew *sabra* was the Israeli name for a cactus, tough on the outside and sweet on the inside. In Arabic, the name can mean perseverance or persistence. Had Amina intentionally chosen a name with both Arabic and Israeli roots? Probably. She had knelt in my mother's Brooklyn living room to say her sunrise prayers. She had claimed me to my history teacher. We had chosen one another, again, after my mother's death, after the sixties had passed.

. . .

In the many-storied, glass-fronted NCCJ headquarters, on an upper floor where we congregated, there was the director, a man, and there were two or three others, men and a woman, who worked with us; they had other jobs teaching in public schools or colleges. They mentored us, asked us questions in such a way that in answering we could learn to trust our judgment. We learned how to run meetings, how to listen to community people, how to show up. We talked *a lot*. We read C. Wright Mills and Michael Harrington. Listened to the LP of Carl Reiner and Mel Brooks and to Oscar Brown Jr. singing about "Rags and Old Iron" and to Miriam Makeba doing her miraculous *click*! Went in a pack to movies like *Lilies of the Field* and *Never on Sunday*, afterward dancing like Zorba the Greek on the sidewalk. We were mostly Black, young, adventurous, each of us stepping outside the families that had raised us. We were in the streets, dragging home bone-tired but still having to finish our homework; we were my first family outside my birth family. Some nights one or another of us would go home with another of us, for safety on the subway or bus or through dark streets with men who made those noises, went home with one another to be together. I remember kitchens and corridors and the sound of apartment doors scraping open. I remember the disconnect the following morning of French class or math class or those steps through the park.

An adult who bridged my experience from NCCJ to SNCC was "Dr. Bob" Johnson, an Antioch College professor on staff at the Brotherhood Camp. Dr. Bob was the son of Dr. Charles Johnson, Black educator, sociologist, and former President of Fisk University in Nashville. I had never heard of Fisk and maybe had not known there were HBCUs, or historically Black colleges and universities. Soon I would meet people from other HBCUs, especially students from Howard University in Washington, DC. Again, as a white girl, my universe expanded. I learned of the Fisk Jubilee Singers. I learned of the Nashville Movement, where SNCC leaders like Diane Nash, John Lewis, Cordell Reagon, and Marion Barry came of age.

Maybe it was Sherron—there we were, calling one another "Sis." We did it in the streets and on the subways and in coffee shops. We called one another's parents "Mommie" and "Daddy." Candy's mother, Theodora, became Mommie T.

We laughed loudly. We were teenagers. We were open to one another.

We developed an analysis of power and a distrust of authority, specifically of government officials who lived too comfortably with injustice. We were death on the unfair. We didn't even have to talk about how race was at the bottom of everything. We wanted nothing to do with accommodation. We loved our own defiance. We loved one another.

I'm not sure what we accomplished in terms of housing injustice in New York City. We learned a lot, but I don't remember lobbying or marching or attending tenants' meetings. We were too young to vote. Thanks to Dr. Bob and others, I was pointed toward the study of sociology, the study of power, which we insisted we must understand. As people, we learned about trust and relationships. We learned one another. Some of us went on to college, some didn't. Some of us became community activists and several pursued lifelong careers of community service and rights advocacy.

There was a *but* (or was it an *and*?) to this "We Shall Overcome" exuberance. Race. Othering. That it was everywhere. That it was sneaky. That it was not going to go away just because a few teenagers had figured it out. I was only six when people had chalked the sidewalk outside our apartment. This had made my mother angry in a way that almost embarrassed me and also made me feel tender toward her and toward us. She had scrubbed away the words before Charity went out, because the words were hurtful and shameful. *Oh, they're just angry about Ethiopia*, my mother would say. I asked what she meant; she nodded toward the funeral home with an Italian name. *The Ethiopians humiliated the Italians, humiliated them*, she said. One of the tiny accretions in the formation of my self, tempered by the presence—always—of Charity in my white child's existence. When we lived in Haiti, the people of our household were called *les americaines*. I knew that this word denoted we were female. From the faces of some who said *les americaines*, I understood they were saying, *You know the ones. A white woman and a Black woman. And two little white girls and no man*. Occasionally, when we were older, my sister and I were accosted by kids who called us shameful names that had to do with Charity.

I was in high school when Charity took a teaching job in Westchester County and moved to Manhattan's Upper West Side to be closer to her rides. She didn't drive. The grown-ups were not telling us everything; it was an honorable breakup, I now think, but one-sided, Charity's choice.

In September, before I began Barnard College, my mother, sister, and I moved to Brooklyn, where rents were cheaper. The last day on Jane Street, the play street, my mother and I loaded the final items into our car. In the late afternoon, tired and grubby, we paused at the Hudson Street end of Jane. It was hot and our windows were rolled down. As we waited to turn left, Jimmy, with whom Shai and I had roller-skated, came to the same corner on foot. He bent down into the driver's side window and I started to say goodbye. He spit in my mother's face and walked away. She wiped her face—the spittle was slimy, so she wiped her hand on her pants—and made the left turn. Did he spit because of long-standing contempt, because of his and others' contempt for an all-female and mixed-race household? *Les americaines.*

Sherron sang in our midst, *White man's heaven is a Black man's hell.* I learned I could breathe in that moment, "White Man's Heaven Is a Black Man's Hell," trusting us to be us in that moment, but at the same time—unease? Fear for myself? Fear for my new self? For our collective selves?

On weekends, there were dark rooms at parties, cigarettes and alcohol, and either listening or holding my own in conversation, feeling glittery except that night an older student was talking with Sherron and a couple of others in a circle around him and when I approached, he shut the conversation down, but I could do that, keep breathing, and move away to mingle and laugh, but when people began to dance, I held back, even as Candy sank into the music. I felt awkward, though I had loved to dance in childhood, had loved being within music. Because: Charity Bailey. Because: Haitian drums at night in the hills. I thought at the time, and for decades, that this awkwardness was because I was white, or more precisely because I was feeling white, my body a declaration of awkward, no-rhythm, uncool *whiteness*. This may have been the case, but decades later, I see also that the difference that was troubling, perhaps even embarrassing, was my own queerness that I had not yet acknowledged to myself.

What did I think and feel when I was teased by Candy and Sherron and Brenda for offering to fry chicken for a day trip? Brenda cackled immoderately. I can only imagine from this distance, but I think I was hurt, though not devastated. What I remember of that evening—we would all sleep at Candy's and board the boat together in the morning—is a sense of *hmmm*. It was in the intimacy of Candy's family's tiny kitchen, from which two adults and four children were fed. We were going to Candy's and my second Brotherhood Camp, Sherron and Brenda's first, on a day boat up the Hudson River. I think what I felt that night was that I was safe; that I was with people who loved me and whom I loved. I laughed. And I shut up. Not shut up like I had suffered egregious abuse but like I was processing, thinking what Brenda had said might be true and that, look, I probably didn't make great fried chicken; in fact, I probably made sautéed chicken and not fried at all, because I had learned from Charity, a New Englander, who never fried anything except occasional Sunday crullers. I felt like someone who was learning to be necessarily uncomfortable.

When Sherron sang in her velvet voice, in the midst of a handful of us, "A White Man's Heaven Is a Black Man's Hell"? My feelings were more complicated than when it was about me and fried chicken. I knew there was a bookstore in Harlem, or maybe it was a restaurant, or maybe it was both, associated with the Nation of Islam. I remember the nation's famous bean pie being mentioned, but that may be a memory of a different time collaged onto "A White Man's Heaven Is a Black Man's Hell." I had no idea what a bean pie might be. I knew people at the bookstore were urging Sherron to join the nation. Made sense. But then, worrying in the night: would Sherron stop wanting to be around if I were there? Later, when Candy and her husband spoke about moving to a Republic of New Africa, perhaps in Alabama, I did sink into despair, even as I accused myself of being self-indulgent and *white*. Not ready to tell myself: *Well, you are white.* Thinking I was an *exemplary* white person. And Jewish, so *not quite* white.

Groping toward the question: what right did I have to be in a Black space?

Maybe something early and formative was at play. I was raised in a school where children were listened to and respected. I didn't have the startled defense reflexes of a child raised in a hostile (maybe only passively hostile) environment where, from an early age, she felt she must defend herself. Maybe? Maybe not. In high school, as an art student, I learned to accept critiques and comments on my work without reflexively defending myself. For one thing, I (private me, inside the public me) did not have to do what my classmates suggested, and for another, they often had insights that hadn't occurred to me, although sometimes they said a lot of words with no content and I learned to identify these (some of the time) and ignore them; these critiques applied to my work, which was me. I think this helped me listen receptively in arenas outside the art studio; I'm grateful for this training. A caveat: when I reached grad school, as a creative writing student, in workshop I received helpful criticism of my work, but I did also see critiques of others' work that were nothing less than bloodletting. I did not have, still do not have, the skills to deal with bloodletting. Although it didn't occur to me in my teens that it was relevant, I was walking around as a survivor of child sexual abuse. This term had not yet entered popular usage. I had no name for what had happened to me and I had no idea what *normal* children might or might not have experienced, just as I had no language to acknowledge that my mother Eunice was on occasion verbally harsh, perhaps even abusive. It was complicated, who each of us was. And is.

We lived on Jane Street. West Fourth Street cut from Washington Square Park through the breadth of the Village, crossing Jane Street. I could walk a half mile east and south on West Fourth to the apartment of Dr. Bob Johnson. My last autumn in high school, I often did so. It would still be warm. I'd walk along, confident in the streets of my childhood, past the laundromat, across Bank Street where my best friend Katie lived, past the studio where my sister studied dance, almost to Seventh Avenue. Dr. Bob's apartment, which overlooked West Fourth, was a hub for SNCC people. There I met Diane Nash and Chuck McDew and Charlie Jones. I had seen Diane's picture in *Newsweek*: a young woman in a shirtwaist dress on the phone, telling Robert Kennedy, *No*, she would not stop the Freedom Rides. She was a few years older than I, soft spoken but steely-willed. She had come to New York to raise money and to get the word out about McComb, Mississippi. That autumn, almost the entire body of SNCC field secretaries had gone to McComb. Diane had been the only woman among them. Not long after, hundreds of Black students had marched in the rural heart of the Magnolia State. The repercussions after SNCC's arrival were immediate. Local activist Herbert Lee, who had welcomed SNCC and taken Bob Moses into his home, was shot and killed in the street in broad daylight by Mississippi state representative Eugene Hurst. Diane Nash, in Dr. Bob's apartment, a college-age girl. I listened to her. I watched her. I couldn't believe I might be in the same room as she. And she was returning to McComb. I went with others to see her safely onto her plane. We walked onto the tarmac. I watched her, young, slim, the most determined person I had ever met, climb the metal steps and step into the Delta plane. A few minutes later, she was gone, but a connection, a personal connection, had been forged between me and a specific place, specific people, in the Deep South.

I had graduated from high school and was attending Barnard. I was learning how to be a Barnard student. I was making the commute with an armload of books, often getting home late at night. "Interested in people," I had signed up for a psychology class, only to discover psychology, at least for freshmen at Barnard, had little to do with people and everything to do with numbers. This was not my only setback that first semester. Between the childhood year in Haiti and my hard work over many years of school, I was proficient in French, so proficient I placed out of French language classes and was allowed to sign up for French literature. In French. Great, right? *No.* The French professor from France spoke so fast, her words whizzed past. I was lucky to catch a syllable here and there, filling in the missing parts as best I could. I had no French critical literary vocabulary. I cried when I went to my advisor and asked to drop the class. But it was not just that I was having to conjure missing French words. I was coming home to my mother, who was thrilled that I would school myself out of financial hardship. I was coming home to an entirely different apartment from my childhood home in the Village. An apartment in which Charity did not live, had never lived. We had moved because my mother could no longer afford Greenwich Village. Not only were there missing words here, in this story of Charity's move as geographic convenience, there were heart holes, but still I carried my books back and forth from Barnard in Manhattan to the small new apartment in Brooklyn. No words for this separation from everything about my childhood, so much of what I thought I was, to a different borough. There was still Dr. Bob's apartment above West Fourth Street. There were evenings with SNCC people. There were Candy and Sherron. A subway ride distant.

The night before Christmas break, I received a phone call: Would I go on a sit-in on the Eastern Shore of Maryland. In two days. I said yes.

My sister and I had always spent Christmas Eve with our father in his chilly English basement on East Tenth Street, with him and the Siamese cat Igor and the shrunken-sized poodle Gigi. Everything about him shrunken and cold. Most years, after dinner and the modest gluttony of present opening, he walked us out to get in the car with our mother and Charity. We caroled friends of Charity's in Harlem and then to the Heilbroners' in the Village. It had been so since we were very young. The Heilbroners' apartment glowed from the lit candles on the eight-foot tree, the pink and gold of damask. Inga, the wife, calling us *Darling* and petting us, and even the German grandmother (as opposed to Fritz, who was German Jewish), who in November baked her Christmas pfefferneusse, who could be a white-haired fury (Inga had found missing kitchen knives under her mother's mattress), who each year whistled the carol "Silent Night" all the way through, a near-celestial sound.

Instead, on December 23, 1961, my mother drove me to the Port Authority Bus Terminal, where hundreds of us bought tickets to other places and where hundreds more arrived. It was cavernous and noisy and dirty, and it always seemed like either boarding the bus to your destination or missing the bus entirely was a possibility. My mother waited with me for the bus to Baltimore, a southern city neither of us had been to. I stepped up into the bus without a thought for my sister, who would go to our father's without me. Having mothered two children, my heart goes out to my mother, whom I left standing on the concrete platform as the bus powered up. We would cross under the Hudson River, drive into Jersey. Never *New* Jersey. I journeyed into the Movement. When SNCC people said "the Movement," there was a barely perceptible pause and drop in our voices, as we named our world, our reason for being, our family, a specific entity so large and embracing, it deserved an upper case *M*, despite grammatical convention.

Hours later, the driver announced Baltimore. We were on the outskirts. I was embarrassed to ask: Would there be a downtown terminal? What if there wasn't? What if Baltimore was just a series of stops outside convenience stores on streets sloping downward until, without warning, we turned upward and left Baltimore behind? Where would I be? I got off with my overnight case, thinking it looked very prissy, maybe meaning *white*. I found the phone number I was to call. When I said where I was, I knew instantly I was in the wrong place, but after a wait on the sidewalk, a car pulled up. I was easy to spot.

I climbed into the car and was greeted with enthusiasm and whisked to an office. A coalition, including the Baltimore Nonviolent Action Group and SNCC, was involved in the planned sit-in. There were two SNCC organizers: Reggie Robinson, who was Black, from Baltimore and Bill Hansen, white, a former Freedom Rider from Ohio. We received desultory training in nonviolent resistance. Reggie had a beautiful laugh and a gleaming smile. Peggy Dammond and her brother Hank from HBG arrived. We were waiting on the go-ahead to hit the road. There was a lot of waiting around in the Movement. It was decided we would arrive in Crisfield too late if we left that afternoon, so we were parceled out to spend the night with local people. Peg and Hank and I went home with Diane Ostrowski. And none of this day of anticipation and dread would turn out to be as big a surprise as Reggie, the man with the beautiful laugh and the gleaming smile in his dark and brilliant face.

The next day, when the convoy of cars pulled up out front, we knew this was *it*. The drivers were older Black men. We were assigned to small groups and would be confined for the duration to our assigned cars. The leader, Reggie, managed to sit beside me and for all the ride, I listened to his voice, rising from a chest I so wanted to lean against. There were no plans to stop. It would be just the few of us in our car, riding past land and houses and people we would never meet. The Eastern Shore was segregated to the max. We would ride hours—across the bay and then down the Eastern Shore past fields and towns to Crisfield, home to Governor J. Millard Tawes. By dusk, when we reached Crisfield, lights would have come on in the houses we passed. In the car, we talked strategy. We learned the plan. We would sit in. We would probably be arrested. We would go to jail. The Chesapeake Bay Bridge spun out over the water, rising toward the sky, the far end barely visible. Although it was the bay and technically not the ocean, I felt that surge I feel when I see boundless water. For 24 hours we'd been in a noisy crowd. Eating from bags of popcorn, eating fries that were lying about. Talking. Calling home. Eating hot chicken from a local place.

Crisfield is a town on the mostly enclosed but also enormous body of the Chesapeake Bay. We filed out of the cars and tramped through the twilight. I was about to step into the newspaper photos and TV news clips I'd seen, sit-inners at lunch counters, sometimes spat on, sometimes having live cigarettes put out on the tender skin at their napes, sometimes pushed to the floor to be kicked or stomped. *Curl up around your belly. Shield and embrace your head with your arms.*

How much planning and support must have gone into this moment when a dozen or so of us approached the City Diner. There were the men who drove us, gassing up their cars and making sure the vehicles were roadworthy, the men prepared to drive back through the night to Baltimore once the sit-in had happened. There were the phone calls to be made after we were arrested—to the press, to the office in Baltimore, to SNCC in Atlanta, to our families, I imagine to a lawyer standing by. If things went badly, there would be other steps to take.

We walked into the cold dusk.

The café door with its swinging "open" sign admitted us to the hush of silenced conversation and the movement of stilling bodies. Everyone knew instantly what this was, a tableau in which each of us had an ordained role. We filed in and took seats at the counter. We were asked to leave. We did not. The manager flipped the sign on the door to CLOSED and called the police. I don't know how long it took for the cops to arrive, though I do know it felt like forever, in that place where silverware was not clinking against china, where the cook stared through the pass-through window, where there must have been Black workers in the kitchen. Where the slightest change in equilibrium as we sat at the counter could have unleashed the white people at our backs.

We began to mutter to one another, little bits of barely voiced words, passing up and down the line.

Reggie and I, without words, which would have been dangerous, answered the question we had toyed with all afternoon: *Might we perhaps be flirting with one another?* And in code, the answer passed between us: *As a matter of fact, yes, we were. Flirting with one another.*

The police arrived with a fanfare of sirens.

We sang our fool hearts out, freedom songs all the way to jail, a stone block building that looked ancient, with three small windows on the second floor, two windows on the first floor flanking the door. We five women were placed in a cell, the floor and walls, as I remember, concrete, the beds metal bunks. The five men were across the hall. Grated openings in the cell doors allowed us to yell or sing to one another. We decided as a group that we would fast. We went to bed. I had never been on the Eastern Shore of Maryland at the butt end of the mid-Atlantic seaboard; I only knew two of the four women in the cell. I had never lain down in a bunkbed in a room with a concrete floor. I had never been locked up. My sister would unpack her Christmas stocking at our father's; its shower of pistachios would stain her fingertips pink. My mothers and my sister would gather in the candlelight at the Heilbroners'. Muni would whistle "Silent Night."

Past midnight, I woke to singing. Below us, a handful of men and women, their faces craning up toward us, held candles and sang carols. In the dark, they looked small, and their voices were soft. They were faculty from the nearby HBCU. After we went back to bed, Peggy, Bonnie Kilston, Angeline Butler, who was a friend of Peg's, and Diane Ostrowski from Baltimore. We must have talked in the dark, five young women not quite or barely into our twenties. I must have wondered about my mother, who would have received a phone call from a stranger. I must have thought about Reggie, whose voice had rung out above the others' as our cells sang across the corridor to one another.

Reggie bailed out to organize local support and to publicize our case. This in the days when telephones and shoe leather were the technology. A week later, we were bailed out. We boarded a bus loaded with Baltimore supporters and were driven to a Black church in nearby Cambridge, where hundreds had gathered. This is the work that had been done while we stayed in jail. The Black community on the Eastern Shore of Maryland had a long and proud history of civic engagement. They had voted and participated in segregated local government since the 1800s; they owned businesses. They had set down long roots. Churches and schools and even an HBCU in Princess Anne.

That was my first mass meeting. The sound and motion, the singing, the exhortations—what a rush. Those of us who had fasted must have been fed; maybe the community had prepared food for everyone. Perhaps those professors who had sung to us were there. When the last song was sung and the last "amen" called out, we boarded the bus and were driven through the night of the Eastern Shore toward Baltimore. Reggie and I sat together, talking and laughing and napping and kissing through the hours, until we crossed the bridge back over the Chesapeake Bay, retracing our route from the time before our arrest. The sun rose as we descended the slow curve of the bridge to earth, the sun at our backs and everything—everything—light filled before us.

One of SNCC's strengths was its organizers' ability to tap existing community resistance and struggle. As the months unfolded on the Eastern Shore, local students took up the banner. Elementary school children organized their own march, despite their elders' misgivings. Gloria Richardson followed her high school daughters into the struggle to become one of the most defiant, courageous, and principled leaders of the era. She was a child of the St. Clair family, business people who had participated in civic life in Cambridge since the 1800s. She had attended Howard University in DC. She was a single mother. Gloria was not to be trifled with. There are photos of her brushing aside the blade of a National Guard bayonet pointed at her face. There are tales of her taking on the Kennedy brothers, president and attorney general, both. Cambridge was less than a hundred miles from DC, too close to the nation's capital for the establishment to rest easy with turbulence and Gloria Richardson at their back door. The participation and leadership of local people was as important everywhere in the South as it was on the Eastern Shore; equally critical across the South was the unwavering, informed, and brave work of women like Gloria Richardson and the women I would meet in Southwest Georgia.

That spring, by the time we returned for our day in court, newspapers and television had broadcast a massive movement in full swing: the Cambridge Nonviolent Action Group, or CNAC, which was similar to both the group in Baltimore and the Nonviolent Action Group, or NAG, at Howard University. The National Guard would spend eighteen months in Cambridge to quell the white violence that had been met with armed Black resistance.

This movement grew out of the community, combined with the work of Reggie Robinson and Bill Hansen. SNCC organizers became icons of that struggle and that time; Reggie exemplified that icon. He came from a Black working-class family in Baltimore. He had been enrolled in business college when he joined SNCC. He was an exuberant Black man in his early twenties. He could stay up half the night drinking bourbon and shooting the breeze with old-timers. He could tell a good story, even as he was helping to rewrite the story of Civil Rights in the United States. He knew the freedom songs and the old hymns. Reggie had the organizing know-how to offer support and guidance on everything from managing a mass march to mobilizing national coverage. Like all SNCC workers, he kept a paper address book worth its weight in gold with entries crossed out and written over. He was meticulous in the records he kept, tireless in working the job: finding and encouraging local supporters. He could size you up, which is to say he could see you in your entirety.

That spring of 1962, it was back to juggling Harlem meetings and SNCC meetings, juggling home in Brooklyn and Barnard, that hour-plus subway ride out of Brooklyn, through the midsection of Manhattan, to 116th Street. That semester, I dropped the statistically minded psychology sequence and took my first sociology class. It was in the Sociology Department at Barnard that I first read Karl Marx. And C. Wright Mills. And Cash's *The Mind of the South*, this last one a big fat nothing to me. During my years in the department, because of what was happening in the streets and jailhouses of the United States, and because of my growing involvement in Harlem and in the South, I came to see that I could not study society and social structure without considering power. I saw how some academics shied away from the subject of power, as if considering it were in poor taste, allowing them to sidestep questions of justice and racial equity.

Midspring of my freshman year, Peg Dammond, Angeline Butler, Bonnie Kilston, and I returned to the Eastern Shore for our trial. We stayed with several generations of the St. Clairs, the Black historic activist family. The trial was *pro forma* and resulted in our being free to leave. As in the arrest, there were bail-related arrangements; the Civil Rights Movement was in part a system of financial and bureaucratic relationships handled by older community members, without which the Movement could not have existed.

What I remember from our trial, what I will never forget, is the arrival of our lawyer, Juanita Mitchell. The courtroom was small and old-boy comfy. Mrs. Mitchell was the first African American woman to practice law in Maryland. I didn't know it at the time, though I could guess the essence of this from her demeanor, but Mrs. Mitchell was the wife of Clarence M. Mitchell Jr., a prominent leader in the state's NAACP. She would become the mother of two state senators and the grandmother of another. Like the St. Clairs on the Eastern Shore and others in every southern state, she was a member of a Black bourgeoisie that often supported and underwrote the Movement. She would have been anathema to many if not all of the white men in that courtroom.

When Mrs. Mitchell arrived, all eyes were upon her. I'm pretty sure she wore a hat. I remember with certainty how she removed her long gloves, loosening the fingers one by one, with all of our attention riveted upon her.

SNCC: Been Down into the South

> Never been to heaven, but I've been told—
> been down into the South—
> Folks up there both Black and white—
> been down into the South.
> Hallelujah, Freedom—
> been down into the South.
> —Traditional, adapted as a 1960s freedom song

In the summer of 1962, Claude Sitton of the *New York Times* attended a mass meeting at Mount Olive Baptist Church in Sasser in Southwest Georgia. The *Times* published his account, a portrait of state-supported white vigilantism. Sheriff Z. T. Mathews and a band of lawmen, and a hostile crowd of white people, intruded upon the mass meeting. At least one of the sheriff's party ostentatiously fingered a holstered weapon; one smoked within the sanctuary. The sheriff strutted up and down, singling out members of the congregation for verbal abuse, and at one point, in classic red-baiting form, accused the Movement of being willing to vote for Castro or Khrushchev (Claude Sitton, *New York Times*, July 27, 1962). This church and two others were soon set on fire and burned to the ground by hostile whites.

I decided to go south that autumn. My decision was both abrupt and a long time coming. Peggy Dammond had gone to Southwest Georgia that summer. Candy and I had been firm: we were northern organizers—city organizers—period. We were working summer jobs and often spoke to one another by phone during the day, and we regularly met one another after work for meetings or just to grab a bite, often pancakes, and sometimes to go to a movie.

That summer I worked at a travel agency across Forty-Second Street from the public library, the one with the guardian lions, the one where in high school I had snuck in to read Gordon Allport on the nature of prejudice and Gunnar Myrdal's 1944 book *An American Dilemma: The Negro Problem and American Democracy*. These library visits were illicit because I was still in high school. They lasted into dark night. I would work in a whispering clump of Music and Art students, there in an adult library, with its high ceilings and murky light, with the invisible weight of the stacks. At first, I didn't understand the books at least half the time; figuring them out was fun. Candy and I shared the excitement of discovering concepts and histories we had not known. Integral to that youngness, that pleasure of discovery, that business of being inside a cavernous and complex building filled with the past, was the night a couple of classmates and I saw John F. Kennedy's cavalcade flick by. We knew from the radio that he would travel Forty-Second Street at a particular time. Before that time, we returned our books and made our way outdoors. It was dark, a deserted business district. It began to rain. A few cars whisked by soundlessly, their headlights big in the rain. And were gone. "We saw the president," we said. "Maybe it wasn't," someone said. "Nah. It was." We were getting wetter. We had long trips home. "Wow. The president," we said. Less than two years later, I was heading south.

My father told my sister, "Faith is leaving me." His response to my going south.

The uncle who had abused my mother when she was a child told her, "Come on, Euni, you can tell me. This going south business. Are you sending Faith away because she's pregnant?"

I arranged a year's leave from Barnard.

I made a farewell visit to Charity.

I spent a night in Candy's family's apartment in the Dunbar. That night, Candy's father was due to return from his annual trip south. In Candy's room with the trundle bed she had shared with her older sister, who was now a mother a few buildings away—with Candy, there was always more than one reality present—we heard him arrive.

"Don't tell Daddy about Georgia, let me do it after you leave," she said. He was a cipher to me, frequently gone to his job in subway tollbooths and at union headquarters but a looming presence nevertheless. *Daddy.* "He's gonna be so mad," Candy said. Because I was part of his family. Because the South. Because I can see with twenty-twenty hindsight, he had spent his life ensuring his family did not have to suffer the outrages of the South. And yet he went back there yearly. *Home.*

"Girls," Mommie T called.

"Come on," Candy said, stubbing out her cigarette.

He had brought home a paper sack filled with assorted stockings from a mill in North Carolina. He pulled some of the light-colored pairs from the jumble and gave them to me. I knew I must not say I never wore stockings or that these were at least a micro shade too light, even for white me. I said *thank you.*

A few days later, Candy came with my family to the airport.

"Don't let any man talk you into going to a hotel when you get to Atlanta," my mother said.

My sister Shai said almost nothing but stood straight-backed like a sentinel. Candy said, "Don't get killed."

"I won't."

"You goddamn well better not."

When I arrived in Atlanta, I had to choose a cab. I wasn't going to accept a cab driver's offer to take me to a hotel. And where in my mother's life had that advice come from? At the curb, there were cabs driven by white men and cabs driven by Black men. None of them were named the White Supremacist Cab Co. or the Right-On Black Cab. What to do? A white driver asked me where I was headed. When I gave him my friend Bobbi Yancey's address, he didn't flinch. He had another passenger, another white woman. I was not used to sharing cabs with anyone. It was approaching midnight. Was Atlanta always this dark at night? *You goddamn well better not.* I was in the South. A night with

Bobbi and Mary King and then a Greyhound. In addition to SNCC staff, the police in Albany would be waiting for me.

My new home would be the SNCC Freedom House, three small rooms: a front room with a couch where the men slept and a kitchen/office with shelves for papers, a kerosene cookstove, and an office corner with a picnic table and benches. Penny Patch and I would sleep in the back room, our bed covered in donated family quilts. Two white girls working to reverse the legacy of segregated racism, warmed by covers pieced by many hands with fabrics from the daily lives of Black Albany, Georgia.

At nineteen years old and new to Southwest Georgia, doing work for which I felt unprepared, letters from home kept me grounded. My mother wrote often, grateful for my letters and urging me to stay sweet and honest with her, that nothing that happened to me could be worse than her imaginings.

My seventeen-year-old sister, a high school senior, wrote of her work for SNCC in New York. Her letters document SNCC's earliest organizational presence in New York City in an office shared with the War Resisters League. She casually refers to "Miss Baker," the influential and beloved SNCC mentor and advisor. Shai's letters give a sense of SNCC outside the South and document the early support of well-known figures like Ossie Davis, Robert Nemiroff, and Theodore Bikel, among others. Although she doesn't mention him in the letter below, Harry Belafonte was a generous and stalwart supporter. In my sister's mention of Penny Patch, I can see the flow of SNCC workers from north to south and back south again, depending on family or academic obligations. Shai suggests the displacement of those who went south and returned to prior northern existences. As well as her work for SNCC, Shai's letters were filled with her life as a dance student at Public High School of Performing Arts, theater life, singing lessons, the life of a late teen in worldly city.

Dear Cif,

I am in our office alone. Miss Baker has just gone home and Bill Mahoney has left to go to the retreat, so now I'm taking off time to write you.

Our Christmas was not the best, but it was tolerable. I, as usual, went to Daddy's on X'mas eve, but this time with Allie, so it wasn't too bad. Then the Mule and I went to the Heilbroners' with Ma, that was fun.

Before I start any real kind of news, I want you to know that I have not forgotten that I am your sister, and that I love you, but as I'm sure you know, writing time is quite scarce. BUT I do love you, honest.

The office here is a cute little thing, not adequate but cute. Bill and I work here most of the time alone, with Miss Baker in and out. Oh yes, before I forget, Miss Baker always asks after you. Our main project at the moment is to get the rally on its feet. The whole project was looking pretty slim, but a Mr. Nemiroff has offered his assistance in the struggle. He's a big name in show biz, a good one. We hope that he will be finding most of the talent for our show. Tonight I and Miss Baker will be meeting with him, Theodore Bikel, Ossie Davis, and others to decide who we want for the show.

Penny called me the other day. She sounds so lonely and depressed. We are going to meet tomorrow after a class of mine. I think I am going to drag her here to work.

I went to church with Carola and Matteo. I went to see "The Lion" with the Mule. We liked it. Carola and Matteo are going on tour in a week for three months, so I will take one more singing lesson a week until they get back. Allie is going to teach at Northwestern this January, for two years. He will be getting his masters while he teaches. I spoke to the Mule's mother last night, she has a nice voice. I spoke to the Mule's grand aunt last night. She sounds nice too. Daddy is going to Switzerland. Aunt Pat and Aunt Marg are going to Europe next month.

Am late.

Love,
Ciffee

In Southwest Georgia, the tent at Sasser was sacred space, a musty canvas tent with wood poles, rickety metal folding chairs on uneven ground, and a kerosene lamp hanging from a crossbar. Do you know how sweet kerosene can smell? The tent stood on the ground of a Black movement church that had been burned by the Klan.

We arrived at mass meetings—in the yellow-and-black Nash Rambler, Rev. Wells's aquamarine-and-cream sedan, Carolyn Daniels's dreamboat Chevy Biscayne in red and white, and assorted pickups and cars. We drove through two-lane crossroads in the dark and out the dirt track to park in the field, a jumble of cars on the stubble. Was there an old chimney or a set of brick steps that had once led up to the destroyed church? One night during hog-slaughtering season, a family gave out barbecue sandwiches from bulging, grease-marked grocery sacks. The pork, soft and sweet, oozing with sauce, was wrapped in slices of white bread. When I bit into mine, I bit into bone. There was a whole pork chop or rib in the sandwich. Bone to spit out. I don't know what others did with their bones, but I sucked mine dry and stuck them in my pocket and settled into the tent that held us against night raiders.

There was an order to the night. A lesson from the Citizenship School on what to expect when people went to the courthouse to register. The voices of the volunteer teachers opening a portal into a way of being that had not been present before. There were reports of trips to the courthouse, sometimes frightening if hostile whites had threatened. The new registrants speaking of what it had been like. Once, when I went to the courthouse with some women, a couple of them dipped snuff in the car. They offered me some and, unknowing, I accepted and just about blew my head off with the kick. I was ready for anything, if I could just catch my breath. I walked beside two Black women into the courthouse where minor mayhem ensued. The woman registrar sputtered. The sheriff strolled by. More and more white men nosed in. Every membrane in my nasal cavity shot flames into my brain. I didn't give a shit what happened. I hurt. My rash dip in the face of danger and my responsibility to the potential registrants was a mistake. What my mother Eunice would have called *self-indulgent*, an indelible connection between the burn of tobacco and danger. The sheriff announced the registrar's office was closing for lunch though it was only ten in the morning. Over the ride to take the two women back to the house in the field—peanuts? probably—the burn wore down to an ache like a toothache, reaching up into my skull occasionally to jerk on a tender thread.

The tent, heavy canvas suggestive of military campaigns, the kerosene lamp hanging at its heart, held us. That tent, with us inside it, stood on holy ground that had been violated but that we reconsecrated with our presence. It was so in the mass meetings in churches. It was so in staff meetings in the freedom house. It was so when we sat in the kerosene-streaked Freedom House kitchen talking, one on one or maybe three or four of us. It had been so with Candy and Amina in Harlem. The seriousness of being with one another, of taking our time and listening and not scoring points, these are things I'd been given by my mothers, Eunice and Charity, lessons I took with me into the field.

In a grocery store, two children overheard white men talking about burning a church. Hearsay of intended white violence regularly swept through the Black community. As a Yankee, I might have discounted the rumor, but for centuries such rumors had functioned to check Black demands for justice; they worked because, often enough, they were realized. After all, I had come to Southwest Georgia because three Movement churches had been torched. After all, Candy Keeling's *You goddamn well better not*. After all, even in Greenwich Village, rumors of intended acts against our household, all female, white and Black living as one, had shaken us.

In staff meeting, we decided Chico and Chatfield would try to trace the rumor to its source. Charley would call Anne Braden in Louisville. I knew she and her husband Carl were antiracist white people whose names SNCC people said with that slight drop of voice that meant: all honor due. Reggie Robinson and Bill Hansen had stayed with the Bradens in Louisville, organizing public accommodations demonstrations. I had spoken to Reggie late nights by way of their household phone. I didn't yet know that the Bradens had been harassed, threatened, and prosecuted in 1954 for helping a Black couple, Andrew and Charlotte Wade, buy a house in an all-white community covered by racially restrictive covenants, resulting in white violence, including a cross burning and a bombing. The Bradens had faced down racist red-baiting and a House Un-American Activities Committee (HUAC) shit show; as a consequence, Carl had served time in a federal prison. As my year in Georgia played out, I would learn how well-earned was the respect paid to Anne and Carl and the organization for which they worked, the Southern Conference Educational Fund, or SCEF, where Ella Baker also worked. The SCEF newspaper, *The Southern Patriot*, carried stories of southern struggle that no one else carried and was read not only in the South but across the United States. I also learned, in part around the issue of working with the Bradens, who were deemed *red* by some, that SNCC stood behind its policy to work with anyone who supported our work, regardless of political affiliation.

Anne Braden walked in the door at 504 South Madison Street, talking and smoking. I took a deep sniff. I missed cigarettes. She realized her mistake and put out her cigarette. Her Alabama drawl was as full of curlicues as her plume of smoke. Barely in the door and Anne's legal pad had come out. Her sharp brown eyes were on Chatfield as he spoke. Who? Where? When? What had the men said? And somewhere in there, she managed to say as an aside, "So you're Faith. Reggie's friend?" Sherrod said I was to ride with Anne to mass meeting. *Why me?* I could have asked, but I knew the answer. I was white. She was white. She had not stopped talking, except when listening to answers, when she became still, so still, those sharp eyes focused on the speaker. I was white, I knew that, but I wasn't sure I liked this woman and I hadn't asked her into my life, which was full already. I knew this was ill-mannered on my part, but that was how I met the woman who would become my mentor and a lifelong political friend. I could write a definitive set piece on Anne, tracing the decades of her work, but it is more true to let her consequence unfold moment by moment and year by year for the four-plus decades until her death in 2006.

Driving through dark Southwest Georgia to the tent in Sasser and back, Anne smoked nonstop. She cracked the triangular driver's-side window and flicked her ashes out with a practiced hand, all the while talking, talking, in that Alabama twang, the smoke flying out over the countryside behind us, past the lynching tree in Lee County and on to Terrell County, and the tent, heavy canvas smelling of everything damp that had ever happened in Sasser, Georgia, and the kerosene lamp swinging from the rafters. Across the tent, I could see Anne talking to a cluster of people. When a new person started to speak, she'd turn her head to look the person full in the face. She squatted down to listen to the two children who had heard the white man make the threat, listen with her eyes as well as her ears. We gathered in that tent, the separation between us and the land permeable. White men could come toward us at any time, drive the dirt track across the fields, their headlights boring through canvas.

Word traveled with Anne Braden to the southern movement: Anne Braden, a sole white woman on the road, leaving her husband Carl and her children in Louisville, but also carrying with her those family people and the world of the Movement, which included Jim Dombrowski, Ella Baker, C. T. Vivian, Mississippi SNCC people, and Georgia SNCC people. She heard with her ears and gathered with her eyes, spun onto her legal pad the story of two children who had heard a threat of a church burning, the stories of the adults in that community. Thought and talked about it driving back to Albany. Smoking and talking, going over what she had heard. During the long drive back to Louisville, perhaps driving all night long to see her children in the morning or to make a meeting scheduled for noon, she would go over it and over it, as if she were talking to someone. Back in Louisville, in the little house where my sweetheart had once stayed, she would sit down at the manual typewriter and write her story to appear with a photo in the *Southern Patriot*, the SCEF newspaper, read by thousands gathered onto a mailing list over many years, dating at least from the time Carl had been charged with sedition and sent to federal prison in the mid-1950s. I came to feel that community of activist readers was mine, those I had met and those I had not yet met.

In addition to her journalism, Anne wrote long letters. I mean typewritten, single-spaced, paragraph-after-paragraph letters, like she was sitting and talking with you, smoking and talking. She worried at ideas and events, searching out the implications for the fight against racism. As I remember her, that was always her focus: racism and the fight against it. She could worry a moment just about to death. I'm sure there are countless people like me with archives of those sprawling and at the same time razor-focused, analytical letters. Even as she was analytical and used her grasp of the history of race in this country to make her point, she was unvarying and unmoving in her devotion to what she felt was critical and morally right. She had grown up in a Christian Alabama family and she clung to those Christian values of love and human dignity. Having been tried in the struggle of selling a house in a "white" neighborhood to a Black family in the mid-1950s, having gone through the HUAC hearing into her and Carl's alleged communism, having lost her job at the so-called liberal Louisville paper, and despite Carl's time in federal prison, she did not lose sight of what we then called *brotherly love*. She could be quick to question those she thought in the wrong. Years later, at a meeting in Birmingham, someone began to sing, "We're in the same boat, brother." It was a popular thing at the time—we are all one in the struggle. "That is ridiculous," Anne burst out, saying the word *ridiculous* in her way of adding Alabama syllables as well as indignation to any English word. "We are *not* in the same boat. Black people suffer oppression more than any white person in this room or outside of it ever will."

Anne was part of a south-wide web of communication that got the word out across the South and also sent it on to the outside world. This communication was key to our survival. In 1962 and 1963, we communicated long distance with the Atlanta office by phoning there collect; Atlanta would refuse the call and immediately call us back. By the 1964 Mississippi Summer Project, SNCC was using WATS, or Wide Area Telephone Service lines. We felt *au courant* about this setup. Any of us could call the WATS line and the charges were automatically reversed to the Atlanta office. These lines were precursors to today's 800 numbers.

People in Atlanta, including Julian Bond and Dottie Zellner, worked on press releases. Nothing was computerized. We sent reports, letters, and press releases through the US Postal Service. Our mailing lists were hand typed and valued like treasure. In the New York office, in the summer of 1964, the mailing list was maintained and fiercely protected by Lucille Perlman and Trudy Orris, each of whom had a child or children in Mississippi. I know at least one SNCC person, Martha Prescod Norman Noonan, who still has her tattered SNCC address book with names crossed out, with addresses changed over and over, year after year. We sent out press releases like carrier pigeons. In the early sixties, Charles McDew often began his press releases about violence with the phrase "hobnailed boots of oppression." That's how I learned hobnailed boots were a thing, and it might have been the first time I encountered the word *oppression*, and with that word, my ability to analyze what was happening, the scope of my thinking, expanded. By the time I arrived in Georgia, the press list was substantial: specific newspaper people, newsrooms, United Press International, or UPI, and the Associated Press, or AP. We used the conventional news structure. In 1964, in the New York office, if we wanted an update on a potentially violent confrontation that hadn't yet been covered in the papers or on TV, we phoned the wire service and asked them to read us their story and they would. In that way, we could learn if there had been casualties or arrests.

Technology has changed in ways and at a pace we could not have imagined; our pride in the WATS line is kinda quaint. Communication may now be faster and wider, but we understood then that communication was critical to our safety and effectiveness; that the wider the circle we reached, the safer we were. Our communication was itself a political act.

Cars were another factor in our safety. In Southwest Georgia, we had the yellow-and-black Hornet, a donated Nash Rambler. The last Ramblers were produced in 1955, so in 1963 our car was not new and was subject to breakdowns in dangerous places. We never had spare cash. I can remember Sherrod stopping at a cheapo gas station on the way out of town. That night, we would cover twenty miles out to mass meeting and back. I can see Sherrod pumping exactly one dollar's worth of gas and unraveling a single dollar from the roll in his overall pocket.

Our cars carried us down every dirt road and every paved ribbon of two-lane road in Southwest Georgia, carried us to isolated wood houses and compounds of two or three houses. When we drove, we declared ourselves. We traveled visible from the highway, across flat, treeless fields, trailing behind us a plume of clay dust or black smoke if we were burning oil. We traveled at night, picked up in the headlights of the armed white men who sat in their cars or trucks at the crossroads where one white man's land butted up against another's. White people owned the land at the crossroads in Southwest Georgia. People talked about the crossroads, a watching place, a place where the road *to* crossed the road *from*. The public way we had to go to get from one place of organizing to another.

One night, driving home from mass meeting, the SNCC car had a flat tire. We stood beside the car in the dark. Sherrod insisted Penny and I change the tire by flashlight while he coached us. Soldiers needed to know how to change a tire. Every car that approached in the dark, its headlights washing over our group of vote workers, might be that one with some angry white men with energy to burn. Penny and I got the flat off and the new tire on. Sherrod checked that the lug nuts were tight and then we were heading toward home.

Sherrod insisted I get my driver's license. City girl, I was ungracious about it. Why should I spend my time learning to drive when I could be cranking out flyers on the mimeograph machine or canvassing; nevertheless, he took me out to practice and drove me to the Department of Motor Vehicles and dropped me off. The building was a squat cinder-block structure. When I opened the door, I was confronted with a room divided in half by a rope strung from the back to the front, where the workers sat at tables. There was a sign at the front of one line: *colored*. Another at the front of the other: *white*. I had not faced this physical choice of where to put my body. I had spent my time on the Black side of town, had ignored the bigger jigsaw puzzle of Albany, a town with white power secured by violence and white tradition. I knew no one in the room. It was just me and the choreography of segregation. I could make no other choice than the one I made. I joined the *colored* line. If I were lucky, my gold skin and dark curly hair might allow me to be coded as *colored*. Sherrod was already irked with me over this driving business; he would like this even less. I stood, isolated, afraid of the white people and apprehensive about Sherrod, moving with the crowd as the line inched forward. I have no idea what I did with my eyes. And then I was at the front. I was handed a form to complete and came to a second choice point. The form inquired: was I *colored* or *white*? I knew I was doing the wrong thing, but coming into that room of people who had done this all their lives, knowingly standing in the *wrong* line, it was inevitable that I checked the box that said *colored*. It was inevitable and I knew Sherrod would be displeased.

And displeased he was. Justifiably. He wrinkled his forehead and shook his head at my pique. I could not use the falsified permit without jeopardizing my safety and that of the project. The project was deprived of a potential driver, and in a crisis, the project might have needed that one driver: me. He was right and I knew it.

But. I was glad I didn't have to go out practice driving anymore. Didn't have to learn to manage a potentially death-dealing piece of machinery when we were already surrounded by the death-dealing machinery of segregation. Mine was the potentially dangerous mistake of a racial and regional outsider, as had been my rash dip of snuff on the way to the voter registrar in Terrell County. As my year in Georgia progressed, I was taught by local Black southerners who understood the risks and who, nevertheless, knowingly challenged the status quo.

I canvassed with the teenagers, gathering after school at Shiloh Baptist. The teens, mostly girls, were full of laughter and indignation and righteousness and tenderness and tirelessly knocked on doors, cajoling the reluctant to admit us, passionately speaking to the importance of voting. The scene was comfortable, reminiscent of my own canvassing with HBG during high school. In the Freedom House, I wrote reports, managed financial recordkeeping as best I could. The first weeks, I was never on the street by myself, and for the rest of the year, I was never on the street alone with a Movement Black man, whose life I might endanger, one of what Sherrod called his Movement Anti-Lynching Measures. Every week, at least on Wednesdays and Saturdays, there were mass meetings in Albany or in Lee County. In November, there was an anniversary celebration of the first mass marches and arrests in Albany. Dr. King came from Atlanta and spoke, giving one of his versions of the "I Have a Dream" speech. Movement people noted to ourselves that the summer before, SNCC member Prathia Hall had delivered a precursor to this speech on the site of one of the burned-out churches. Sherrod designated Prathia to speak for SNCC at the anniversary, which was, for 1962, a female-affirming choice.

Fifteen-year-old Joann Christian was one of the students who canvassed with us, rode with us to outlying mass meetings at night, canvassed in Lee or Terrell Counties on weekends. She was one of many, most of them girls: Joann and her sisters "Dear" (Lavetta Marie) and James Zenna; the sisters Shirley, Patricia, and Marian Gaines; Vera Giddings; Mamie Nell Ford; Eddie Maude McKendrick; and others. The backbone of the Southwest Georgia Movement was women, and often those women were girls barely into their teens. Any one of these youngsters could lead the singing in a mass meeting of hundreds. They followed in the footsteps of Bernice Johnson, who was away at Spelman

College in Atlanta. She had been expelled by Albany State for marching. Bertha Gober, an Albany State student who was arrested with Blanton Hall in the local Trailways bus station for attempting to use the "white" waiting room, had also been expelled. Bertha went on to work with SNCC in Atlanta. In the spring of 1963, after white officials canceled access to all federal food programs to the Black citizens of Greenwood, Mississippi, Bertha wrote the Movement anthem, "We've Been 'Buked and We've Been Scorned."[1]

The Albany teenagers went to school and church and participated in other activities of family and community life. When school let out in the afternoon, they walked a mile or more to the Freedom House. They walked everywhere. Albany was divided by a conventional squared grid of streets and avenues, but this grid was superimposed upon a shape in which roads flared out from the center, like the spokes of a wheel. Perhaps this configuration came from Albany's beginning as a center for the cotton trade with roads from nearby towns and plantations leading into the center of Albany and back out the other side. Overlaid upon the square grid and the spokes leading from outlying towns was the configuration of segregation: Black Albany and white Albany, unmarked on maps but known to all. Sometimes in the afternoon, I walked out one of the diagonals in Black Albany with Joann, sharing homemade fried sweet potatoes nestled in a brown paper bag. In the SNCC office at the end of the teens' walks after school, they might talk race and justice or argue politics and tactics with the SNCCs, or we'd meet at one of the Movement churches, probably Shiloh Baptist, and canvass. They'd walk home in the dusk. Maybe help prepare dinner, eat with the family, do homework. The next morning, they'd get up and do it all again. On weekends, they'd load into Rev. Wells's car and canvass in Lee or Terrell County. Unless they were in jail for demonstrating. I think every one of these girls went to jail at least once. They finished high school, and most if not all attended college.

Joann's family lived at the five-points intersection in Black Albany, diagonally across from their cousins, the Gaines family. Joann was placed by family at intersecting roads coming from other towns and crossing Black Albany to the white side of town and then on to other towns. She was a junior high school girl

[1]. "We've Been 'Buked and We've Been Scorned," composed by Bertha Gober; released online November 12, 2014; recorded by Northern Harmony on *Northern Harmony Live* (1998). https://northernharmony.bandcamp.com/track/weve-been-buked-and-weve-been-scorned.

in bobby socks who listened to the talk—ideas, history, inspiration, strategies, jokes, and tall tales—in the SNCC front room and began canvassing the year before I arrived. That momentous November 1961, when hundreds of Black Albanians marched and went to jail, Joann was among them.

The month of the first Albany Movement anniversary, Joann Christian and a few other teenagers went with us to the south-wide SNCC meeting in Nashville. I was a passenger in the car heading up a major highway with two or three teen activists when the driver said, "Police coming up behind us." We fell silent.

One of the girls squealed.

And then another.

"A Black policeman," one of them said.

"I've been marching and picketing for Black police," another, perhaps Joann, said, "but I never thought there could actually be such a thing."

Joann's life for the last 60 years is rooted in the fight against racism. She was one of six Black students who integrated Albany High School, where she faced the same and worse hate speech and harassment than she had in the county jail. Stalwart as he was, Rev. Wells attended Albany High football games with the six, joining them as he always had, while epithets and objects rained down upon them. At the end of that year, Joann was so exhausted and traumatized that she needed Sherrod and another Movement worker to support her as she walked out of Albany High for the last time. She married another SNCC activist, Bob Mants. They moved to Lowndes County, Alabama, where in 1965 not a single Black person was registered to vote, although Black people constituted 80 percent of the population. Lowndes was a notorious site of racism, but, as was almost always the case in such places, it was also the site of courage and struggle. The first Black Panther Party in the United States was founded in Lowndes County.

When we were creating *Hands on the Freedom Plow*, I visited Joann in Alabama. She and Bob had raised their children in *the rurals*, as Carolyn Daniels called not-towns. Joann was teaching students the same age she had been when I knew her in Albany. She was teaching in Selma, "Bloody Selma," the site of the Edmund Pettus Bridge. She was teaching both Black and white students in integrated classrooms as she had once imagined but never had had a chance to enjoy. I wanted Joann to be present in the book by women in SNCC, but she said *no*, she was not going to write a piece. She did agree to my coming from Maryland to interview her. In Lowndes, we sat outdoors. Bob may have been in and out. She said a friend of hers down the road was out of town. Joann had arranged for the two of us to talk there. She said she wanted to talk out of her grown children's hearing. She and Bob had never shared the full story of their experiences in the Movement because they did not want to embitter their children.

When *Hands on the Freedom Plow* was published, including Joann's story, Bernice Johnson Reagon arranged a daylong conference at the Smithsonian. Joann and Bob came. Joann spoke. And her children were there to hear her story, to bear witness to her power and vision. I am happy that *Hands on the Freedom Plow* corrects the conventional narrative, which is that Albany, Georgia, was Dr. King's failure. The Albany story has its roots in intransigent Black survival and informed resistance in the Jim Crow South, which gave rise to not only a mass Movement but was fueled by a community's political understanding and demand for autonomy. I believe it was this community power that prompted the highest authorities in the land to go after the Albany Movement.

That autumn I was in Georgia, my sister came from New York for the SNCC conference, so my home life and SNCC life converged. SNCCs from all over the south were there, including the Mississippi staff, including people whose names I had known but whom I had never met, another convergence. That was when I met Dorie Ladner, intrepid Mississippi staff, and I finally met Albany's own Bernice Johnson, who had been away at Spelman. I will never forget the first time I heard Bernice sing. She stood alone. When she opened her mouth, the largest, most daring song rose from her lips, in some ways the weighted pauses as powerful as the voiced words, the words slipping from high to low and rising back up: "Up above my head, I see freedom in the air. . . . There must be a God somewhere." I had never imagined someone my own age, not yet twenty, could fill a room with such force.

When we returned to Albany, it was back to canvassing, report writing, financial records, talking with the ministers and Goldie Jackson in the Albany Movement office two doors down, talking with northerners who came through, spending afternoons with Mississippi workers or other field staff on their way to Atlanta. Marion King, wife of Slater King, who had been pregnant and kicked to the ground by police and had lost her baby, was a member of the alumna chapter of the Black sorority Delta Sigma Theta. The Deltas began a voter registration drive based in the building around the corner from the Freedom House, and much of December was consumed with working with them on the campaign. Though we SNCCs were the wild-eyed radical youngsters on the front lines, we also, time and time again, cooperated with the more established organizations and individuals in the Black community, some of whom had been doing this work since before we'd been born.

In January, when temperatures were frigid and the tiny gas heater with its glowing ceramic elements could not touch the cold, we got a call to attend a meeting at the Southern Christian Leadership Conference (SCLC) Dorchester Center on the Georgia coast, a long diagonal drive north and east across Georgia, one of those nighttime rides, fraught with potential danger from cars bearing hostile white people or the police. Inevitably, halfway to our destination, we needed a break. We left the highway and slipped through a night town, until we found the Black community and a building with lights on that looked like an after-hours club. When our racially mixed group walked in, the place stilled into silence. Sherrod promised we would use the bathrooms, buy something to go, and be on our way. Back on the highway, we drove toward a destination written on a piece of paper from a phone conversation, until we arrived after daybreak. We were greeted at breakfast by A. Philip Randolph, president of the Brotherhood of Sleeping Car Porters; Roy Wilkins, executive director of the national NAACP; James Farmer, executive director of the Congress of Racial Equality, or CORE; Dr. King of SCLC; our own executive director, Jim Forman; and Bayard Rustin, who worked with SCLC. We SNCCs, including Southwest Georgia, Mississippi, and Atlanta staff, had been summoned to help plan the proposed August 1963 March on Washington.

Between meetings, we walked the grounds of the center, a hundred or so acres of flat, coastal land graced with old oak trees. The ocean's presence made me feel I was in a timeless place, despite the harrowing night before, despite planning a march that would bring a quarter of a million people to Washington, DC, to demand jobs and freedom. The ocean made me feel safe, a part of something so much larger than any of us individually. I was unaware of the parallel between the demands of 1963 and the demands immediately following the Civil War, when this land I was walking became an educational center for the formerly enslaved and which was now a center for its equivalent, SCLC's Citizenship Education Program. I had read of the Freedmen's Bureau but had never walked on land where the bureau had done its work. I now walked it in the company of my SNCC cohort.

In late spring 1963, Movement teenagers, including Joann Christian, picketed a Little Harlem store that was owned by white people and employed only white salespeople although the clientele was entirely Black. The picketers demanded the store hire Black people. They were arrested, including Joann, who went limp on the ground when she was arrested. The police dragged her down "Freedom Alley," behind the jail. A policeman stood his full-grown male weight on her legs. She kicked him in the place of male vulnerability. He went to the hospital. As was usual with Movement juveniles, she was moved to Camilla Jail, far from family and far from the community adults who were in jail in Albany. In Camilla, Joann was held on a separate floor from other Movement juveniles. The police told her she was on death row. Sixteen years old. They locked a police dog in the cell with her. She told herself if it was her time to go, it was her time to go, and turned over to sleep with her back to the dog. When she was released and driven home to Albany, the Klan rallied blocks from her home (though Black and white Albany were eons apart experientially, geographically they were in one another's backyards). That evening, a white SNCC summer volunteer heard Joann and her family's names shouted over the microphone to the fevered KKK rally.

. . .

From nighttime mass meetings, people gathered on the poorly lit sidewalk outside the church and marched through the business district of Little Harlem, past the bus station, across Oglethorpe Boulevard, which divided white from Black Albany, into downtown and a few blocks farther to the police station. They were arrested, filling the large "Black" side of the jail. One Wednesday, I joined the marchers. At the jailhouse, I was separated from other marchers and held in an office, where as many as five white policemen crowded in around me, felt me up, looking for contraband and finding my toothbrush in my brassiere; they pulled back before it went further. As I was walked back to the two white cells on a short corridor, I could hear people on the Black side calling my name, asking if I was all right. I was locked into the women's cell, a space with four metal bunks hanging from the wall, two on each side, the toilet at one end and the barred entry on the other. I joined Joni Rabinowitz and Joyce Barrett, the other white SNCC women. The next morning, Chief Laurie Pritchett came to inspect me, the newcomer. The other cops felt free to come back and stand at the bars to talk with us, especially late at night. One night when I slept on a lower bunk, with my head toward the corridor, a cop squatted down by my head and intimately spewed hatred toward me, a race traitor. We were in jail for a week. We fasted. Some of the time, other white women were jailed with us. A woman going through cold-turkey withdrawal was taken from the cell periodically, perhaps to be grilled about us. There was also an angry woman in a filmy green dress. She had driven through town at breakneck speed, running lights. She had been in the jail before. She had never had a driver's license, though she had been driving for years. We were released, hungry and dirty. Sherrod insisted we stop at a doctor's for venereal disease, or VD, tests. I have no idea why he insisted on this for all the women staff. The doctor was an unkempt white man who practiced over the Little Harlem pool hall. After we'd gone home and showered, Joann's mother, Odessa Mae, brought us her chilled banana pudding. The coolness, the floral and sweet bananas, the all-forgiving whipped cream. I had never had such a thing. It was heaven after a week in Chief Pritchett's jail.

When we left the Dougherty County Jail, I didn't know I was sick. We stepped out of jail into full-force Southwest Georgia summer, flattening, but we had a dozen summer volunteers about to arrive, an orientation to design, beds and meals to be found in the community. Some of us were living upstairs in the clubhouse owned by the Deltas, who had been working on voter registration since the winter. Down the street and around the corner, some of the men still stayed in the Freedom House, until the night hostile white people shot into it. And the heat. With the heat and the pressure of the work and the fear, I could barely finish my work, but as a group we did what we had to do and held an orientation for the volunteers at Koinonia Farm. The summer project was launched, with volunteers in the community, families feeding them each night, canvassing, mass meetings. I felt such shame that I was weak and badly focused. McCree Harris of the Albany family that included Freedom Singers Rutha Mae and Emory took me in. Carole King and Marion King paid for me to see a doctor, a recent graduate of Meharry Medical School at Fisk. I don't think he was thrilled when I showed up, and I imagine he had good reason, confronted with this white woman's body he was trained and ethically obligated to treat, but whose body, barely covered by a medical gown, posed a threat to his own safety. He did take blood samples, but I have wondered if he sent them to the state lab. In 1963, I believe the blood samples would have clearly come from a Black doctor while being labeled "white"; however it happened, I never received word of the results.

It was a relief when Sherrod assigned me to go out to Lee County with summer volunteer Martha Prescod and photographer Danny Lyons. A half hour of sitting in the car, watching the cotton and peanut fields flow by. Danny was one of a cadre of SNCC photographers who had been trained by Richard Avedon. We were going to meet with a Movement family, a farmer and his wife and children. I didn't know Martha, but we'd talked a few times at Koinonia, enough that I'd enjoyed our conversations, two non-southerners finding our way in this Deep South world, one white and one Black, comfortable talking about issues and ideas, veering from big-world ideas to the personal, not unlike talking with Candy or Amina or Peggy back in New York.

Martha, Danny, and I stepped up onto the porch and entered the country house, Danny first, then me. I turned as Martha came through the door. Backlit, an opaque silhouette, erect and slim, her unpressed hair an aura, passing from the outdoors sun into the dark house. Unreadable. Danny caught with his camera that backlit second of passage and possibility.

. . .

It was a summer of repression and terror. Dogs set on Black children in Birmingham, Alabama. Demonstrators arrested en masse in Danville, Virginia. NAACP leader Medgar Evers assassinated outside his home in Jackson, Mississippi. One night, the Freedom House was surrounded by police cars with squawking radios. Most staff and summer volunteers were already in jail. In a surreal moment, we were trapped in the Freedom House in Albany, Georgia, speaking with Sherrod who was at a SNCC benefit in Carnegie Hall in New York City, while police "cherries" splashed red across the Freedom House windows behind which we huddled. We snuck out the back door through the backyards of Black Albany, terrain we knew better than the police, Black Albany terrain our underground railroad. We could hear panting police dogs, see the headlamps of the police cars speeding through the alleys. Eight or nine of us took refuge in Shiloh Baptist.

At night, Mr. James Christian, Joann's father, and Mr. Monroe or "Cuz" Gaines, sat on the front steps of the church that had so often burst with songs of the Movement. They sat with shotguns across their laps. James Christian was a military vet; in World War II he had been stationed in France. The Klan in their pickup trucks circled the church in the moonlight. We turned off the lights so they couldn't see us. Fully clothed, we stretched out in the dark church listening to the trucks and murmuring to one another. One night, after the Klan had gone home, SNCC worker John Churchville played jazz on the church piano, laying down a different track to obscure the trucks' revving.

In the dark church, Martha and I sat talking quietly in the pews. I loved Martha's unwavering love for local people and their courage. Martha and I talked for hours, two young women—I was twenty and she younger than eighteen—building a friendship that has lasted more than five decades. When Martha had first arrived in Albany, Sherrod had received phone calls from Martha's mother, threatening to sue him for causing her underage daughter to be carried across state lines, an act with the very ugly name of white slavery. It had been hard enough for me to come south with the full, though frightened, support of my family. Martha's strength of will awed me, even as I saw her vulnerability. Like everyone, she saw my physical weakness, but only she asked about it. I had noticed Martha sometimes slipped out of mass meetings, when she was so tired she just had to sleep. She would slip into a SNCC car and sleep, despite the circling police and the Klan.

What happened in Albany, especially during the summer of 1963, radicalized me. I had arrived in Southwest Georgia a well-informed and *together* white liberal. To me, liberals believe the system can be changed through a give-and-take that leads to reform. In January that year in Georgia, I had heard Bayard Rustin apply the word "revolutionary" to our work. In 1963, I claimed that title, and it was Southwest Georgia that gave me that clarity. I left Georgia bitter and cynical.

I don't have room to suggest the courage and understanding of power relationships shared by the people of Albany; there is a shadow side to the community's Black militance in the white supremacist repression it provoked, an underrecognized chapter in the story of the Southwest Georgia Movement, a Movement too often dismissed as *Dr. King's failure*.

In November 1961, the year before I went south, Albany was the scene of the first mass marches and arrests of that era's Civil Rights Movement. The nation watched on TV as hundreds, including Dr. King, were arrested and thrown in jail. After Dr. King's time in jail, he brokered a deal with the white *city fathers* downtown: he announced the Black people of Albany would honor an injunction prohibiting them from marching onto the front pages of newspapers and the national evening news. The white people of Albany would no longer have to endure the Movement's presence on shows like *Meet the Press*. A *gentlemen's agreement*.

When the people of Albany, the marchers and the chanters and the singers, Miss Corinne the Black Avon lady, the schoolchildren, the students at Albany State, the men who guarded Movement spaces, the women who dipped snuff and went fishing on the banks of the Flint river, the women who cleaned white people's houses, the women who taught Black children in segregated schools, the men who preached in Black pulpits and those same preachers who drove Black people to work in rickety buses donated from up north during the boycott of city buses: those people were pissed, and they weren't shy about saying they would be enjoined from *nothing*. The people of Albany had an attitude. A reputation of defiance. They let nobody turn them 'round.

By the summer of 1962, arrests of over 2,000 Albany Movement members had been made. They had made a name for themselves. The white name would have been *uppity*. The true name was *righteous*.

From the earliest marches in 1961, the Albany Movement had documented instances of police and citizen harassment and persecution of its members. Laurie Pritchett, chief of police, charmed national press and officials by claiming to meet demonstrators' nonviolence with police nonviolence. It seems there was a deal that if the police in Albany were not egregiously violent, the federal government would leave official white Albany alone. Though it was documented and submitted to the proper authorities that fifteen-year-old Joann Christian was brutally dragged up a flight of stairs during an arrest; though it was documented and submitted to the proper authorities that Rev. Wells was dragged by his genitals during an arrest; though it was documented and submitted to the proper authorities that Marion and Slater King lost their unborn child after Marion was kicked to the ground by police, for over a year, the affidavits and phone calls and petitions went to the US Department of Justice and nothing was done about the brutality of white Albany against its protesting Black citizens.

And then. And then. In Washington, Robert F. Kennedy himself announced that the Albany Nine would be prosecuted. You might think these nine were police and others who had persecuted and harassed Movement members, but the Albany Nine were nine leaders and members of the Albany Movement. They were deceitfully charged with tampering with a juror in a federal case. Such announcements were usually made by local officials, but Bobby Kennedy, admired by so many white liberals, chose to make the announcement himself, demonstrably throwing his weight behind the prosecution of the Albany Movement, while his Justice Department took no action concerning the documented complaints filed against local white authorities and citizens.

In an apparent attempt to intimidate activists, more than fifty Black citizens of Albany were called to testify before a grand jury in the government's case against the Nine in Macon, a drive of over 100 miles. Among those called was Joann Christian's littlest sister, James Zenna, so young and petite she needed a step stool to speak into the mic at the hearing. No action was announced to address the wrongs perpetrated against Joann Christian, against Rev. Wells, against Marion and Slater King, against the dozens of others whose rights had been violated: the right to protest; the right to live without fear of physical and economic reprisal; the right to vote, the right to secure religious sanctuaries.

The federal government, especially the Kennedy administration, is depicted as a friend to the Civil Rights Movement, but Southwest Georgia tells a different story, a story of the federal government allied with local counterparts to suppress a mass movement for social justice. When in defense of the Albany Nine, the coffers of the Albany Movement had been drained, and key members traumatized and at least one bedridden, the federal government blithely dismissed all charges, but no restitution was paid to those who'd been forced by subpoenas to enact this federal charade. The details of the persecution of the Southwest Georgia Movement are difficult to locate and verify. The usual sources of Movement history are mostly silent on the subject.

In the days of approaching winter during COVID-19, I look at the sky outside my window. Some days it is moody and dull, flat. Other days, it is an azure that suggests all things are possible. My view of the sky is through intersecting tree limbs, reaching across and upward, seemingly without regard for one another and certainly without regard for me, sitting behind the finely gridded screen. Today, the sky was flat and deep, not a performing blue, not a blue with an audience in mind. Today's blue gives slightly to the body of my presence, holds me, does not lose its balance or shape because of me. This is the depth of community over the generations. This is how the Albany Movement did not fail.

SNCC: New York Office

That summer that ended with the prosecution of the Albany Nine, I had been sick since June, when we had gone to jail. The summer volunteers eddied in and out of the office, canvassing and trooping back to report, going by foot in groups to eat with local families; after the police had begun a dragnet, picking up SNCC people all over Albany, we had taken refuge in the church. At summer's end, in the city of Americus, SNCC workers Don Harris, Ralph Allen, and John Perdew were arrested and charged with sedition, a capital offense; they could lose their heads if convicted. Liz Holtzman, one of C. B. King's summer law interns, arranged for a couple of people to lobby in DC on behalf of the Americus Three. I wasn't any use in the field, so I was one of the two sent north to lobby. When I protested, our lawyer, C. B. King, said the Movement needed me to go, that I was perfect for the job, that I was phlegmatic. When I looked at him askance, he said, *unflappable*.

But I don't want to, I told him.

We need you to.

That is how I left Albany in August 1963.

After lobbying in DC, a few bizarre days in which, unlike my life in Georgia, I lived with and saw nothing but white people, I caught a Greyhound bus home and my mother had me in a doctor's office almost as soon as I walked in her door. Within days, I was diagnosed with hepatitis and banished to my bed.

No 1963 March on Washington for Jobs and Freedom for me.

During my banishment, Candy phoned.

"Sis. They're killing the children. Birmingham. Four little girls. . . ."

I jumped up to do . . . what? And fell, useless, to the floor.

By the end of September, I was back at Barnard, though hepatitis weary: the subway back and forth, classes, evening hours to study in the library with classmates Augusta or Gussie Souza, Denise Jackson, Juanita Clarke, and Adaeze Otue. Gussie and Denise were also sociology students. Fairly often, I clandestinely spent the night in Denise's dorm room to avoid the late-night trip home to Brooklyn. During one fire drill, I hid in the closet in Denise's room. How emblematic of that year: the shelter of Denise's friendship, the potential danger in the room when neither of us knew whether it was a drill or a fire; the fortunate outcome that I was not trapped on an upper floor in a fire.

Barnard and SNCC converged in the lobby of Lehman Hall, which housed the library and sociology classes on the upper floors. The FBI had phoned, insisting they talk to me about the Albany Nine. I spoke to a Movement lawyer who advised that I did not have to, but in my overwhelmed state, I didn't feel strong enough to say no. I insisted on a public meeting place. They suggested Barnard's campus, and I suggested the lobby in Lehman Hall, so we met there between classes, my classmates rushing around us. The two FBI men wore nice suits and shiny leather shoes. They wanted to know whether it was the white SNCC worker Joyce Barrett or the white SNCC worker Joni Rabinowitz who had picketed a store in Albany. One of the fed's goals seemed to be to spotlight the presence of Joni Rabinowitz on SNCC staff. Joni's father, Victor, was counsel to the nation of Cuba; raising this connection was a strategic federal move to paint SNCC and the Movement with a red brush. The autumn before, when I had arrived in Albany, US military planes had flown from Turner Air Force Base outside Albany to patrol the air above Cuba. The Cuban Missile Crisis. I had been working in Dawson when the store in Albany was picketed and had no knowledge of where Joni might have been. I told them I had heard the white woman in question had been Joyce Barrett.

SNCC had held summer projects in Southwest Georgia in 1962 and 1963, and in 1964 was planning, along with other Civil Rights groups, a summer project in Mississippi. Beginning in January, much of our work in New York was preparation for that: strategizing, fundraising, recruiting. In April, the drag of the hepatitis began to lift. I would work in the New York SNCC office that summer. The long, hot summer began early—two hundred Civil Rights demonstrators were arrested at the World's Fair in the spring. I remember demonstrators jamming subway car doors and people being caught in the squeeze. That's how the whole year felt, caught between the squeeze of sociology and the New York SNCC office and the tunnel-screeching momentum of Southwest Georgia in my heart.

Julie Prettyman, who directed SNCC's New York office, assigned me to process a direct mail campaign. I had no idea what that was, but SNCC was as audacious and innovative in fundraising as it was in the field. In connection with the Mississippi Summer Project, Julie and a group of powerful friends of SNCC raised $350,000, a large portion of SNCC's budget that year, the equivalent of a couple million or more today. Dependable cars were essential to the safety of staff and volunteers for the 1964 summer project, so much of the money went for that.

Among the volunteers to leave the Ohio training for their assignment were James Chaney, Mickey Schwerner, and Andy Goodman. Arrived in Mississippi, they were abducted, and for much of the summer, they were not found. The disappearance reverberated through every aspect of our work. Schwerner and Goodman were both New Yorkers. I remember coming out of my office one day and seeing two older adults, a man and a woman pressing close to one another. Someone told me they were Mickey's parents. They and the Goodmans and hundreds of other parents of summer volunteers did heroic work that summer, not only seeking justice for the three missing men but also raising money for the project and using their considerable influence to publicize the truth about Mississippi.

One afternoon early in the summer, I sat at a table opening return envelopes from the direct mailing. Julie had taught me to line them up and work through each row quickly, as she taught me so many things, including how to write a personal bank check. There was no air-conditioning in the SNCC office on Fifth Avenue, just above West Fifteenth Street. The window in my room was higher and wider than I was, and on the hottest days, when we flung this window open, the sounds of city traffic would rush in, the papers would fly, and I would feel like I could be swept up and out the window. When I'd go home, my bare arms would be stubbled with soot and sweat.

I sat at the table with ranks of return postage-paid envelopes before me, recording the donations. Based on a printed code on the envelope, I could track from which mailing list the donor's name had come. Some of the envelopes were returned by racists. At least once, the envelope contained a printer's metal plate, for which we had to pay a huge sum of return postage. Occasionally, there would be suggestive brown smears on an envelope. The majority of these hate returns came from Harry Golden's *Carolina Israelite* newspaper. On all of the envelopes was printed a black-and-white photo of volunteers at the Ohio training, a blurred, randomly selected image of a row of faces, which included Andy Goodman. At least once a day, I would open an envelope on which Goodman's photo had been circled, and written beside it would be something like, *We got him.*

Despite the grim narrative of the summer of 1964, there were moments of joyous solidarity. One day I opened an envelope, pulled out the enclosed check, took up my pen to record the info and almost fell out of my chair. It was a check for one thousand dollars. I had never seen such a thing. And. It was a check from Leonard Bernstein, conductor of the New York Philharmonic. I ran down the hall, flashing the check in excitement, perhaps bumping into Lucille Perlman or Eve Osman, the guard dogs of our mailing list, the file drawers with thousands of handwritten names, addresses, and recorded donation amounts. I would have run on to Julie's office and several of us might have gathered around to exclaim.

All summer, we worked. Trying to find people or news of people: phoning the wire services AP and UPI and asking them to read back to us a story from Mississippi, within which we hoped to find information of life or death that had not yet been published. Crowded night meetings with the parents—imagine, parents whose so-young children might. Might. Night tutoring in Harlem in a church basement. Buses. Subways. Walking long blocks in low heels and a damp cotton dress, running an errand, perhaps hand delivering the draft of a news release to someone on Manhattan's Upper West Side, maybe a family, who lived in the same building as the Goodmans, with a child in Mississippi. Maybe in the sweaty daytime, picking up or delivering mailing lists to an industrial building blocks from public transportation, a nearby boat on the Hudson River sounding its horn. Hurried phone calls to Candy, who was working somewhere else in the city. Brushing past exuberant clusters of High School Friends of SNCC, one of our organized support groups, in the office corridor, at least one of whom, Ted Gold, would die in a Weather Underground explosion on West Eleventh Street a few years later. Talking to my mother as she smoked and tipped her ashes into her enameled ashtray, so small it fit in the palm of her hand. And a fire engine wail nearby or a shout in the street. Gloria Richardson, from the Eastern Shore of Maryland, came to town for meetings. Julie had found her a place to stay off Fifth Avenue. Julie asked me to accompany Gloria to where she was staying. We arrived at the building and were taken around back to the freight elevator. In retrospect, Gloria probably knew what was what. I definitely did not know, I'm embarrassed to admit. The elevator deposited us at the apartment's back door, the maid's entrance to the home of the wealthy liberal family hosting Gloria. Another afternoon, I escorted two women from Mississippi to

Washington Square Village, where they were staying before driving to Atlantic City, New Jersey, for the Democratic Party challenge. It took the three of us a while to get into the building. The two women were Mrs. Fannie Lou Hamer and Mrs. Annie Devine, two heroes of the Mississippi struggle.

In Mississippi, stymied by racist violence and voter suppression by the white mainstream Democratic Party, in preparation for the 1964 nomination of a presidential candidate, local Mississippians and summer volunteers organized a statewide primary under an alternate party, the Mississippi Freedom Democrats (MFDP). More than 80,000 Mississippians joined the rolls of the new, racially diverse party. Ella Baker addressed a late-summer MFDP convention in Mississippi, where Fannie Lou Hamer, E. W. Steptoe, Victoria Gray Adams, Rev. Ed King, Aaron Henry, and Annie Devine, among others, were chosen to act as an interracial group of electors to the 1964 Democratic National Convention in Atlantic City. They demanded the MFDP delegation be seated instead of the all-white Democrats. The floor fight over the seating of the MFDP representatives was epic, with Lyndon B. Johnson (LBJ) weighing in forcefully and viciously in favor of the white regulars. A compromise was proposed, to offer two seats to the MFDP, but they turned it down. This unsuccessful fight for a voice for Mississippi Black people in national Democratic politics provided the momentum behind the subsequent fight for the Voting Rights Act of 1965.

I went to Atlantic City for a day with the parents of a brother and sister who were both Mississippi Summer volunteers. The father was a doctor, and the car was a boat that rolled regally from Manhattan to Atlantic City. Once there, I went looking for my people. Like everything about that summer—its ambition, its vision, its tragedy—the Atlantic City operation, run out of a few rooms with some bedrooms in the back, not unlike the Freedom House in Albany, Georgia, was staggering. Phones rang and were answered, legal pads filled with info, pickups and drop-offs arranged, transports to the convention floor taken care of, consults with Democratic Party supporters and with lawyers taken care of, and reporters attended to. When Mrs. Hamer gave her riveting speech to the credentials committee, the word among SNCCs was that LBJ, still in DC, watched her on TV and raged that he wanted that (expletive) off the TV screen. He called an impromptu press conference to draw attention away from the Mississippi challenge and its spokeswoman.

Candy said on the phone, "There's a neighborhood group forming. It's tentative, but I think it could work. They've been meeting for a little while." She had dropped out of college, was working at NYU. So much was so bleak. She had been to Andy Goodman's funeral with me.

I said, "Maybe I could come to a meeting."

She drew in her breath. "No, Sis. I don't think so." It was a local thing, she said—and did not have to say I was not local. It was a Black thing and I was not Black.

In SNCC's small New York City office in 1964, I could look out on the city where I had grown up, streets I had walked with my black spaniel, Fifth Avenue where a bit farther south I once had seen Eleanor Roosevelt, all the tallness of her, hailing a cab in front of her posh apartment building. I had ridden the Fifth Avenue bus past B. Altman's, where Peggy and Hank Dammond's mother Ellen worked, and past the lions in front of the Forty-Second Street library, a few blocks north of the swanky Plaza, the hotel where I had interviewed to attend Oberlin, the apartment buildings on one side, the green of Central Park on the other, including the zoo, and further north veering west onto 110th Street and following the southern hem of Harlem, but not entering. I knew the city intimately, but it had changed, was changing, and so had I. I stood at the window and looked out and looked some more, until someone in the office called my name.

Not far from where the Fifth Avenue bus would turn west, skirting the hem of Harlem, a blond woman was photographed screaming, hands raised to her mouth, not unlike Marilyn Monroe in *The Seven Year Itch* but also not like Marilyn Monroe in *The Seven Year Itch*, because this was a white woman standing in an intersection in Harlem in the middle of an uprising—the press called it a riot—and simultaneously the summer of the Mississippi Summer Project. Maybe she hadn't even left the car, but I remember her as standing in the middle of an intersection, in the middle of the rage of that summer when Chaney, Schwerner, and Goodman were murdered and when James Powell, a fifteen-year-old child had been shot and killed in Harlem by a New York City policeman. Perhaps they saw not a child but a fifteen-year-old Black man? And that difference made it OK to shoot him.

That woman's image across the pages of New York City newspapers: a white woman in an intersection where she didn't belong. How many narratives can flow from that woman in an intersection during a rebellion? The racist cliché spins this as a story of a (civilized) white woman in danger at the hands of rioting Black people who window smash and loot, somehow not citizens in the same way as her. An alternative: Black people rose up against a history of injustice in the context of the killing of a young Black man by the racist police and everything else about that summer and the centuries that led up to it. This was a Harlem thing. A Black thing. That woman shouldn't have been there.

No, Sis. I don't think so, Candy had said.

I rode a subway into Harlem during the six-day rebellion; I rode standing in a car where every seat was taken by white—as I remember it—police in uniform, the blue serge pressed and pleated and buttoned, the mahogany riot sticks holding within their gleam that distinctive sound the sticks make when struck against a curb.

I had lived my life in spaces where I, a white girl woman, was not expected to be. Haiti, for instance. Southwest Georgia, for instance. Etcetera. Etcetera. Was I different than the people in the auto in that intersection? I believe the people in the auto in Harlem would have protested, they *didn't know*. They could go *anywhere*. Whenever. Because they were *white*.

The year before, in Georgia, outside the SNCC office, Willie Ricks had yelled *Black Power*. Ricks had been arrested and was on a jail detail—chain-gang style. He had yelled *Black Power* despite the guard standing by with a shotgun.

By the time I left Georgia, the term *Black* had edged out *Negro*, which had replaced *colored*. The N word burned like a brand.

I had been one of the four known as *les americaines* in Haiti. *Les americaines*, Jewish and white and woman and child and divorcée and Black and music teacher and two women without a man.

Before I could read words, I had watched my mother scrub away chalked epithets outside our building on Sullivan Street, leaving a wet and unblemished spot without the history of that bit of racism.

I had heard my New Hampshire aunt, my father's redheaded sister, call my mother *the Jewess*, surely an admonition to her little nieces staying with her in New Hampshire. *Don't act Jewish.*

I had heard other Southwest Georgia staff call one another the N word and knew that was taboo to me.

I knew I loved Charity Bailey.

I knew when we moved out of Jane Street, a boy who had been my playmate, leaned down into my mother's open window and spat in her face.

I knew: Charity.

I knew: women without a man.

I knew: my mother and sister and I had been called N lovers.

Black power thrilled me. Because Charity. Because Haiti. Because Candy Keeling, and Sherron Jackson who was becoming Amina Rachman, and Reggie, and and and, but I also knew, as I had known not to pick up the practice of using the N word in banter, that I did not belong to Black Power, though I might like to. I knew I was loved by many and that I loved many. I had been invited in but not born into what it was to be Black. The day of Malcolm X's funeral, I could not be with Amina, who had been Sherron Jackson, as she rode in the cortege behind her minister.

I know others who have stood at this point and made a principled decision that racial identity politics were not the decisive factor; I know some standing at that same moment felt class was the definitive element, but I knew from inside my body and from inside my childhood that race stood at the center of everything; as W. E. B. Du Bois had said, "The problem of the twentieth century is the color line." Into the twenty-first century.

Black Power, shouted proudly by Willie Mukasa Ricks in 1963, was the antithesis of the default in the United States—white power—that default so universal it did not need to be spoken aloud.

This is not to say that Black Power and its consequences for me did not hurt. I was sad, as in I felt I was entering exile, no longer having access to the emotional and political geography that was home. With my mind and in my heart, I celebrated *Black Power*. It was so apt and so timely. I had neither felt entitled to work with SNCC nor entitled to be part of the rich relationships and work that I had been allowed. I knew white people who were so hurt, they never got over this separation, described themselves as having been expelled by SNCC. I think they felt that SNCC and the Movement for racial justice was *their* Movement. They felt entitled.

Did the elaborate but unspoken protocols of my childhood—the chosen silences that encircled my mother, my sister, Charity, and me—shape my response to Black Power? Those childhood silences existed at the same time as the unspoken rules about where we did and didn't go in one another's lives. I never went to Rhode Island with Charity to visit her family, although I did go with Charity to Harlem on Christmas Eve and on other occasions. It wasn't clear cut, any of it. Like when Jimmy spat at my mother; did he do it because we were Jews or did he do it because Charity was Black, or did he do it for both/and? Part of Charity's separate world had to do with race, but she also moved in a circle that included people identified with the left. I think, in retrospect, my mother Eunice was skittish when it came to the left and may have avoided or even been unwelcome in parts of Charity's circle for this reason. Which is not to deny that my mother enthusiastically supported causes that were considered leftist. Charity's TV show was almost canceled by NBC in the midfifties because the studio said that both my mother Eunice and Charity had engaged in activities deemed *prematurely antifascist*, McCarthy-era shorthand for *communist*.

There were warm associations for me with what Ricks had shouted, *Black Power*—associations rooted in my childhood. Charity's pride in Haiti. *It's an independent nation*, she would say. *They fought for their freedom and they won.* She, like other Black intellectuals in the 1930s, had gone south, in her case to Bluefield, West Virginia, where I would one day live on a hilltop facing the hilltop upon which stood Bluefield State Teacher's College, the Black college where Charity had once lived and worked. She was the grandchild of people who had been enslaved, people who had bought manumission papers and traveled north to Providence, Rhode Island, where she was raised, a Yankee.

And there was Candy Keeling and there was Amina Rachman, and there was Reggie, and SNCC staff and community people of Southwest Georgia. There was the history I had learned at Little Red School House, history pieced together for us by our teacher Mimi Levy, because there were no textbooks, history which she called Negro history because, well, 1950s. And I took that history in with the hunger and trust of a ten-year-old, took it inside me, so, as ten-year-olds, when we danced to the song "Sometimes I Feel Like a Motherless Child," the muscles moving me were this history. And the names I learned at home and at school and in HBG. Dred Scott. Harriet Tubman, Frederick Douglass, Mary McLeod Bethune, Ralph Bunche, Jackie Robinson, Paul Robeson, Emmett Till, Diane Nash, Herbert Lee. And the amazement and delight my ten-year-old classmates and I felt at the end of that year when the *Brown* decision was handed down by the US Supreme Court. That decision, despite the serious flaws that have become apparent as the decades have passed, opened a portal for me to step into history with the expectation that I could change it.

There was my appreciation and there was context, which could add layers to understanding a time, exposing racial, feminist, and class dynamics at work. The context for SNCC had been a racist segregated world upheld by state authority, white Christianity, and cautionary power narratives of violence. The context for SNCC also had been generations of previous Black struggles, including the generally unacknowledged work of Black women and members of the labor movement, as documented in the book *At the Dark End of the Street* by Danielle L. McGuire. As SNCC grew, white supremacists focused increasingly upon the organization. The persecution of Movement leaders in Albany is one example. By the summer of the 1964 project and the Harlem Rebellion with the white woman in the crossroads, the United States had been home to never-ending racist violence since the 1600s. In 1964, racist murders, phony arrests, and vilification of the Movement in the media not only persisted but intensified. In the next few years, many white supporters, including long-term Jewish supporters, stopped supporting SNCC. The deaths of SNCC people continued after I had left New York; for instance, in 1970, Ralph Featherstone was blown up in a car traveling on Maryland's Eastern Shore.

By 1965, SNCC was an organization with its back against the wall. The oppression had been there since the beginning and did not originate in the years after 1964, which is why, on a jailhouse work gang back in 1963, Willie Mukasa Ricks yelled, *Black Power*, and Kwame Ture was still yelling it on the Meredith march in 1966.

We were an organization under the gun, despite the Voting Rights Act of August 1965.

A year after the Mississippi Summer Project, Carol Rogoff, with whom I'd worked in the New York office, went south to work in Mississippi. From letters I wrote her that summer, the sense of struggle in the face of daunting and confusing odds emerges.

July 9

. . . If I'm incoherent, it's because of a couple hundred high school students who are 1. folk singing, 2. eating lunch, 3. collating a mailing, 4. getting ready to go soliciting, in, out, and on top of me. In other words, things are the same EXCEPT that Barbara, Erin and Charlotte and Prathia are now on staff. Yeah, Prathia's working in the office behind my partition and I think she and the HS kids are going to have a gun-battle by the end of next week. Constancia is presiding over the front desk, assistantly administering. . . . No fund-raiser has been hired. . . .

I guess Micky told you about the HS kids. Chain-in, conference, National HS SNCC, Bedford Stuyvesant.

Courtland [Cox], Bob [Moses], [Walter] Tillow and that group are in and out of the office. I went to a Peace Group's meeting with them last week. God all the squabbling. Awful. I'd forgotten about the "old" left.

The parents have set up a phone in Stephen Wise Free Synagogue. Alan Reich's father is temporary chairman. They're going through the same old hassles, and it's great to see the old parents like the Zwerdlings finally telling the new parents, "like it tee igh is."

[Paul] O'Dwyer (younger) is possibly coming into the chain-in case as one of the lawyers.

August 18

Things are not good, not good at all, I can't put my finger on why, but Civil Rights just isn't good business this year. I guess for those who were only peripherally involved, like contributors, the change in the tone of voice of the mass media has had a strong effect, and maybe for those who have been more involved, problems on a nationwide and especially northern level has [sic] become more pressing. At any rate, SNCC is not pulling people the way it used to up here. Also, I guess, we have finally settled down to a long-range community organizing program in the south; crises are no longer as important in what we're doing, and it's difficult to convey the relevance of what we are doing to those who aren't there. What we are doing has somehow changed character (a good thing, most of the time), and we're still consciously projecting the kind of image that was good publicity during the Freedom Rides. Or something.

I should be leaving around the first of Sept, and the way things look now I don't want to stay here part time during the winter, even if asked. What are your plans? One faintly interesting possibility is that Riverside Friends of SNCC, together with Manhattan Committee for FDP might open a store front on the west side this winter. I don't think SNCC could pay me to work out of there part time (I haven't mentioned it to anyone), but it might be a good thing. What I want, what I was doing before I started working with SNCC (many, many sad years ago), is to work on the small-scale local level in New York. As important as I see political wheeling and dealing, and as much as it interests me from a distance, what I personally want to do is work on the idea of building the community in a city setting. So it's about time I got back to that, I think. I was half-way, half-assed going do that this summer, and then I unknowingly and innocently and without intent wandered into your office, in which location I was foully propositioned by you [note: when Rogoff suggested Holsaert work in the SNCC office the summer of 1965, a joke].

As far as me personally, I moved in with H. . . . , which is interesting. I have no idea how it will work out, but it's nice. My new address is. . . . My mother lost her job at the beginning of July and hasn't found another one yet, so that's great too. Shai is in Canada with the Kismet cast.

WRITE ME, tell me what you're thinking and doing.

Two additions add context to these 1965 letters:

Significantly, though filled with foreboding, neither of these letters mentions racial animosity within SNCC; though those tensions were present and building, they were not high on my list of concerns, or I would have mentioned them to Rogoff.

In addition, in spring that year, I underwent an illegal abortion. I spent the month and a half before the procedure in a private hell of pregnancy-dread and then the abortion, arranged by a friend of my sister's, took place on the kitchen table in an apartment. A woman inserted rubber tubing into my cervix and instructed me to remove the tubing at home when I began to bleed. She explained that introducing the foreign tubing and air would prompt an abortion. A few nights later, when I had a raging fever, my sister called my mother and then our family doctor, Fritz Heilbroner, who with his wife Inga was celebrating his fortieth wedding anniversary at the theater. Around midnight, my sister and I met my mother and the doctor at his office, the man who had cared for me since childhood, the man whose fingertips I can still feel checking a swollen gland in my neck when I was very young. That night he checked me with his gentle hands, gave me a shot of antibiotic, and sent me home. For a month I forced myself to walk for hours in our neighborhood to drive any remaining tissues from my womb. And going to school. And riding the subway back and forth. And laughing out loud and long with Candy and Amina. And studying in Lehman Library with Gussie and Denise and Ada and Juanita, but not telling a single person, except Candy, what I was going through. And receiving letters from Joann Christian's mother in Albany, Georgia, who was learning to read and write at the SCLC Citizenship School and who signed her letters to me, "Your Mother in Christ, Odessa Mae Christian." And one evening in the first-floor bathroom in Lehman Hall, I expelled the frank red clot that told me the abortion was finally complete.

My final year of college, it was war at home, and US involvement in the war in Vietnam was heating up. The war to colonize Vietnam had gone on for decades, with the US first involved in the mid-1950s. Tellingly, in August 1964, coinciding with the discovery of the bodies of Chaney, Schwerner, and Goodman buried in an earthen dam in Mississippi, the Gulf of Tonkin incident escalated US involvement.

The man I would soon marry qualified as a conscientious objector to the war in Vietnam. Michael Simmons, a SNCC staffer, was convicted of refusing military induction and served two and a half years in prison; Michael went on to become a lifelong staff member of the American Friends Service Committee. Earlier, James Lawson of Nashville, scholar, SNCC mentor, and practitioner of nonviolence, had been a conscientious objector and served prison time during the Korean War. More recently, David Bell, one of the 1963 summer volunteers with whom I had worked in Southwest Georgia, was imprisoned as a conscientious objector. There were countless others, including Muhammad Ali. It was the Black men I knew, or knew of, who served time. The day before we married, tens of thousands across the United States marched against the war in Vietnam. We marched with them down New York's Fifth Avenue.

It was so hard in the final year I worked on SNCC staff, the final year before I moved to New Mexico, to know how to continue to define myself as a person working for social change who was at the same time defined by gender and race. A person who loved and desired social justice and human dignity but understood the power amassed against us. A person who understood that neither justice nor dignity for all in the United States could be achieved without taking on the issue of race.

New Mexico and Detroit

In 1965, when President LBJ proclaimed, "We shall overcome," it made me sick.

My husband and I moved to Santa Fe as if we could move anywhere without an ancestral relationship to that particular *where*. We could move anywhere—we post-Nazi-Holocaust Jewish children, children with broken ancestral ties to any particular land, wandering Jews who did not belong by lineage to a land.

I went about the business of marriage, employment, pregnancy and birth, though the just-past years festered.

Before my husband and I moved to Santa Fe, Charity came to a farewell dinner. My mother was flustered. I was flustered, torn between myself as daughter to Eunice, as daughter to Charity, and as wife. I could not be with Charity, quiet and close as we had been when I was her child. Charity handed me a parcel. "Open it." Inside, her patchwork poncho pieced from dove gray and dusky pink and shimmery black, the surfaces smooth and pebbled and nubby. It bore the magic of Charity sweeping into the classroom when I was four. For decades I wore this gift, wore it from New York to New Mexico to Detroit to West Virginia, and for many more years I kept it among my winter clothes but never wore it. It was a garment that someone else would wear, a garment to shelter another's life. I thrifted it.

I left New York, and my sister moved to India to dance *bharata natyam* with Mrinalini Sarabhai's company in Ahmedabad. My blue aerogram letters rarely reached her, and hers did not always reach me.

To stay in touch with the world as I had known it, I read SNCC's *Student Voice* and SCEF's *Southern Patriot*, experiencing long distance SCEF's work in Kentucky, experiencing SNCC's work with the Black Panthers, journeys to Africa, and the 1967 position paper against the Israeli invasion of Palestine during the Six-Day War. I agreed with and was grateful for the statement, but it caused mainstream ritual outrage against SNCC. The mass media excoriation of SNCC for the statement promoted a separation between SNCC and its long-time ally, the liberal Jewish community. The meaning of the word *excoriate* comes from removing part of the skin, skinning.

After a period of no communications from SNCC, I realized I must have been removed from the mailing list or that there was no more mailing list. The Detroit Rebellion on our small black-and-white TV screen: more than forty people killed, most of them Black. Thousands injured. Thousands arrested.

Thousands of buildings burned. The white, gray, and black flickers from Detroit so similar to the flickering of Vietnam. When my son was born in Santa Fe, New Mexico, I was twenty-five. I had left the grief and anger and confusion of New York, and/but all of those had come with me to the Land of Enchantment.

We prepared for a holistic Lamaze childbirth at the Catholic Maternity Institute, a quiet and gentle place run by nuns, but we were foiled when pneumonia brought my contractions to a standstill the night of January 8, my birthday. After hours of labor, the nuns bundled me into the Institute's VW Beetle and drove me a few blocks to St. Francis hospital, where in the dead of night a doctor eased my son from my body. Santa Fe for me was like that: the bad taste of national betrayal and the amazement as I made the transition into motherhood and my own adulthood.

The war in Vietnam ground on: television, newspapers, our breakfast, our bedroom, on the phone with my mother.

Liz Sutherland (now Betita Martínez), with whom I'd worked in the New York SNCC office, lived near Española, New Mexico, not far from Los Alamos, birthplace of the atom bomb, and on that fouled ground, Betita and her teenage daughter Tessa worked in support of the Land Grant Movement, based on centuries-old Spanish grants of land that did not belong to the crown.

We stood in front of the Santa Fe Post Office once a week bearing placards against the war. There were meetings where people smoked cigarettes and had affiliations dating back to the 1930s. As I remember it, the group was entirely, or almost entirely, Anglo, in a state with a large Chicano and Chicana population.

Events in Georgia and New York had repercussions in Santa Fe. My husband lost his job because he had been arrested in front of the courthouse in Foley Square back in New York City at a demonstration I had helped organize.

Someone had contacted his employer, the State of New Mexico, and he had, as a consequence, been fired. My boss at the Santa Fe welfare department called me into her office to ask me about this, as *someone* had phoned her. When our son was born, my husband was unemployed. Despite feeling not only isolated but exiled, a very personal experience, my husband's situation was not unique, as similar repercussions happened to countless others in the late sixties and seventies.

A friend helped my mother, whose sewing skills included no more than mending, to weave yellow blocks out of fine yarn to create a receiving blanket. A blanket to receive our baby. To each corner, my mother affixed an embroidered red strawberry, a finishing touch to mark the occasion for which even she had no words. Later, in Detroit, when we were expecting our second child, Charity helped her piece a baby quilt of disparate patches of bright cottons, rough and smooth side by side, striped and floral and African, outlined in small yellow featherstitching, with a lavender peace symbol at its center. Vietnam. Charity imagined my mother could do this, so it was a gift from both of them.

1968. Uprisings at Columbia University. Uprisings in Paris and across Europe.

Jonah = *dove* in Hebrew.

On television and radio, the spigot of national news opened twice a day; no continuous urgent feed. I sat on our nubby gold-colored couch, nursing my four-month-old, when I heard: Dr. King had been assassinated. I saw the news at the same time as the rest of the country. How could the assassination and my brown-eyed infant both be true?

Dry-ice vapors came on me as they had on the Haitian verandah. I lived in a marriage and I had no idea what a marriage should look like. I tried to remain myself with a partner who called me a *dilettante* for my politics, who called me *twitch* for my innate femaleness. Vestiges of myself as my mothers' daughter lay within me, invisible to this world of blue-blue New Mexico skies and evergreen mountains, lit each autumn with gold aspens.

I ran to be a delegate to the state Democratic Convention. How easily a small group of us overwhelmed the precinct meeting. I won. Does not feel great in retrospect, this outsider takeover. I was still nursing Jonah. Coincidentally, my mother was visiting. Throughout the day of the convention, my husband and mother brought Jonah to me in the gym where we were meeting so the baby could nurse. I had never seen so many sticky, empty mini liquor bottles piled into and spilling out of the ladies' room trash, a spill of soft bribery. The party powerful chose who would go to Chicago and I did not make the cut.

We headed north and west to places we had read about: the Grand Tetons, Glacier, the West Coast from Oregon down to San Francisco and back home by way of the Grand Canyon. I sat in the passenger seat in front, lifting our son in and out of a collapsible bed, basically a box with sides that folded in upon themselves. He lay there sleeping or murmuring to himself, less than fifteen pounds that on impact could have flown through the air and into the windshield, but we didn't know any better. Un-seat-belted, I held him against myself and nursed him, his cheeks flushing in the heat and kernels of sweat sprouting on his nose. And he didn't. Get jettisoned.

At night we stopped at motels, ten or fifteen low-ceilinged rooms shoulder to shoulder, a few yards from a two-lane highway. We carried the baby and his collapsible crib into rooms where we could hear the voices and the shenanigans of our neighbors. We heated canned food on a hibachi outside our door and retreated indoors to eat, where we sat on the tufted bedspread and watched the evening news. There we were, not at the Democratic National Convention.

The counterculture Yippies had proclaimed: "Join us in Chicago in August for an international festival of youth music and theater . . . Come all you rebels, youth spirits, rock minstrels, truth seekers, peacock freaks [sic], poets, barricade jumpers, dancers, lovers and artists . . . We are there! There are 500,000 of us dancing in the streets, throbbing with amplifiers and harmony. We are making love in the parks . . ." There we were, with our infant son in the room with painted cinderblock walls, semitrucks roaring all night, and we'd get up, carry baby and crib out to the car in the cool morning, and spend another day on the road, sometimes pausing to walk through mountain lands or open prairie.

Ten thousand demonstrators in Chicago. In a cloud of tear gas, police clubbed and beat protesters, journalists, and bystanders, in neutral grays on the TV screen. The police were determined to enforce a curfew. No making love in their parks. CBS evening news anchor Walter Cronkite, hardly a voice of the left, proclaimed, "The Democratic convention is about to begin in a police state. There just doesn't seem to be any other way to say it."

The protesters chanted on television, as we watched at 6:00 p.m. and 10:00 p.m. A car might pull into the motel parking lot, its radio blaring, laughter, car doors slamming, a room door shutting.

The next day. Again. Mountains. Or perhaps prairie. Or moonscapes of rock. Magnificent skies. Spectacles. Separate and apart from the three of us in the speeding red Falcon.

Eight Movement people were arrested in Chicago.

One night, the hibachi put to bed, the baby sacked out, the taste of dinner on our tongues, we watched as the name of Julian Bond, my SNCC brother, barely older than I, was put forward as a nominee for vice president of the United States of America, although he was seven years too young to serve in that position. A protest nomination from Wisconsin, and the convention microphones were turned off before another delegate from Wisconsin could second the nomination. The prairies and one-time seas and fossils, the moonscape Badlands, silenced.

We pulled into our driveway on Agua Fria Street in Santa Fe. Early September, a grand jury investigated the protests at the Democratic National Convention. The grand jury would meet dozens of times into the spring of 1969, before the Chicago Eight were charged with crimes associated with the convention.

My husband applied to the School of Social Work at the University of Michigan in Ann Arbor.

I had a miscarriage.

1969. Six years after I'd left Southwest Georgia; five years after the murders of James Chaney, Mickey Schwerner, and Andy Goodman; four years after the assassination of Minister Malcolm; three years after SNCC came out against the war in Vietnam; two years after the US Supreme Court handed down its Loving decision declaring laws against interracial marriage unconstitutional; one year after 2,500 US citizens camped out on the national mall at Resurrection City.

Cocooned in the red Falcon on our way to Ann Arbor, Michigan, baby in my lap, awash in all that had happened, I daydreamed about what lay ahead. Martha from the summer in Southwest Georgia and Denise Jackson Lewis from Barnard lived in Detroit. Martha, who never had an idle thought and who knew about and had perspectives on history and power. She knew where everyone in SNCC had been and where they were, all recorded in her dog-eared, pocket-size address book. And Denise had sheltered me in her room and chuckled at my jokes and gone to Mississippi the summer of 1964, and had been studying at the same table in Lehman Library the night I knew I had expelled *the products of conception.*

Ann Arbor, sedate and white.

The motor of our red Falcon blew up. The snazzy red Falcon was towed away in a clank of chains and groan of gears. We bought a used black Dodge whose paint was dull and blistered. On Detroit's west side, we found an apartment, the upper floor of a house on West Thirty-Third Street. Our Polish landlady showed us around—a large eat-in kitchen with linoleum floor, a small bathroom with slubbed-over enamel paint jobs, a small bedroom for our son, one for us, a narrow living room, and a room with a balcony overlooking the street. A day later, as we were moving in, the landlady climbed the stairs to tell us she had sold the house. To a minister. She paused. The minister was a Black man. That was fine with us, we said. Soon, we realized our new landlord was the only Black person on the block; most residents were Polish American, sometimes related to one another. In these households, the breadwinner often worked in the auto plants or related industrial jobs. Only two years since the Detroit uprising, our new landlord must have been a local upheaval within an era of upheaval. If there was trouble about him, as outsiders we didn't hear it and lived above his apartment without incident for two years, by which time the residents of that block had become overwhelmingly Black.

As my husband began his first semester, the trial of the Chicago Eight began. My husband's life was centered in Ann Arbor, though there were reverberations of unrest there, including the presence of a group called the White Panthers. Jonah and I were in Detroit, learning the Polish bakeries, which on Fridays carried a braided bread (*not* labeled challah); the commercial rush of Livernois Avenue; the stores and traffic of Michigan Avenue, where with my son on my back I might catch a bus downtown to nearly all-white protests against the war in Vietnam. From the pages of Detroit's independent political paper, the *Fifth Estate*, I learned the city before I experienced it, finding my way to demonstrations and to meetings of mostly white groups such as PAR, People Against Racism.

My husband's social work placement was with the UAW, the United Auto Workers. I think this is why early one morning I found myself on a dawn picket line at the Fruehauf Trailer plant. I remember a chain link fence, the imminence of sunlight, and the cold hard work of walking the line, the shouting among familiars back and forth. There may have been a trash barrel burning for heat. The beams of the trucks coming in and out of the yard mesmerized me. The trucks' tires were taller than we were. Union women in their bundled coats and scarves, their boots, steam puffing from their mouths, defiantly kicked at those tires. The trucks kept coming.

At meetings or demonstrations, I learned of other meetings and other demonstrations and met people, including people I'd known at Barnard who were now associated with a Marxist Humanist group founded by Raya Dunayevskaya, who had once been Lenin's secretary. I learned of DRUM, the Dodge Revolutionary Union Movement, an organization of Black workers. I, child of Greenwich Village, felt the excitement of this new place—blintzes at Hamtramck's Workingman's Co-op Cafe, Hamtramck home of the Dodge Main plant, Hamtramck with its consonants aligned in a way I had never before seen, aligned in a way I might have thought unpronounceable but that was straightforward on local tongues. This was not New York. There was a group of SCEF supporters, mostly older than I, with whom I organized a fundraiser at which Anne Braden spoke. I began to attend SCEF board meetings in Louisville. I had Martha and her family and Denise and her husband John. There were continuities.

I had eaten a soufflé only once in my life—couldn't imagine preparing one, the recipes full of admonitions—yet when my baby, husband, and I arrived at Martha and Silas's apartment for Sunday brunch, that's what she was making. Those Sundays, while Martha assuredly folded egg whites into creamy custard, we might chew over recent events and what they meant, because the meaning of history and power was on our minds. Weekday afternoons, Martha and I sat in her apartment with our babies and talked. And laughed. Maybe a prerequisite for an organizer should be their chuckle; chuckles assume the listener will catch the chuckler's meaning. Of course, chuckles can also express condemnation—Martha is capable of those chuckles for people unfortunate enough to earn them. During the soufflés and the talk, while absorbing the slight weight of our toddlers drinking from cups we offered, I felt how after the police violence and the burned-out central cities and the betrayals by the government, we were knitting ourselves back into the fabric of our lives as they were meant to be.

In Chicago, at the trial of the Chicago Eight, Black Panther Bobby Seale was denied representation; in public, in the courtroom, Seale was bound, gagged, and chained to his chair, the mirror image of abused Black men during slavery, an image broadcast on the evening news. Seale was removed from the case, which was then called the Chicago Seven. What was it Walter Cronkite had said about a police state?

I worked at REP, the Radical Education Project, originally a Students for a Democratic Society (SDS) project. We produced print materials for the Movement, including a pamphlet I wrote, "Having a Right-on Baby." I learned to lay out, print, and distribute pamphlets. I rode across the bridge between Detroit and Windsor, Canada, to transport illicit cartons of *Our Bodies, Ourselves*. The

REP office, less than a mile from our apartment, was on Michigan Avenue on the second floor, above the web press, a machine as big as an elephant run by the Detroit Printing Co-op. The press produced gorgeous color posters of women with infants on their backs and guns across their torsos. Also on the ground floor of the building, the always-locked metal door of a white man whom none of us knew. I didn't even know his name to say *hello*.

Jim Forman of SNCC moved to Detroit to work with the League of Revolutionary Black Workers.

I attended my first SCEF board meeting. These meetings were gatherings of southern activists and their supporters who drove into Louisville in beater cars and trucks from across the South and the North. The weekend meetings flowed from analytical to passionate, studded with details I could hear nowhere else, stories that defined us, stories with which I could identify. I was in the presence of my contemporaries but also in the presence of the generation who had come before us: the Bradens and Modjeska Simkins, for instance. Ever present was the principle that southern organizing was groundbreaking and that all of us—whether organizing pulpwood cutters in Louisiana or coal miners in the Appalachian Mountains—shared assumptions about justice and race and class; that we might each have different approaches to our work but held a few tenets in common; that we shared a history of opposition that could result in repression; that we honored our elders and treasured our children; that we did not aspire to join the mainstream power structure.

For that board meeting, I left my son behind in his father's arms for the first time and boarded the bus, alone and excited. In Louisville, after an all-night journey in close proximity to strangers through a landscape I didn't know, I stepped down into the Louisville terminal. Carl Braden bought the two of us breakfast, which we ate in the bustling terminal, before going to our meeting in two crowded rooms separated by pocket doors, where people spilled into the hallway and sat on the stairs going up to the second floor. That space: domestic space converted by necessity to a workspace for serious and sometimes dangerous political work.

For another meeting, I drove from Detroit to Louisville, Jonah not yet three and by my side, my daughter *in utero*. Downstairs, during the day, we reported and debated the pulpwood cutters; democracy in the United Mine Workers; the Welfare Rights Organization (WRO); amnesty for Walter Collins, a Black draft resister in New Orleans. Over the coming decades, at these meetings I would meet long-time SNCC people like Bob and Dottie Zellner and Dinky Romilly, and new political friends like C. T. Vivian, Modjeska Simkins, and Fred Shuttlesworth. Upstairs, on the night of that particular meeting, I watched over Jonah, who slept fitfully and woke whimpering with a fever, while Anne worked through most of the night in the next room. Now, I wonder whose crib had been sitting in those attic rooms? Relic of whose childhood, remaining in that building where the past and hope for the future converged?

SNCC workers Ralph Featherstone and William "Che" Payne were driving to attend court in Maryland. SNCC's H. Rap Brown had been charged with arson and incitement to riot. A bomb beneath the car's floorboard exploded. Featherstone and Payne died instantly. Although the media and law enforcement officials, most prominently the FBI, were quick to claim that Featherstone and Payne had planned to plant the bomb, that was never proven. Family and Movement people said from the beginning that the government—possibly the new COINTELPRO—was responsible. The press coverage is riddled with the word *militant*. The word was used then the way the word *terrorist* is used now—an attempt to delegitimize Black activists and their work.

When Martha, who is nothing if not thorough and meticulous and wholehearted, heard of the deaths, she began to wash a smudge on the kitchen wall, perhaps a random distraction at first, but then she washed the contiguous margins, and so on and so forth, until she had washed every inch of kitchen wall. As if a smudge on the wall were the problem. As if the problem could be attacked with a scrub brush and soapy water. Martha's erasure—the loss of everything or the possibility of beginning again? That is the opening within which we raised our toddler boys and waited for the births of our second children.

. . .

The trial of the Chicago Seven dragged on. Notable supporters took time to be present in the courtroom, both to witness the proceedings and to affirm the seven were members of our community. At night, some of those supporters traveled to share their insights and indignation at the "trial." One night, such a delegation came to Detroit. We sat on the balcony, in the first or second row, looking down upon the speakers. Among them were Anne Braden of SCEF, Bill Kunstler, one of the lawyers for the seven, and a parent whose child had gone to Mississippi for Freedom Summer. The crowd was enthusiastic, much clapping and cheering and stamping of feet. In my lap, Jonah, who was about a year and a half, was swept up in the excitement. Still riding the wave of partisanship, when silence fell over the auditorium, Jonah continued to clap his hands and for good measure let out a peal of laughter that sailed into the open space. Bill Kunstler looked up and smiled. "I haven't heard a sound like that in months," he said, before the evening's noise rushed back in. The sound of home, breaching public space.

Because 1970 was dangerous for people in the Movement . . . and and and . . . the five or six of us at REP went for target practice in the countryside. I was terrified for the baby in my belly, what it might do to the drums of her tiny seashell ears, but in a field outside Lansing I shot a gun for the first and last time in my life.

Sun and dust motes drifting in our office, a man and woman visited REP. Their son was underground. He had known my coworkers before SDS separated into the Revolutionary Youth Movement and the Weather Underground, the latter formed after an SDS basement bomb factory had inadvertently blown up a Greenwich Village townhouse. The SDS people who lived in the townhouse had fled and gone underground, including my elementary school classmate, Kathy Boudin. When I heard the REP visitors' last name, I understood that they had been parents of someone (this very same son) who had joined Mississippi Summer in 1964. When the parents and I saw one another, they recognized me and I recognized them. I had known their son.

. . .

Martha knew local parks where our families had picnics, setting out blankets and food, the little boys running in the grass. We began childbirth classes, a room full of women on the floor, beached below our bellies, our breasts falling to either side, husbands hovering. In those third-trimester weeks, Jonah was in daycare in basement rooms in a co-op on the Wayne State campus—either my husband or I worked there one day a week, supervising snacks and nap times, walking down the street to watch the assembly line at the nearby Vernor's ginger ale plant. If you've ever walked with a two-year-old, you know it's mandatory to stop at every dandelion, every bit of dog poop, every rock. These were mostly children of white hippies. At least one coworker, charming and imaginative with the kids, was often stoned. One of the children, a featherlight three-year-old, would climb onto her crib's guardrail during nap time and walk barefoot around the top rail. It was a pretty sweet place. Martha enrolled her son Silas. There was ugliness. Black boy. He was watched overscrupulously by parents. Martha withdrew him. Looking back, I should have spoken to the other white parents. I think my *feeling* that I was not like other white people allowed me to act as if I bore no culpability for the hostility of white grown-ups toward Silas, a three-year-old.

Night. I was alone guarding the REP office. Through the windows facing Michigan Avenue, police lights strobed through the dark. Several police cars had pulled up directly below the office. As we'd agreed, I took the shotgun from its secure spot. I stroked my belly where the baby lay, feeling a hurt I could barely breathe through, though as agreed I stationed myself at the top of the enclosed staircase that ended in our barricaded door which opened into the entryway, the Movement press on one side and the unknown white man on the other. I heard the police on the other side of the door. Though I held the gun in my hands as I'd been taught, I knew immediately and without question, I would never shoot another woman's child. Not even a policeman.

The police did not storm upward toward me.

They were after the white man, who, it turned out, used his space to produce loaded dice.

. . .

In December 1970, Chicago Black Panthers Fred Hampton and Mark Clark were murdered by police who shot through a door into the mattress where Hampton lay sleeping. The next Sunday, with members of the Detroit group People Against Racism, or PAR, I attended a church in a white suburb, Dearborn. We were expressing outrage at the killings in Chicago. I sat in that pew with the others. I was more than eight months pregnant. The handful of us were outsiders and I think everyone in the sanctuary knew this. I steeled myself. Was it hostility I imagined? Was our presence alone enough to make us provocatively worthy of retaliation? Our showing up was righteous but foolhardy. I think it unlikely we changed any minds or hearts that Sunday morning, but who knows? There must have been some, perhaps teenagers, who weren't sure about what they'd been taught about race, but they may have never known any white people who stood up in support of Black people. Our presence may have heartened them. There may have been congregants who had also had run-ins with the police and maybe we gave them pause. At the time, youngish and self-righteous, sitting in that church on that Sunday was mostly about me—my anger and helplessness in the face of Hampton and Clark's deaths, as well as my political correctness—and not so much about the congregants, their thoughts and feelings, into whose midst we had come.

The apartment was small. A romping and shouting three-year-old and his cat could make quite a bit of noise and consume a lot of air space. Because she was small, and growing slowly, I continued Carmela's midnight feeding. I would lift her from her crib and nurse her in the living room, the apartment quiet. She was a sipper and player, so it took a while for her to finish. She would smile at me and even pat my breast companionably as she nursed. One night I realized this wasn't about eating at all. Smiling, cooing, patting my bare skin, she was having a ball. She had me to herself in the dead of night. As spring came on, we moved Carmela's crib from our bedroom to her brother's. Mornings, she would haul herself to her feet and laugh and laugh at the wonderful sleeping boy across the room. *Haha*, she'd exult.

. . .

I thought I was a self-determining adult. Despite the chaos and oppression around us, my children would be children of the new way. I would love them; they would love me. That would suffice. Our mornings would be soft and bright like sun on the worn linoleum. My children would grow in the shadows cast by the old ways, the ways I fought, but they would be loved and they would be safe; my children would not be harmed. We had moved out from under the harmful generations. My hubris. Me. A survivor of child sexual abuse, twitching with old fears, dread was my middle name. Even when my children were in elementary school, I would look out the night window on the point of land above Middle White Oak Holler in West Virginia—the gleam of the moon was soft, but I was filled with dread.

West Virginia

West Virginia, where I raised Jonah and Carmela, the whitest place I had ever lived, a place where no one whom I had known in SNCC resided, a place where my mother visited only once before her death. We had had many visitors in Santa Fe, quite a few in Detroit, but almost no one came to West Virginia. To New Yorkers, the move to the Appalachian Mountains put us beyond the pale.

We drove from Detroit, south and east across Ohio, down the West Virginia Turnpike to a place we had never been. *Caution, this is a modern two-lane highway. Proceed at your own risk*, read the sign. Five men had died constructing this road. Mountains towered above us, in places the rock face bald due to strip-mining. We crossed bridges high above slim chains of rivers. We swerved through harsh turns dictated by the land. Ponderous semitrucks tracked up to our bumper and zoomed around us, or roared toward us from the other direction. On the hills, the weighty trucks slowed to a crawl, motors straining. Snowbirds from the Detroit we'd left passed through West Virginia, trekking away from Midwest winters and toward working-class bungalows in Florida.

We passed a roadcut seamed black with coal, our destination's heart. Later, when I taught in a two-room West Virginia school, a student's father would haul into the school an armful of coal. With his black-seamed fingers, the father would point out flurries and constellations of fossils. Told the children the fossils had lived so long ago they couldn't imagine it, that there had been seas over the land in which these trilobites had lived. That the black coal had once been green plants.

West Virginians worked for black lung recognition and benefits, for democracy within the United Mine Workers, for welfare rights, and for women's and family health. Among them were long-time activists, for instance Cliff Bryant, who as a child had known the strikers' camp up Cabin Creek, who would have known miners were massacred in a similar camp in Ludlow, Colorado. West Virginia activists included children of coal miners who might be in their twenties and had gone to West Virginia State College, an HBCU that was becoming increasingly white in its student body; Marshall University in Huntington; West Virginia Tech, a long-time center of coalfields activism; or West Virginia University. Among the activists were former VISTA workers who had grown up elsewhere; some of them had gone to work in the mines.

The activist women of the coalfields canvassed, petitioned, lobbied, marched, confronted politicians, joined one another in women-centered organizing, fed, and fought side by side with men in a period characterized by outsiders' occasional interest, publicity stunts like that of the Kennedys in the 1960 presidential election—a sort of poverty road show. A grassroots revolt was in progress, largely unacknowledged by outsiders, although Barbara Kopple's 1976 Oscar-winning documentary *Harlan County, USA* did capture this time when tens of thousands engaged in wildcat strikes and demonstrations.

Like the southern antiracist struggle, which had drawn upon a many-centuries' history of resistance to vicious and state-enforced white supremacy, people in the coalfields had a long and honorable history of resistance. Both in the Deep South and in the southern mountains, I saw communities that drew upon old institutions and perspectives: the church, the NAACP and similar groups (a significant number of the southern-born women in *Hands on the Freedom Plow* had come up within NAACP youth groups or parallel church groups); in the mountains, Cliff Bryant, who as a child had marched with Mother Jones, had joined the wobblies for life; sometimes when I drove up Cabin Creek, I would see him hitchhiking, his red IWW neckerchief eye-catching. In meetings,

I felt the force of militant working-class politics with their roots in European struggles.

The Movement I experienced in West Virginia in the early seventies through much of the eighties crossed state lines and married supposedly distinct struggles. Wild cats and campaigns that surrounded me in West Virginia were one with movements in East Kentucky, Southwest Virginia, and Tennessee, much as the Movement in Southwest Georgia gained its power in part from the larger southern struggle, to which Southwest Georgia, in turn, had given weight. Mountain movement politics shared members and ideas among the UMW (United Mine Workers) and WRO (Welfare Rights Organization). Nationally, WRO was a predominantly Black and female organization. The connection between Welfare Rights organizing and organizing among insurgent mine workers led to a powerful creativity and solidarity between two organizing traditions. The third source of Movement momentum in the mountains was the movement for women's and children's health care.

Only months after our arrival in West Virginia, in the spring of 1972, a Pittston Coal Company water impoundment in Logan County broke in the middle of the night; a slurry dam deluge—a wall of water up to twenty feet high—let loose upon miners and wives and children and schoolteachers and family dogs and chickens; the beater cars and trucks parked in yards were lifted up and slammed into the sides of houses, or the vehicles were lifted and carried downstream to be set down askew and athwart someone else's driveway; water covered the length of Buffalo Creek Holler. Throughout the twenty-four hours preceding the break, federal inspectors had been checking the dam. They had watched the hourly rise in water level until it lapped at the lip of the dam. They had warned the company, which had already amassed innumerable safety violations. Famously, the drowning mother of a *miracle baby* made her way from the raging waters as close to land as she could get and threw her baby up onto the bank. The baby survived, but the mother drowned.

Pittston Coal Company. One hundred twenty-four people dead.

I drove into the coalfields in my red VW squareback, passed through the checkpoint at the mouth of the holler, and drove through the wreckage to the Citizens Commission Hearing. The commission was formed when it was clear the miners and their families would not receive justice from the official commission appointed by the governor. Over six hundred claimants received over $13 million in a settlement covering, among other things, neurological and psychological damage.

My baby daughter was with me as I drove up that holler. Arrived, I sat in a folding chair among a crowd of Black Lung activists, members of Mine Workers for Democracy and Welfare Rights members, my daughter on my back, her warmth resting on my back, her plump legs against my upper arms. I was straining inside myself for the cadence of mass meetings, the music of Harlem, the keen understandings of New Mexico and Detroit. Inside me at Buffalo Creek. With me on winter mornings when I drove over the mountain to teach at Caretta Elementary, a WPA gothic structure. When I put my children to bed and when I roused them in the morning. That cadence stayed. *Test me*, I'd say going over the mountain. *Test me. I have not forgotten my mothers. I have not forgotten Harlem. Not Southwest Georgia. You cannot put me anywhere, where I will forget.* Driving the hills, bending over my children, unable to sleep and listening to tree branches skittering over the roof: my mothers, Candy, Amina, Joann Christian. *Here.*

Women's liberation was in the air. I joined a women's group mostly of ex-VISTA workers, other miscellaneous political outsiders, and a couple of born West Virginians. We defined ourselves as *not* being middle-class consciousness raisers. We were in our midtwenties to midthirties. Some people in the Movement were now ten years younger than I was. A couple of us in the group had children and a couple of us were intentionally child-free. I don't know if the group dissolved over this, but I stopped attending when my need for childcare became an issue in the group.

I was invited by Karen Mulloy, who with her husband Joe worked for SCEF's Mountain Project, to join a statewide women's group of *political* women. Of all the women's groups I've joined, this one had the most lasting effect upon my life. We ranged from the rough-and-ready Frye booted to more sedate-looking wearers of Clark's Wallabees, clad in plaid shirts and rough sweaters and schoolteacher turtlenecks. All of us wore jeans. We were teachers, antipoverty warriors, general agitators, childcare workers, and at least one lawyer. One of us, in the next year or so, would visit China with a political delegation. Some of us were single and living alone. Some of us were involved and living with a partner. Some of us were married. Some had kids. Some did not. Some of us worked as organizers, and all of us were involved in organizing. One of us worked in the lab where Dr. Donald Rasmussen, or Dr. Raz, evaluated miners' lung capacity to determine a diagnosis of black lung disease. Dr. Raz traveled all over the state, displaying the preserved lungs of miners who had died of black lung. In our women's group we learned the rollercoaster history of that diagnosis—since the 1800s, depending upon the United States' political climate, it has been defined as a disease, subsequently ruled not a disease, and as a result of tens of thousands of miners engaging in wildcat strikes from one end of the coalfields to the other, not only was black lung once more officially a disease but a disease compensated for by the federal government. At least one member of our women's group was present when the US president signed black lung compensation into law.

We read *What Is to Be Done* by Lenin. We read about "barefoot doctors" in Mao's China and debated whether those among us who were thinking of medical school should think, based on questions of class and power, about nursing school instead. We read, kind of ad nauseam, Doris Lessing's *The Golden Notebook*. We strenuously critiqued Harry Caudill's *Night Comes to the Cumberlands* and Jack Weller's *Yesterday's People*. Karen Mulloy helped produce an *Appalachian People's History Book*, partially funded by SCEF.

Most of us had been raised outside West Virginia. We fit the profile of settlers, white people who take as a right the ability to move freely and possessively in a geography that does not belong to us. None of us were coal miners, though at least one of us was the daughter of a miner. A couple of us worked for the mine workers union, and many of us worked in support of the Black Lung Association and the Movement for Democracy within the United Mine Workers.

West Virginia's people were more than 95% white. For a while, one of our group's members was a Black woman who worked in childcare and whose husband worked with Dr. Raz. After a group member at a weekend retreat gave a presentation on self-defense, in the spirit of women's self-assertion and capabilities but with resonance with the racism of self-defense rhetoric, this Black member stopped attending.

While two Black students were shot by police in Baton Rouge; while the Rockefeller antidrug laws, which were a major building block in the criminalization of Black communities, were enacted; while Shirley Chisholm ran for president; and while the Combahee River Collective of Black feminists was launched, the group in West Virginia was focused upon the passage of the Equal Rights Amendment and the *Roe v. Wade* decision, black lung, and democracy within the union, as well as issues specific to the coal industry, which increasingly relied upon markets as far away as Japan. I felt good about the work that engaged our group, though at the same time I wanted more. Our discussions were like the afternoon sky I watched as I crested a hill on my drive home from school, the pale winter gray. I could see dimples and sinkholes and even the lashing of a dragon's tail inside the smooth winter gray, an implied eruption of everything. I missed everything that had come before, but here I was, in a political world almost entirely populated by white people. Since the time I had been four, my family's life, and therefore my own, had been a declaration about race.

Women's health was our third focus, equal in urgency with welfare rights and the mine workers. *Our Bodies, Ourselves* had been published in 1970, the year of Carmela's birth. Within the women's group, one of us was already a nurse, and two others entered nursing school. *Roe v. Wade* was decided the year my daughter was three, the year I left her father. Grassroots women organizers in West Virginia were fierce and articulate advocates for women's and children's health. The two currents of a movement for women's and children's health merged at an Appalachian regional conference, when women organizers in the coalfields saw Dr. Elinor Graham, who was pregnant, publicly insert a speculum and invite us to view her uterus, within which resided her anticipated twins. Women canvassed for women's health and abortion rights; Eula Hall and other coalfields activists in Eastern Kentucky opened the Mud Creek Clinic in Bethel, Kentucky. In Charleston, a women's health center opened—among its organizers were members of our women's group. For years until the opening of the center, an informal underground network had been transporting women to New York City for abortions. Women associated with the women's group were also involved with the UMW-associated Cabin Creek Clinic near Charleston and the New River Clinic near Beckley.

· · ·

I took a teaching job in McDowell County, where roadside signs proclaimed the county the *Heart of the Nation's Coal Bin*. Caretta Elementary was a WPA gothic structure, set in bottomland in a curve on the road that corkscrewed its way through the mountains to Southwest Virginia. There were seven children under the age of eight in my class and all of them had failed a previous grade. There were three sets of siblings in this small group. Two children were Black and one was the daughter of a retired white coal miner and her Black mother; everyone knew this, as the teachers were quick to tell me at recess. None of my students could read. Our only textbooks were discards the principal gathered up from other classrooms. The small class was housed in a narrow space, partitioned from a larger room.

One day there was a knock on the door; it could have been children selling raffles on a candy bar; it could have been the reading teacher; it could have been the principal; that day it was none of those but a tall, dark-skinned woman. I stepped out into the corridor. She told me she was Madeline James. Her grandson Eddie was one of my students. His mother was dying of cancer. She wanted Eddie's teacher to know. And she wanted me to call her if he was having trouble.

This is how I met one of the great women organizers of West Virginia, in the corridor outside my classroom in a tall-shouldered WPA gothic schoolhouse, in bottomland, where not long before white children had gone to school in this building and Black children had gone to a school at Warrior Mine Holler down the road. Some of the Black women with whom I taught had begun teaching in segregated Black schools. This history stood in our midst, always. One of the graces of Welfare Rights organizers like Ms. James is that they stood within their history and they acted upon it. They knew both in terms of facts and figures and in terms of embodied history, where they had come from, the injustice they had experienced, and the determination they felt in light of their history to make things better.

I spent summer vacation days driving with Ethel Brewster, a white welfare rights and women's health activist. Ethel was the wife of a coal miner who was active in the black lung and UMW struggles. Ten of her sixteen children had been born at home. She understood the role women played in maintaining their families' health and how women did not control their own reproductive health. Those summer afternoons, we went from house to house, speaking with women about health and welfare rights and the federal Early and Periodic Screening, Diagnosis, and Treatment program for young children. Ethel and I drove up and down the hollers of Logan County, sitting and talking, leisurely, leisurely, in a manner I had learned in Harlem, a bit of gossip, a bit of information, cups and cups of instant coffee, sitting on couches in front of TVs on which soap operas played. Cigarettes were smoked. Children ran in and out with urgent requests, or maybe for the little ones to snuggle into their mother's or their auntie's side. A hungry teenage son might come in from his shift in the mine. Nothing deterred Ethel Brewster. Like the others, she went to meetings in Charleston or Fairmont; she lobbied legislators. People in her community called her when there was a crisis: a house fire, a broke down car, a sick baby, a daughter in trouble.

Madeline James and Ethel Brewster were two among dozens of grassroots organizers in the black lung movement and the move for democracy within the UMW and the dozens who organized around welfare rights and women's and family health, movements which crossed state lines, particularly between Eastern Kentucky and West Virginia. They included women and men, Black people and white people, born West Virginians and outsiders such as former VISTA workers. They attended statewide and regional meetings and lobbied in Washington, DC, but their primary focus was their grassroots communities.

Helen Powell, a Black woman from Glen Jean, West Virginia (featured in the National Park Service's "African American Heritage Tour" of West Virginia's New River Gorge), was one of these organizers. I met her at a statewide meeting and participated with her in the West Virginia Rainbow Coalition (of which she was treasurer); she worked and organized at a state, regional, and national level. Her obituary reveals the breadth of her work and legacy: She was the granddaughter of the first Black sheriff in Fayette County. At fifteen, she had helped her father gain compensation for injuries sustained in the mines. She worked at the grassroots but also served as president of the state and national Black Lung Associations and, in 1972, drafted amendments to the federal black lung bill that opened benefits to thousands with black lung and their families. Through correspondence courses, she became certified as a paralegal and, in 1988, received an honorary doctorate from West Virginia University. She was chair of the Southern Appalachian Labor School and a board member of the New River Family Health Center.[2]

Helen received many more honors and organized in many other projects, but what I remember, in the end, is the energy that gusted through a meeting when she arrived. And I remember how when Helen arrived, my preschool daughter would shout, "Helen," and Helen would say with a grin, "Carmela," and then Helen would snatch up my child in an embrace as big-hearted as her love of social justice and the people of the coalfields.

In the context of the women's group, in the course of our reading and disputing and eating tomatoes from one another's gardens and cold Bulgarian cucumber soup and homemade breads so heavy they could have sunk a ship and slices of watermelon, I faced an aspect of myself that I had been trained, and had allowed myself, to ignore. Maybe first there was the meeting when two women, older by at least a decade than most of us, attended. They, like most of us, were outsiders. They were lively, literate, had a grand piano hauled up a dirt track to their mountain house. Their energy felt different. After they left, though I can't remember details, maybe for obvious reasons, someone raised the issue: the two women were a couple. The problem. The two women were a couple. I have to say I did not have a light bulb go off in my head, a light bulb to illuminate what this might mean for myself. Who—me? What did it have to do with me? I imagine I watched silently as the group (as I remember it) decided to discourage the two women from returning. What I felt was like the shifting interior of a winter sky. My learning and changing about this took place over some time and continues today.

Only in my late seventies, in correspondence with Kate, my childhood best friend who was dying, have I come to understand how I was formed to be an invisible and self-governing lesbian child.

But that was later.

What did happen in the women's group is that I fell in love with another member, a woman. There were *unspoken* protocols in the group: to allow *unthreatening* affection and intellectual intimacy among members, there was

---

2. Information from Helen's funeral service: http://sals.info/wp/wp-content/uploads/2016/07/helen-powell.pdf.

to be no lesbian *stuff*. To say it was simply a matter of my falling in love with a woman, made my falling in love with a woman an ahistorical event, side-stepped the issue of was I inherently *that way?* In my mind, my falling in love was just a mundane, girl-meets-girl sort of situation. An individual aberration is probably how I saw it. In those days, I wrote and received letters through the US mail all the time: from my mother, from my sister in India, from SNCC friends, from the mother of my elementary school classmate Kate, from Candy and Amina, and from members of the West Virginia women's group, including my crush. Much as had happened going to that sit-in on the Eastern Shore of Maryland, an unspoken dialogue developed between this woman and me: *were we flirting with one another?* As in 1961, the answer was, *Yes, as a matter of fact, we were. Flirting with one another.*

In the 1970s, repression had an enormous appetite. This loving of mine, this self, had been repressed back two generations into my mother's early years between the pandemic of 1918 and the *Great* Depression of the 1930s. I grew up in a household headed by two women. After my earliest years, there was no man present. I was a mother with two young children and found myself in love with another woman. Not only was it legally impossible to be a lesbian and a resident mother, it was illegal, on grounds of *moral turpitude*, to be both a lesbian and a teacher in West Virginia public schools.

My woman lover, my three-year-old daughter, and I lived in Boone County. My son, who was six, had chosen to live with his father. My lover, daughter, and I shared a house with David and Susan Greene, who had come as VISTAs to West Virginia from Ohio (Susan) and Long Island, New York (David). Susan had finished nursing school and was working at the medical center in Charleston, twenty miles away. David worked in the mines in the next county over. Sometimes when he went to work in the county on the other side of the mountain, he would take an old coal mine one-lane tunnel from our side to Cabin Creek on the other. If he met a vehicle coming in the other direction, one would have to back up to let the other car pass. What happened in those seconds when the two drivers silently negotiated which car would back up?

We lived with David and Susan, who was pregnant, in a tall, narrow, hand-built house on a point above bottomland. There was no road to the house. We parked our cars beside the two-lane road and either we walked up a dirt track through the woods, across the Butchkos' yard to the house we rented, or we walked across the bottom past the house of a renting family and up a steep path. We hauled groceries and laundry and Carmela and David and Susan's baby Josh. My family slept in an upstairs room that we reached through a door and up an enclosed staircase. The only plumbing in the house was a spigot in the downstairs kitchen. In our room, we had an improvised toilet: an upended produce crate with a hole cut in the top and an enamelware bucket below. Carmela learned to use a "toilet" in this setup.

In the spring of 1974, women from our group and others demanded the Council of the Southern Mountains devote an issue of its newsprint publication, *Mountain Life and Work*, to women's health in Appalachia. The special issue opens with photos and an interview with Ethel Brewster and Madeline James. They told of Ms. Brewster's many home births. Ms. James's thirty-two-year-old daughter was misdiagnosed in the early stages of cancer—the doctor told her she was allergic to washing powders, like Tide. Ms. James's daughter died eight months later of breast cancer that had spread to her ovaries. Both Ms. James and Ms. Brewster spoke about the need for birth control (and not the pill, which clinics were pushing at the time), prenatal care, choice of safe childbirth, care from doctors who treated women with respect, and the need for a connection between the welfare system and women's health.

The interview with Madeline James and Ethel Brewster created a structure and perspective for the rest of the issue: care for the elderly, which must include not only the medical aspects but housing and community support networks; there was an analysis of the medical system, problems with the fee-for-service structure, medical incompetence, issues of discrimination against what were then called *minorities*, and lack of continuity and coordination of care.

The publication was remarkable for its breadth and humanity; it spoke of Appalachia, but it spoke to the poverty and pain of lives from one end of the United States to the other. Sadly, so many of its concerns and insights around family health, the welfare system, discrimination, the need for paid work for women, and housing are still with us, and not just in the mountain South.

. . .

My mother lay in a bed in a New York City hospital from New Year's 1974 into the spring. I took a leave from teaching. I was working at a two-room school in Prenter, where I taught the primary students and the principal taught the upper elementary students. The school was set in a bottom, reached by almost ten miles of winding not-quite-two-lane road, much of which wound beside a creek. The road passed through the cluster of houses in Prenter and then climbed the mountain behind town and crossed over to the other side of the county. The creek was usually low and placid. During a heavy rain, a woman who lived beside the creek would watch as it rose, and when it reached a certain level, she phoned the board of education and the school buses were called to take the children home before flooding made the road impassable. There were, at most, thirty of us in the white wooden building. The classrooms were spacious, and the windows large. At lunch during good weather, children flocked around the building, or walked home in twos and threes, or hung around in the large office, talking with us grown-ups. Within a few years, the school would be closed. *Mountaintop removal*, or strip mining on steroids, stripped the mountain above Prenter, resulting in avalanches of debris and a moonscape scraped clean of vegetation, raw with obscenely copper-colored runoff, and the sludge ponds of mountaintop removal. The water contaminated. Cancer rates soaring.

The principal had a garden outside my classroom window. I remember rows of potatoes. In addition to we two teachers, there was a secretary who answered the phone and, I imagine, filled out forms expected by the board of education, which seemed a million miles away. There was a cook who prepared meals from government surplus foods. My students were country children. One student flushed the toilets over and over—she didn't have indoor plumbing at home and it was a novelty to her. The books, as they had been in McDowell County, were odds and ends, some of them leftovers from other schools with the names of their earlier schools stamped on their fronts. I hope I helped the children of Prenter, as well as the earlier classroom in McDowell. I had no training, only the memories of my extraordinary elementary school and a belief in my students' dignity and worthiness. I think they thought I was nice. Nice, but peculiar.

. . .

During the season of my mother's dying and my new love, my mother's relationship with Charity was on my mind. Always. I wanted an epiphany, a meeting across the generations. Lesbian mother to lesbian child. I wanted this from either or both of my mothers, as I tended Eunice's failing body in Lenox Hill Hospital. I sorted through my memories, looking for clues to *who* my mother and Charity had been.

I remembered a primal scene in Haiti when I was seven. We were schooled, without a word being spoken, to never discuss this aspect of our shared lives: we lived with both our birth mother and another woman. And my father's redheaded sister, a businesswoman with whom my sister and I spent elementary school summers, lived her entire adult life with one woman. We didn't talk about that either. When my friends entered the boy-crazy years, I was so clumsy and misdirected, I just knew there was something lacking in who I was. I didn't think I was queer because *we* in my family didn't think such things. Writing this section, I've been imagining an alternative ten- or eleven-year-old self. She is with me while I write. I conjure this child—sturdy, active, maybe even brash, loving the pretty clothes her family could hardly afford—in correspondence with Kate, who had been my best friend from the time we were nine or ten, through high school. In our seventies, she had battled leukemia for more than three years, had entered a hospital isolation ward in preparation for a stem cell transplant during the same month in 2018 that I sat by the hospital bed where my daughter lay close to death. Correspondence unfathomable.

In 2020, approaching the end of her life, Kate asked some of us to write snapshots of our memories of her. In addition to memories of tootling on our recorders and walking our dogs and candy stores in Greenwich Village, I made a glancing allusion to my self-conscious awkwardness at square dances in Vermont, where I spent summer months with her family. She had been *boy crazy* personified. Mentioning my awkwardness was a door I cracked no more than an inch, but my friend stepped through. She named the difference between us, wrote about how it had been a bit intimidating. Up until then we had been two wordy-nerdy, horsey little girls. And at the age of seventy-five, that plucky girl me who had misnamed herself *ugly, clueless, plump*, took on the naming of herself. Young lesbian. Young queer. There had been no adults affectionately noting and therefore honoring my secret crushes, no models, no figurative big sisters to applaud me and laugh at me and give me a hand back up when I stumbled.

In West Virginia, adults asked my son, *Do you have a girlfriend?* when he was in early grade school. My daughter: *Do you have a boyfriend?* I don't like this early and inappropriate insistence on boyfriends and girlfriends for children, but as it existed in its heteronormative form, it did not and had never included me. Kate's letter acknowledged the ten- or eleven-year-old I had been. The correspondence between me and my dying friend bridged the gap between me as I am now and that ten- or eleven-year-old nascent lesbian in a way that neither of my mother figures had been able, before my mother Eunice's death in May 1974, when I was thirty-one.

In seventh and eighth grade, I thought I was *ugly*. I thought I was *plump*. I thought I didn't know what to do, I thought boys were a strange country to which I did not have a passport, to the point of taking out library books, boys' fiction about basketball and such, things about which, as an urban femme, I did not have a clue. And I found the books to be honest, to have nothing to do with me and who I was, but if only I knew how to talk to boys, like my sister, a fabulous girl-boy flirt from a young age. Imagine if I could have said, "I might be a lesbian," a word not spoken in my household until I was in late high school and then always about others. Several times, my mother Eunice did tell me other people were lesbians—for instance, one of my favorite elementary schoolteachers, who could have been held up as a role model but wasn't. Imagine if that eleven- or twelve-year-old girl could have had an honorable, a proud name for who she was? What if, among many others, those of us who found our lesbian selves—I'm naming myself, Amina Rachman, Janice Robinson—could have taken on that honorable name, *lesbian*, as each of us had taken on the names mother, or aunt, or teacher, or Jew, or Black, in addition to the name of woman. Just who we were, out there in plain sight, for the young ones to see and model themselves upon. And decades later when the lens had become more refined and more complicated, what if I could simply have been. A little of this. A little of that. There have been men I loved being with and whom I loved; no doubt, however, that the center of my emotional and sexual universe has been women.

For a ten- or eleven-year-old girl: I imagine you running free. Not tomboy free and throwing balls and hitting things with bats free, but girl free. Your hair, curly and rampant and frightening to your mother who is the daughter of "respectable" immigrants, is loose in the outdoor air. Your lungs are full of sunshine, your legs strong. You run like you are a freedom fighter resisting the Nazis, a hero. You carry that you are descended from people who were enslaved in Egypt. You carry that the chosen mother you love unconditionally is the daughter of free people brought from Africa and enslaved in the United States. You love the purple-and-black plaid skirt that flares out from your waist and wear beady earrings that brush against your neck. You do not have names for yourself except free and happy and articulate and good and the words you and your childhood friend once owned: wordy-nerdy, horsey.

After Susan and David moved to their log house, my lover, children, and I moved up Middle White Oak Holler, across the dirt road from the Hagers in their double-wide, a classic holler winding up the creek between two shaggy hills, where, as they say, *If you stand on one hill, you can holler across to the one opposite.* We bought that little house and a hefty acreage up the steep, timbered hill behind it, for $19,000. We got the type of loan you get to finance a car. If we had gotten the sort of loan with which people buy houses, we would have had to deal with my children's father's residual claim to the property.

That asbestos-sided house perched above the road prompted me to file for divorce. As a result, I discovered the legal strictures that could constrain me in matters I considered private. A lawyer friend from Charleston offered to help. He said our worry would be the matter of integuments. I know that in biology integuments shield and hold together an entity: skin and membrane. By contorted reasoning, this applied to common marital property. My soon-to-be former husband had an integumentary interest in the property. My friend said under West Virginia law, because I had minor children, I probably could not get back my *maiden* name. That would have to be a separate petition to the court. With this provision, the state of West Virginia thought it was protecting minor children from the trauma of last name ambiguity. If a mother remarried, she could legally take her new husband's last name, so I'd say this provision had more to do with the woman than the children. My lawyer friend and I walked into the room at the courthouse in Madison. The usual family court judge was not present, and a judge from a different division was sitting in. Present were the judge, the court recorder, my lawyer, and me. I don't remember my former husband having representation. Everything was *pro forma*. As we rose to leave, my lawyer said, *Oh, and my client would like to return to her maiden name.* Offhand. The substitute judge did not know any better and agreed. The court recorder got red in the face, shook her head, shifted back and forth in her seat, but the judge ignored her and approved my paperwork. I had my birth name back. Or rather, I was returned to my father's last name, but it was the name I'd had since birth, through Harlem and SNCC. In the parking lot, after congratulating me, my lawyer friend said, *The name change can't be taken as a precedent. If we make a big deal of it, you may lose this judgment. It was a fluke. A trick we played on the way things are supposed to be.*

Living up the holler, I might write: Evening loneliness walks up the holler pretending to be someone's best auntie, the one with the green corduroy jacket, her eyes taking up residence inside your autumnal heart. When all you want is to be indoors and to look out upon the chilly holler, and mercy is extended to you in the form of artificial light. The children play in the back room, and if you are to eat, you must prepare the meal as the dark deepens and the loneliness is winning. You have to.

Sometimes the dread grasped me so tightly, to pull away from it, I slipped free from myself into vacant cold.

Twenty years past Southwest Georgia. Martha Prescod Norman insisted that despite my jam-packed, survival-level life, I absolutely must get in my car and drive the five hundred or so miles to Southwest Georgia for an Albany Movement reunion. Martha was right. It would be the last time I saw Bertha Gober, who had been jailed with Blanton Hall in the first Albany sit-in. For the reunion, students from Albany State had prepared classes on the history of the Movement. The young woman presenting mentioned Bertha Gober and Blanton Hall. Bernice Johnson Reagon gently interrupted her. Nodding to Bertha, who sat with us, Bernice said, "Bertha Gober is here, sitting with us at the table." It was a moment of life stepping in and taking book learning by the hand. It was the last time I saw Mama Dolly Raines, rare Black landowner in Lee County, successful farmer and midwife. She had taken us into her home and sheltered us when no one else would. Like Monroe "Cuz" Gaines and James Christian in Albany, she sat vigil over our sleep with her shotgun.

After the rage and shifts of the 1970s, I took a year off to write. As a schoolgirl, I had written at least one novel during the years of walking up and down those steps to the High School of Music and Art. Somewhere, I may have those spiral-bound notebooks that I never showed anyone. Child of parents who had read to me since before I can remember, parents who at times made their livings editing—scrutinizing, dismantling, and reassembling the words of others—writing was something I did; unlike my painting and drawing, I did it without instruction. Occasionally, a teacher might have singled out something I'd written, but mostly writing was simply a thing I did. I felt how I did it for me and I felt how I did it because of family, because of allegiance to something I'd inherited. Words were what we did.

I struggled. Typewriter, not an expensive one but not so flimsy it skittered across my desk as I typed. Things we no longer fight with: snarled ribbons; white correction fluid; jammed keys; fingertips dirty from carbon paper; illegible copies. Those pages were essentially inert, mistakes and omissions embedded in the paper, leaving a smear of erasure or a blob of correction fluid if I tried to fix them. Worse than the mechanics was trying to dredge the incisive and polished from inside me where there was a confounding swampy mix, or was it a mess of . . . nothing? Was that all I held? Nothing? I had made my way into Barnard College with clever words reflecting nimble thoughts, a use of words and grammar that I might have thought was a gift, but it was more accurately good language manners. The language of a well-trained child of bookish parents. My only other language mode seemed to be the language of verbal fencing, the lethally placed *point*. I was good at that. But. What did I have to say? How to span the gap between the fog in my mind/heart and the intractability of sentences tapped on paper? In the *Nation Magazine*, I saw an ad for a writing program at Goddard

College in Vermont. Because the program was low-residency, I could simultaneously work and raise my children in West Virginia and work on my writing, going to Vermont for ten days each in the summer and winter.

I needed space to assimilate the upheavals: the violence against my community over the last twenty years; Charity's death from an aneurism earlier that year and Eunice's death five years before; the turmoil with my lover. I needed outside air to breathe, needed to get my bearings. Late summer I set out by car. I love road trips; this one began in the West Virginia mountains, through New York City (unknown to most people, where I'd been raised), to Amherst, where my children were with their father for the summer, and then, Vermont. I had spent teenage summers with my best friend Kate and her family in Vermont, but Goddard was a new Vermont.

Soon after my arrival, we entrants gathered in a lounge, perching on chairs and couches, some of us on the floor for a welcome from the director, but my real welcoming was that night's faculty reading. The poet's work could have been in another language and even from another constellation, a constellation where I instantly wanted to reside. There they were on the stage, one by one, in their entire beings, living their work. Sometimes the force of their language made them spit out the words like droplets. Faculty in the program are now burnished elders, but in those days many were literary whippersnappers and firecrackers.

Many fellow students were as clueless as I, but others already knew this writer's way of being. Many already knew the names and the work of our faculty. I did not and went home to a semester mentored by Frank Conroy, whose name I had not known until then. I went to my first week of workshops, where students critiqued one another's work: Avoid the verb *to be*; it makes your language *passive*. *Sentimental* is *bad*. In this vein, it was OK to be critical of and otherwise shun writing about children and mothers. Giving emotions to trees and landscapes was *bad*. Emotions were best when the writer created a world in which the emotions could be intuited, but where they were never named. We read *Lolita*. Nabokov was *good*. What was I to do with my six-year-old self who had been sexually used? When we returned home to write, our weekly critiques of the reading list we had drawn up with our mentors must use *critical language*.

I drove home and began working on a novel set in the southern struggle. From the one-room US Postal Office at Racine, West Virginia, I sent regular packets of my writing and my bibliographic annotations to Conroy; in return, he sent his responses. He had his job cut out for him with me: I had no vocabulary of literary criticism. I didn't know what I was doing. I kept writing.

I returned to Goddard by train in January snow and drove up there the following summer. The situation at home was tough, but we were still together. We moved to Charleston, the state capital. I wrote a thesis on Katherine Anne Porter. Goddard College went bankrupt and closed, including the MFA program, but in the summer of 1981 the program reopened in a new location, Warren Wilson College, a small liberal arts school outside Asheville, North Carolina. I drove there to begin my final residency. I had written most of my novel. There was a question from the program board: Would it perhaps be better for me to submit just a section of the novel, a section I could better revise than the entire work? A faculty member read the novel in its entirety and said, as I remember it, that, although rough, the novel taken as a whole had an integrity that a selection would not. I am grateful that the board at Warren Wilson overrode their reservations and generously accepted the reviewer's recommendation. I treasure those words that recognized that integrity lies within an entirety, even if that entirety is rough.

The month I finished the MFA, my lover of nine years left. I spent at least a year weeping on the living room couch; though I went to work and put meals on the table, I didn't do much else. It was not fun for me, but even more I regret how much not-fun it must have been for my teenage children. I was working an organizing job and later teaching for Kanawha County Schools. At night in my bed, while the flamingo-lit face of the electric clock kept watch, I closed my eyes to suggest to my body it might be a good idea to get some sleep, but instead I was driving Boone County roads in the dark, pitching over the crests, careening toward roadcuts, listening to pelting sleet on my car's roof. Eighteen months later, coming out the other side, I realized some of the road's pitching, the careening, the pelting was early menopause. For my mother's generation, menopause had been the beginning of the end, metaphorically and medically.

What I felt was how much I had liked my periods, their reliability, their message: all is working as it should. No longer true.

Carmela's anger at my abject weeping, day after day. What's a middle school girl to do? She had her own stuff to deal with. She said, "Why can't you just be friends, like everyone else?" Maybe I couldn't be friends *like everyone else* because the heart of who X and I had been had not generally been acknowledged. The child lesbian in me was still unnamed. If who we had been had not been acknowledged, it was not possible to assimilate that loss and move on. How could I move on from something with no social presence? There were the moments like when I told the mother of Carmela's friend, "X moved out this weekend," and that mother said without missing a beat, "You'll need a job." I'd been working through a humanities grant, teaching writing in the schools. Not enough to support a household by myself; children of divorce and their resident parent experienced a severe loss in household income, so that a fifteen-year-old boy is told no, his mother cannot buy him new jeans this month. That woman, mother of Carmela's friend, who offered me a job, understood the bones of the situation, but we didn't name the heart of the matter: I had lost the romantic, passionate, shared head of family, nucleus.

December 3, 1984, two years after my partner had left, in Bhopal, India, at a subsidiary of Union Carbide, massive and lethal amounts of the gas methyl isocyanate, or MIC, leaked into the atmosphere, killing fifteen to twenty thousand people. The only other place in the world where MIC was manufactured was in the Kanawha Valley of West Virginia. That plant was in a primarily Black community outside Charleston and adjacent to the HBCU West Virginia State. Local residents formed People Concerned about MIC, which conducted research, interviewed community members, made formidable appearances at public meetings, and lobbied. They were a coalition of community members and organized labor, including the state AFL-CIO, which led to some contentious meetings. One of the group leaders was Mildred Holt, a Kanawha County Board of Education administrator. Mrs. Holt had been active against the earlier right-wing textbook strike. She embodied two elements of Black leadership I'd seen on the Eastern Shore of Maryland, in Southwest Georgia, and in West Virginia: she was a woman (enough said) and, by her carriage and dress, was in the lineage of the Black middle class who had supported and joined the struggle, either behind the scenes or, as with Mrs. Holt, front and center.

In the media, the gas leak at Bhopal was described in one of two ways: it was either the Bhopal tragedy or it was the Bhopal disaster. To me, the first framed an act of inexorable forces beyond human control; the second was caused by avoidable human error. The same had been true at Buffalo Creek, where the flood that killed one hundred twenty people was either an act of God or a result of human corporate error; the companies had a lot hanging on the distinction.

In 1986, the year Jonah finished high school, Linda Conway, a kindergarten teacher in rural West Virginia, rumored to be a lesbian, resigned under duress after prolonged public condemnation and harassment, including a demonstration of four hundred people against her in her rural county. The accusers *knew* she was a lesbian because she wore pants to work and had at one point lived with a woman. As a kindergarten teacher, she spent time on the floor with her students and skirts would have been awkward. The newspaper stories alone would have been enough to send lesbians and gay men, not just teachers, far back into the inaccessible reaches of their closets, with the door slammed shut behind them and locked from the inside.

The targeting and harassment and forced resignation were egregious enough, but the argument in Conway's defense by *friends*, including a feminist organization and its spokespeople, was worse: They *defended* her by saying, *Many teachers wear pants. Wearing pants does not prove she is a lesbian.* A devastating defense with its unstated assumption: if the teacher were a lesbian, a pox on her. Instead of: *Yeah, she could be a lesbian—nothing the matter with that. She has a right to teach if her pedagogy is sound and she honors her students' rights to respect and safety.*

I fell in love. With the boss. A married woman with daughters of her own, each about ten years younger than Jonah or Carmela. Parenting a middle schooler again, this time a girl who, if she had been able to stay in her home county, might have been a cheerleader, but in Charleston, she was an unknown. A girl whose mother, though Vicki and I were tight-lipped about our relationship, had been *ruined* by me.

Oh.

And.

Vicki and I were outed at work. I thought the fact that I was in bed with management was the scandal and knew this would have horrified my antiboss mother. The outing was gradual, beginning with rumors, and rumors of rumors, people turning aside when I entered a room, and ended with written accusations from staff (former friends, two of whom had recruited me to the agency). In the end, a few staff members wrote the board at least a dozen letters about our relationship, each more adamant than the last: I should go.

Early in this process, when I was feeling under attack and isolated, it was unbearable that Candy Keeling and I had been out of touch. I'd last seen her in New York City, a New Year's Eve weekend in my forties, when I'd spent a chaotic night with her at her parents' apartment, surrounded by children and children of children I had known. As fluffy toddler nieces and Candy's own daughter Noni bumbled in and out of our conversation, Candy took a paper napkin and wrote on it her address and phone number in Lorain, Ohio. So I would always know where she was. The next morning, Mommie T, Candy, her son Kuma, and I ate breakfast at Wilson's Bakery and Restaurant at 158th Street and Amsterdam Avenue, before Mommie T went to work, still at Harlem Hospital, and Kuma and Candy walked me to a bus stop. As the bus carried me away, Candy and Kuma stood on the sidewalk, their faces craned upward. *Goodbye.* Over the years, Candy and I had occasionally lost touch. Even that New Year's visit, back in New York City for a few days, from memory I had dialed Mommie T's number, Audubon 6–8832, and gotten Mommie.

That beleaguered day in the office in West Virginia, missing Candy, missing who I had once been, I dialed the Ohio number Candy had scrawled on the paper napkin, and once again, Mommie T picked up the phone. Candy had had a stroke. I sat in my shared office with three others who before the outing had been warm colleagues. I would not weep in front of them.

. . .

The next morning, in a nervous sweat inside my winter coat, I drove north into horizontal snow through West Virginia into Ohio, to Lorain, where I sat with Mommie T and Candy's daughter Noni in the house whose address Candy had given me that morning in Harlem. I inhabited Candy's home space for a little while before going with Mommie T to the nursing home. Candy's wrists were tied to the bed rails and she struggled to rise to sitting and struggled with her tongue, but her face above the institutional gown was electric with recognition and then she gasped, "Faithy!" Mommie T brushed Candy's hair back from her face, hiding the bald spots. And we managed without much language to breach the years and infirmity to name people, to be those two gallant teenage girls we once had been, the girls Mommie T had once called her *golden girls*.

Through a spring of increasing acrimony at work, I drove to visit Candy, visited through spring, through Noni's black prom dress, through tomatoes and corn in Ohio farm stands, through late summer corn stalks gathered in sheathes. After Noni finished high school, Mommie T moved back to Florida, where she planned to find a place for Candy. I visited once after Mommie T had left. I found Candy asleep. Staff rolled her over and changed her diaper, placed her on her back, tucked the sheet tight across her chest and allowed me into the cubicle. I could see bald patches on her scalp. Her skin was ashy. Her eyes remained closed. "Hey," I said and took her hand. When she didn't respond, I tugged and said her name. We would have our small jubilee of shared names and words, the bridge we had constructed over the months from where she was to where I was, from where we had been to where we were. When I tugged a bit harder than was nice, Candy cracked one eye open and then it fell shut. The photos of her mother, her children, her brothers watched from the wall. After I had sat there for a long time, I left and got in my car. As I turned out of the facility's parking lot toward the interstate I thought, "She's drugged."

To think, Carole Anne Keeling Gordon: being managed.

In Charleston, despite resistance by the board chair and others, the campaign against us persisted, with increasingly strident letters to the board from a few staff attorneys, including longtime friends of mine. I feel the campaign stemmed, of course, from their homophobia but also from their sense that I, perhaps perceived as a communist (though—hah!—no communists in West Virginia would have had queer me), exerted too great a control upon Vicki. The scheming demonic leftist, but they chose to say lesbian instead of leftist. That would be more damning in that place and at that time. Several of the accusers called themselves feminists and a couple were active in feminist organizations. This makes it even more ludicrous that they focused their energy on my bad influence upon Vicki through our sexual involvement, rather than focusing upon Vicki as a boss exploiting a subordinate. It still gives me pleasure to remember saying to one of those feminist attorneys during a heated exchange, "If my relationship to Vicki bears that much weight, when I am forced to leave, I should get health insurance just as you might from your spouse." The feminist lawyer's response was, "Not in your lifetime." After a season of letters and investigations and late-night meetings, the board of directors asked me to leave. Actually, not asked. Told. They did also ask one of the instigating attorneys to leave. And a few months later, Vicki too was gone.

Buzzy phoned to say that after being transported to Florida, Candy had died.

The funeral was in the heart of winter, a nasty wind coming off the Hudson River. From its address, I guessed the funeral home should be at the foot of a park below one of those outcrops that stood guard over Harlem. I had never brought a white companion to this avenue down which Candy and I had raced on college mornings. The city was excavating and building a subway, the sound of jackhammers brutal. Up the hill was Wilson's Restaurant, and if it hadn't been so cold, I might have proposed we swing by there, but I kept Wilson's in the invisible geography in my heart. Approaching the funeral home, a memory approached. Street corner and memory dovetailed. Of all the corners in New York City, of all the corners in Harlem, Candy's funeral took place exactly across the street from the parish house where Candy's and my friendship had begun.

Candy's casket was a flare of red and white flowers. Her face metallic and tired. No makeup. A blousy dress. She wasn't wearing her own shoes, which would have been broken by her merciless limp. She had not walked in a long time; neither dress nor shoes were her own.

A young man carried a week-old baby, its story furled in receiving blankets.

A woman knelt beside the casket, lowered her gray head, and clasped Candy's still hand.

We were all seated and quiet when Mommie T arrived, erect lion woman in a jacket of long-haired fur. In shades, her lips pooched, Noni beside her in a long black-and-white checked coat, Kuma in a pewter suit. A bewildering array of trim handsome men, each with a neat, beautifully shaped head balding at the crown. Handsome men. The kid brothers.

On the way to the cemetery, Vicki and I rode with family. They discussed who had moved to Englewood Cliffs, to Atlanta, to the West Indies. At 151st Street, the car inched down the cemetery drive at Trinity Catholic Church. Someone in the idling car said for Candy's dad, there had been so many people the cars snaked from the top of the cemetery to the bottom. I saw headstones dated in the 1700s. People followed one another on foot down an outdoor staircase into a grotto.

Mommie T arrived embedded in her cluster of men with Noni in the long checked coat.

An empty stretcher with a spray of flowers.

When they were offered, I took one red carnation, which I carried for months in my car's sun visor and after that placed its husk in my jewelry box filled mostly with junk earrings like Candy and I had bought on Eighth Street in the 1960s.

In the multipurpose room at Mommie's old apartment building, they served greens, couscous, chicken. In the cinder-block room, we could have been at one of those War on Poverty events that had made Candy laugh with derision. Vicki and I sat across a white-papered table from a woman with gray eyes. Vicki wanted ginger ale and reminded me we should already be on the road. I fetched Vicki's drink and on my return studied the gray-eyed woman.

"Oh my God," I said, "cousin Judy."

"Taste this." Vicki thrust her plastic cup at me.

Judy said, "Faithy, I thought I'd never see you again."

I sipped Vicki's ginger ale. Definitely spiked. West Indian rum in the afternoon. "For Candy," I said, "and for Mommie." Across the room, Mommie T stood on her pretty legs in her spike heels. She took a drink from a plastic cup and threw back her head to laugh out her grief. She took the tiny baby and jiggled it up and down.

"This Yankee needs some coffee," Judy said, and when she returned with a cup, she made a face, "Instant." With that smile that had turned teenage boys to mush, Judy turned to Vicki. "So tell me about your children." She took a pen from her purse and wrote the names of the girls and their birth dates. She wrote on the paper tablecloth, in big letters, the names of her own three children.

Mommie T had been walking from table to table, the baby in her arms. She met my eyes and made her way to us. "I'll sit with my girls for a minute," she said. Buzzy set her amber drink in its paper cup on the white paper, beside the names of Judy's children.

"You look fine," I said. And we both heard the unspoken *for Candy*.

Mommie T stilled her mouth with a cigarette. "You know, last week Buzzy got into Candy's computer. Faith, it was all there. Two years ago, she had a plan for those teenagers she was working with. She had it all mapped out. All the details." I imagined Candy's ideas glowing on the screen. An ember from Mommie's cigarette burned a pinhole in the paper tablecloth. She took a drink.

"Candy was the idea woman," Judy said.

"I'll have Buzzy print it out and I'll send it to you," Mommie T said.

"It won't be the same," Judy said.

They talked about Mommie T's plans to rent out the Harlem apartment to return to Florida.

"And that book?" Mommie T turned to me to ask. I said I hadn't written it. Vicki caught my eye.

"We have to get on the road," I said.

Mommie took a sip. "That West Virginia," she said.

"Mommie, don't cry," said the middle brother.

She secured her troublesome eye. Against my shoulder, she said, "Don't you girls forget me." I caught the plural, which could have meant me and Vicki and Judy, but I knew Mommie T meant me and Candy. I touched her cheek. Proud and stylish warrior. How I loved her.

"Go back to your West Virginia, then," Mommie T said, handing me to Vicki.

My entire working life, I have been able to move back and forth from freelance to full-time, from boards of education to nonprofits. I was a careful and thoughtful worker, and that was important because I was not a career anything. I was a person who worked and, when she could, took time off, twice doing so for an entire year, so I could write and organize. I had raised my two children and paid off my $43,000 house in Charleston in this manner. When I was "let go" from the disability agency, I was nearing fifty years old; my employability factor had lost some glow. I had no idea what was in my personnel file at the agency largely staffed by former friends.

Within months Vicki had been managed out of her job. At the agency, she had overseen lawsuits against state hospitals and county boards of education. Before the agency, with a master's in special education, she had taught in the public schools. Her advocacy work at the agency did not make her a desirable potential employee for school systems, so she was unemployable. Jonah was a junior at Berkeley and Carmela a pre-apprentice at the Washington Ballet in DC. People who had been in and out of my house as friends, close friends, during my children's childhoods were ranged, both covertly and openly, against us. When I told Carmela about one instance, she gasped: *So and so of Carly?* Carly was a dog for whom we had cared when her owner, my friend, was out of town. Carly was an obnoxious dog and my kids disliked her, though I can no longer remember exactly why, probably for doggish things like strewing scavenged garbage all over our house. This is how it felt: people we'd known so closely we had cared for their dogs, even if those dogs rifled through our garbage, were no longer our family friends. For a year, I, who had been one of West Virginia's political potluck queens, was invited to only three friends' homes. Most people may not have exactly shunned us, may have assumed that other people were still seeing us, but people, including many who had been in the women's group, were no longer available to me. I can see we may have made mistakes, but we didn't do anything that merited the loss of close to an entire friendship circle and the necessity to move out of the state where we had lived much of our adult lives. It's the scenario that in those days kept adult queer people in the closet and turned spirited eleven-year-olds into *ugly, plump, inept*. We left West Virginia because Vicki's teen and preteen daughters lived with us and we needed to feed them. Except for a short stint at an oppressive leftish organization in DC, I never had full-time work again.

Vicki and I were halfway moved from West Virginia, the state where we had thought we'd live out our days. Vicki and her daughter Amy, a high school freshman, had moved to the Washington, DC, area, where Vicki had taken a job with a national disability advocacy nonprofit. After years of trying to get a college-level teaching job, I'd been offered a one-semester adjunct position in West Virginia, so I stayed behind for those four months. I had rented out my hilltop house. During the week I lived in Charleston with my sister-friend Colleen. Fridays, I'd pick up Erin, Vicki's eleven-year-old, from her father's in Braxton County and the two of us would drive to the DC area for the weekend. It was a choppy time. One week Erin dreamed that I picked her up to go to her mother's. We traveled north on I-79 and east on I-70 as usual, heading toward our turn onto I-270 and Vicki. But. Our turn had disappeared. There was no way to reach her mother.

Colleen, with whom I had been in a writing group for many years, with whom I'd been through a few breakups and start overs—hers and mine—lived in a row of brick houses built before World War II, narrow homes with high ceilings. My life and Colleen's had mingled. In her house I could taste past Thanksgiving dinners, hear writers' group back-and-forths, see variegated origami, smell the snuffed match when she'd lit the tiny gas heater.

One such night, Colleen hollered upstairs to me, "Phone." I took the call in the corridor, holding the Bakelite piece to my ear. It was Carmela in California. There was little in the way of greeting before she said, "Sometimes we must hear things we do not want to hear." A sentence or two later, "I am breaking all contact with you. Do not call me. Do not write me. I will not see you." For seventeen years: she could not be found, not even on the internet, except for one errant church bulletin.

West Virginia moved into a space that had been occupied by New York City since 1966: *The home back home.* West Virginia, where in the spring forsythia blooms on abandoned hillsides that once sheltered small, hand-built homes. The place where Madeline James and Ethel Brewster and Helen Powell and Cliff Bryant and David and Susan Greene fought like hell for the living. The place where 78 died in the Mannington Mine disaster and 124 died at Buffalo Creek. The place where I came out. The place I lived when my mother died. The place from where Maggie Anderson and Diane Gilliam and Crystal Good and Marc Harshman write their poems. The place where each autumn up Middle White Oak Holler I went in on a hog to be slaughtered with my neighbors Haredee and Betty Hager. The place where I lived with my children and raised them the best I could. The place where I found love with Vicki Smith and her daughters. The place where my dogs were named Shimmer and Charlie and Puppy and Terpy and the cats were Jasper and Shadow and Squeaky and Ginger. Where I taught at Caretta, Prenter, Wharton, Racine, what is now Mary Snow Elementary in Charleston, Herbert Hoover High School, and Stonewall Jackson High School and for two years in the early eighties researched and visited schools in a historic statewide school refinance case that argued that all children were entitled to a free and equal education as provided in the West Virginia Constitution. Like all who must leave, *home back home* was indelibly part of me.

3
Find a Home Place

Sundered

I couldn't believe, but I had to believe—I might never see my daughter again.

I couldn't bear music. Shut it down.

For seventeen years, she was a buried seam, a strata resting upon what had gone before, supporting all that came after.

Layered, 1991–2009

Carmela's memories included sexual abuse by all in our immediate family, as well as instances of ritual abuse, and those memories alienated her from us. Made us strangers to one another. Except that we could never entirely be strangers, could we?

She had moved to California, where her brother lived, though she had no contact with him. With few exceptions, like when Jonah ran into her in the elevator of his office building, none of us saw or talked to her. That time, Carmela was working at a call center and was on her way to Taco Bell. Jonah said she seemed as lively as ever; she disappeared again, leaving that job and melting back into the wallpaper of San Francisco. Once, he saw her walking jauntily near his job at Virgin Records; she was wearing an embroidered or knitted cap, Peruvian, he thought. There were other inadvertent intersections, but that was it. She had been born long enough ago that her Social Security number had not appeared on either her school records or her birth certificate. We could not trace her. I did not know whether she was living or dead. I made new friends who had never known Carmela, friends who wouldn't have known of her existence if I hadn't mentioned it. Old friends stopped asking if I had heard from her.

Carmela had been absent for three years. Vicki was working at a national disability rights organization in DC; our daughter Erin was living with us and in middle school; I was working as an adjunct teaching English at a community college in Maryland. One spring morning, I hurried across campus to my class. The college had repaired a bit of pavement the week before. I saw workers remove the "wet concrete" sign and thought, *I can be the first person to walk on the new pavement.* I stepped forward onto my right foot, which slid out ahead of me. The foot twisted and all of me, from my hip upward, fell onto that leg, breaking hip and tibia. In the hospital, a hole had been drilled below my knee from one side of my leg to the other and a rod inserted to hold me in traction. The rod was removed before I left the hospital, but a steely sense of having been breached against my will persisted. Sent home, I toggled between not doing anything because I hurt and doing things that hurt so that I could keep doing anything at all. I was fifty-one.

This pain mixed with inertia became muddled with missing my girl child. Beached on my bed at home while Erin was at middle school and Vicki at work, I felt unmoored. The featherstitching around the bits of who I was had frayed. I couldn't sleep in our bedroom, as climbing stairs was impossible, so our bed was moved to the first-floor dining room. Vicki and I had been expelled from West Virginia. Nothing was as I had thought it would be.

I received a letter from Penny Patch, with whom I had worked in Georgia, inviting me to join a group of women who were writing a book about their experiences in the Civil Rights Movement. What joy, to think that despite my being moored and inert, I might share my SNCC story, such a vital but invisible part of who I had been. And still was.

I reread Penny's letter. The women writers were all white. Joining this book tempted me—a public affirmation of my identity. I spoke to a couple of Black women friends, and each time I felt queasy describing the project, until I understood I could not place my memories of working with SNCC, a predominantly Black and Black-led organization, in a book without Black voices, a book about SNCC centered on the white experience. I wrote a long and overly self-righteous letter to Penny and sent it off but also sent copies to a few Black

Movement friends, notably Amina Rachman from my time in Harlem, Martha Prescod Norman Noonan, and a couple of others.

In response, two Black SNCC women convened a meeting to launch our own book project. I had spent time with one of the two in the field in Southwest Georgia; the other I knew primarily by reputation for her work out of Atlanta. Our editorial group of six included three Black women and three white women. We included no southerners and, though half Black and half white was an improvement over entirely white, it did not represent SNCC's racial makeup, which had been predominantly Black. At least half of the editorial group had not worked primarily in SNCC's grassroots field projects. At times, I think I should have yielded my place on the editorial team to a Black woman, a southerner, a member of a field project, but I did not.

Outsiders and some of our SNCC brothers had written about women in SNCC, though not on a scale proportionate to our presence in the work. SNCC men had been written about and had written about their work in their own words, but our book . . . we would create a book in our voices, not oral histories but the active voices of SNCC women themselves, choosing what to include and shaping our words as we saw fit. Always, consent to suggested editorial changes would be required before being carried out. We would address those parts of the history as we had experienced it, which outsiders had gotten wrong or omitted. We would be present.

We would title our book *Hands on the Freedom Plow: Personal Accounts by Women in SNCC*.[1]

Fully present, we would bring forward our contested history. Easier said than done, especially as we swelled from a group of six editors to a group that included more than fifty contributors. Like a disparate group of adult cousins at an extended family Thanksgiving, each of us brought her nineteen-year-old self to the table, and that nineteen-year-old self, who was also her sixty-plus-year-old self, would be seated next to a cousin who was also her own

---

1. Holsaert, Noonan, Richardson, Robinson, Young, and Zellner, eds., *Hands on the Freedom Plow: Personal Accounts by Women in SNCC*, (University of Illinois Press, 2010).

nineteen-year-old self and at the same time her sixty-plus-year-old self. Many histories, accurate, contested, and otherwise.

Within the editorial group, each of us had come to SNCC as part of her personal trajectory and viewed her time in SNCC from her own vantage point. Although the work we had done was various and geographically far-flung, I had not expected our sense of the meaning of our work to be not only diverse but also contradictory. Didn't imagine our shared experiences would not yield a universal story of SNCC women. Because each of us cared deeply about her version of our shared story, because to each of us our version was integral to our sense of who we were and who we had been, without shared trust built upon relationships, disagreements and animosities were inevitable. Having lived and worked and loved people in Southwest Georgia, I was determined the names and stories of the women of Southwest Georgia be declared. I was committed to righting the historic wrong of labeling the Southwest Georgia Movement *Dr. King's failure*. Others in the editorial group may have been adjacent to or participated in projects that validated the *King's failure* analysis.

If I have the true version of shared history, other people's versions must be wrong. To stay with the tension of disagreement, to be generous with one another, to listen, to think of a way out of that right/wrong box requires respect. In a different piece of writing, I once described an afternoon sitting with Martha while we each nursed our newborn babies. I described us as two revolutionary women. I have loved that word, *revolutionary*, since Bayard Rustin used it during a meeting planning the 1963 March on Washington. First, in my post-McCarthy world, that word was not used, and I loved how he routinely and without apology used the word. It sounded so perfect in his particular cadence. Imagine my surprise when Martha, upon reading my words, explained that she doesn't use the word *revolutionary*. In consequence, I could have hated myself or hated her or felt crushed. Because I had known her for many years, had in fact nursed the infant Carmela while she nursed the infant Joe, I trusted her. Martha proposed an alternative word, *radical*, which allowed us not to be stuck in disagreement. This is a small example, but it suggests that to write respectfully about others, trust is important, including the trust that an alternative can be found.

. . .

We contacted about one hundred potential participants who met these criteria: their work had been specifically with SNCC; they had worked at least for part of their connection to SNCC in the South; their experience had included more than the 1964 Mississippi Summer Project. The first response to arrive in its manilla envelope was from Annette Jones White, Albany (Georgia) state homecoming queen before her expulsion from school for joining a march with the Albany Movement. Our book took its first breath with a queen of the Movement. The responses kept coming. When we looked up from the growing pile of papers, we realized white women were responding in disproportionately high numbers compared to their presence in SNCC. We got out more dog-eared address books with penciled entries erased and rewritten over decades, got out lists of SNCC reunion attendees. We made phone calls. Responses came in. More than fifty women would appear in *Hands on the Freedom Plow: Personal Accounts by Women in SNCC*, or more simply, *Hands*. The book would be published fifteen years later in 2010, but we were a long way from publication in the early days of 1995.

We six editors felt there was a handful of women who were essential to our work, but they did not or would not write pieces. Among these was Joann Christian Mants. The editorial group decided we'd break our own rule that all contributors write their own pieces, to conduct a few interviews, including of Annie Pearl Avery of Alabama; Gloria Richardson of the Cambridge, Maryland, Movement; and five women from Southwest Georgia whom I interviewed. Consent is a word with two syllables that bears the weight of power and illuminates where that power resides. Though we heard these women's demurrals and wanted to honor their desires, we also felt the book would be untrue without their stories. In a choreography of consent, we asked: Would they consent to being interviewed? With the exception of McCree Harris, who died before she could do so, the interviewees took the transcripts and shaped them into pieces of their own.

In Alabama, Joann Christian Mants took me to the house of a vacationing neighbor; she and her husband, SNCC organizer Bob Mants, had not told their children, all now adults, details of their Movement life, including the mistreatment Joann had experienced at the hands of the police. They did not want to make their children bitter. The story Joann offered the world felt like contraband when she gave it to me.

. . .

During the years of my daughter's absence, walking down a street or sitting in a meeting, perhaps a meeting of the six contentious editors of the women in SNCC book, when the longing for Carmela was too painful, I would finger my clavicle, sounding a pool of yearning, comforting myself as I imagined her child self had needed to do. *When will I see her?* The answer *never* was untenable.

Writing about being my daughter's mother, I try not to use phrases like *in Carmela's experience* or *Carmela feels that*. . . . With that language, I separate myself from what she has told me, putting her in her narrative place, subordinate to and dependent upon my perspective. Maybe this is disingenuous, because in actuality I am in charge of the narrative. I do say, *Off with their heads*, to hundreds of omitted storylines. As much as possible, rather than saying, *In Carmela's experience, she is subject to hostile bumping and verbal attacks*, I will say, *In the street, Carmela is bumped into and heckled*. I will use her words as I remember them when I can do so respectfully. Tricky, because it is my memory of her words. Tricky, because I don't want to steal her words. In the end, this writing is about me, the complicated mother of a complicated daughter, each of us a many-layered person whose life is at times unbearable.

In Georgia, I had learned a practice of singing while fighting. Like the ocean's edge, the place that is both sand and water, the place increasingly one or the other until it is only one, my understanding of what has happened is not a single narrative, not singing or fighting, but both.

Within the enormity of geography, if Carmela and I were facing the Atlantic, behind us would be the land, or what will happen to each and both of us. Ahead of us, the sea's possibility. From the East, the sun rises over possibility and sets on the far side of what has happened. It rises from the far side of what has happened and sets over possibility if we are on her coast. We may not both be on the same coast at once.

In the time when the government had begun to arrest and charge us with sedition, conspiracy, and subversion, when the outcry in the media against us was that we were militants, in that time after hope, I would dream, night after night, that I ran from pursuers. I couldn't see them, but I knew them. Beneath my feet were rabbit holes that could snatch me by the ankle and throw me to the ground. I could keep on running because David Greene and I ran side by side. We could hear the pursuers' feet thud and the whisper of the grass against their ankles. David and I were *we*, fleeing, with so many others. The power of *us* rose into the soles of our feet and raced upward to our hearts. The power of outwitting *them*. Running until *they* dropped out of sight because we were swift and powerful.

I was working on *Hands*. Teaching as an adjunct at two area colleges. Being with Vicki and her younger daughter. Recovering from the broken hip. Meeting new, mostly queer, friends from DC, many of whom we met through the Lesbian Rap Group at the Whitman Walker Clinic. Visiting my son in San Francisco when I could. He met and married Beth and had two sons. After Jonah's first was born, we tried to contact Carmela through the church on whose internet site she once appeared, but word came back that she did not want to engage. She was approaching her midtwenties. She had said, *Sometimes we must hear things we don't want to hear.*

What I *knew* about Carmela was what I imagined, based upon what I had known or thought I had known. Year by year, I cast a line forward, projecting who she might be. Into her twenties and then her thirties; into my fifties and then my sixties. Except for a single San Francisco church bulletin, she kept herself off the internet. She had gone west to dance with a company named Contraband and had herself become contraband. She could have been anywhere, but most years I thought or imagined that she was in San Francisco. Once, once, in the 1990s she appeared working behind the counter in a Takoma Park, Maryland, coffee shop just blocks from where Vicki and I lived, but she wouldn't or couldn't speak to me and was not seen there again. She was apparently connected with a church; though when I returned to their web page, she never was named there again. We hired a detective with inconclusive results. Was she safe? Was she dancing? Was she alive? Out of my longing, I constructed an evolving series of best guesses.

Later, Carmela would tell me that during the years she was absent, from 1991 into the 2000s, she worked as a modern dancer and arts administrator. Like most who work in the arts, her life and work were marginal to financial security and government machinery like social security. She was active in sexual abuse survivors' and child sexual abuse survivors' groups, as well as survivors' performance groups. She danced until late into the night, went home to apartments or single rooms, where she might eat ramen and watch TV and get up the next morning to do the same. She worked as an usher in a San Francisco theater that brought in Broadway shows and musical comedies; she was in the world of theater and dance as she had wanted since childhood. Living above Market Street, she had had a little cat. She went to the same taqueria in the Mission District, La Cumbre (the summit), as her brother, but they didn't cross paths there.

On September 11, 2001, she received a phone call saying both her brother and I were dead. On the evening of 9/11, she phoned my Maryland phone number and we spoke briefly, our last phone contact for more than a decade. I was sitting on my couch in Takoma Park, chatting with my friend Imani and . . . Carmela phoned. Although she had phoned and talked to me the evening of 9/11, she simultaneously *knew* we were dead and wore mourning for the year that followed.

In the Morgantown, West Virginia, Social Security office, the woman looked over my employment history: public schools (in 1972 my first full-time West Virginia teaching job had paid $5,700/year), freelance editing, community creative writing classes at the Job Corps and elsewhere, advocacy for persons with disabilities. She said, "Honey, no way you can earn enough to increase your benefits. I'd take it. I'd take it now." And so I did. I was working on *Hands* and teaching writing classes from home and taught a couple of classes at West Virginia University. I'd fly out to see Jonah in California, and after he met Beth, to see the two of them, and when their sons were born, to see them all. In 2008, we moved to Durham, North Carolina, into a 1947 house, two stories with rooms as small as those in 1940s Greenwich Village apartments. We brought with us three West Virginia cats, Chevy, Cricket, and Shane, and everything from pots and pans and laundry baskets and bureaus to photo albums with black paper pages, some of which my mother had assembled more than six decades before.

• • •

I was at Martha's in Maryland to work on *Hands*. We met at the home she owned with her second husband, Allan S. Noonan, outside Baltimore. Martha had known Carmela as an infant in Detroit. She and I had ushered in our second infants together, had nursed them side by side. When Carmela absented herself from my life, Martha knew my long loss. With her ability to work with complexity, over almost two decades Martha had been supportive of me in the loneliness of a mother who has lost her child—but maybe not lost forever. That trip, I had driven from snow-hammered West Virginia to Martha and Al's. After a night in their guest bedroom, I had come downstairs to the kitchen, which, when the sun was out and snow was on the ground, was airy and brilliant. I felt gratitude to be inside and gratitude for insulation against the cold. I was at home, because we had been girls together.

Martha is not an email enthusiast, so I felt self-indulgent when I moseyed over to my laptop, casually eased my butt onto the barstool, and fired up. My screen came to life. I had an email from *Kenneth Johnson*, whom I didn't know. The subject line read: *Photos attached*. I was on one side of seventeen years. I clicked open the email. I was on the other side of the seventeen years.

The email was signed *Carmela*.

"Oh my God," I said.

"What?" Martha was stirring oatmeal.

On my screen, images of a baby with hazel eyes. She had sent her son to me. A baby in an infant seat set on the floor, proof not only of himself but of his mother's existence, because inside the margin of the image of the baby, a bunioned foot. A sliver so small, if it had been a voice, it would have been a whisper, but I would have known that foot by its fraction anywhere. The only other foot like that was my sister Shai's. Michael was a fine baby of many faces: grins, serious stares, a mouth stretched up and then down. And those riveting eyes. I treasured above all that sliver of bunioned foot and the knowledge that she, specifically Carmela, had sent this to me, specifically Faith, her mother. She wrote that I was not to respond to the email, which was from her husband's (her husband!) account.

Over the next years, in December or January, I received emailed photos from Carmela: Carmela, pregnant again, pushing a stroller with a black dog grinning beside her; the birth of her black-eyed daughter with the mischievous smile. Carmela was including photos of herself, my whole, adult daughter: after Cami's birth, Carmela dark-haired and smiling against a cerulean wall—how much she looked like her brother, who had aged from the man in his early twenties when she broke contact; Cami in her stroller, enveloped in a white blanket, her dark eyes, her baby mouth smiling, a strawberry of a baby girl. Carmela allowed me to answer once a year to her street address in Brisbane, south of San Francisco, but wrote she could not handle more than that. I was a controlled substance. Back in Fox territory, where I was the overwrought intruder. Feeling guilty, I googled the address: a small house on a hillside with a view of a large body of water. It was more than I had known about her for so long. Each year in November, I began to wait for the email. *What if she doesn't write this year?*

One of my first months in Durham, I stood on the *activist corner* at Main and Gregson, standing vigil for Palestinian rights. I had read about the vigil in the local independent paper. I knew no one. I looked at the black and brown and white faces, some young and some as old as me. Strollers. Picket signs. Clusters of people familiar with one another, chatting. Rush hour cars driving by, blowing horns in solidarity, passengers in other cars yelling slurs as they passed. People stood at each of the four corners where the streets crossed. I had been on such rush hour corners all my adult life. I was with my people. How to meet them?

In September 2008, days after Carmela's daughter Cami's first birthday, Jonah phoned, so upset he could barely speak. My tender-hearted son had been phoned by a police lieutenant. With her two children, Carmela had left home. The police were searching the ditches beside the roads in Brisbane. Jonah was beside himself. I phoned the lieutenant, who told me nothing, except they were looking for Carmela. Later, Jonah and I learned that they *had reason to believe* that Carmela and the two children were in a domestic violence shelter in San Francisco. For seven winter months, during daylight hours, the three were required to leave the shelter, her pushing the double stroller. Cami still breastfeeding. The authorities resorted to sterile, passive language: *had reason to believe*, for this new way Jonah and I were learning to live with not knowing enough about Carmela. Seven winter months. In court, the husband's divorce lawyer hounded Carmela, hammering at questions of a possible pregnancy (the father's family wanting to claim *their own*), demanding details of her physical health, including poor vision and poor hearing, and her mental health.

"Hello. This is Carmela."

I became a mother whose daughter was no longer absent. Seventeen years, more than half her lifetime and nearly a quarter of mine. I was in Durham, a new town, a new state, approaching seventy years of age, having left West Virginia, where I had thought I would live until I died.

She had been given a phone. She talked for forty-five minutes.

I was a mother who had heard the voice of her daughter. A real-time daughter.

At a writers' conference in Chicago, I met Durham poet and musician Shirlette Ammons. The next day, which was cold and stormy, Shirlette came into the airport waiting area with a woman who, without my knowing her name or having exchanged a word with her, was nothing but embodied charisma and joy. I discovered her name was Kai Lumumba Barrow. Over those stranded airport hours, Kai and I discovered our many connections, and it felt like I was both connecting with this magical person and that I was reconnecting with my actual self.

Working with Critical Resistance in New York City, Kai had written a paper proposing a Harm-Free Zone (HFZ), where racist prison culture and our prison-dependent economy were abolished. As in *no more prisons*. None. I understood the racist harm of the school-to-prison pipeline, with its roots in the Reagan era, and its more recent roots in the 1994 crime bill, 356 pages providing almost $10 billion to fund prisons. The roots of this drive to control what were portrayed as dangerous and criminal Black people lay in the history of the slave patrols and other measures that followed slave uprisings and revolts. Bill Clinton was president at the time and bears responsibility for this travesty and the decades of brutality it has caused, but Senator Joe Biden had worked most of his political career, including working with arch southern segregationists, toward such a bill. I knew our police- and prison-dependent social structure was wrong and could even tell you why it was wrong, but I had never imagined that a nation could abolish, as in eliminate, dismantle, and never use again, its prisons. Until Kai Lumumba Barrow.[2]

Kai invited me to a Durham HFZ meeting at the Stanford L. Warren library in the Hayti community. Other than Kai, I still knew no one. For many hours, the group met, though now I can only guess what we talked about: probably a history of the HFZ, Durham's school-to-prison pipeline, our personal stories. It was as pivotal as my first meeting in a church with the Harlem Brotherhood Group, almost fifty years before. I entered a world of astute, passionate, political, sometimes sharp-tongued, laughing-out-loud, mostly queer, mostly Black women, some of whom had brought their teenage children and their toddler grandchildren with them. There was food, great big pans of it, that a group called SpiritHouseNC had prepared. I met Alexis Pauline Gumbs, who had just that morning driven from Atlanta. Alexis, with whom I would write poetry in a community of women. Alexis saw who I was and who I had been. I had found my people.

When she was still living in shelters, Carmela saw Jonah and met his wife Beth and their two boys. Jonah had just turned forty-five and hadn't seen her, except for accidental sightings, since he was in his late twenties. Beth had never met Carmela, and their sons—elementary school age—may not have known she existed. There were a couple of photos taken that day. After their pizza, Carmela loaded Michael and Cami into the stroller. In the parking lot, they said goodbye and she disappeared into the dark without a trace. Again.

Every phone call I received from Carmela felt like a holiday gift. I was dazzled by the fact of her voice over the phone, her giggle the same as when she'd been a teenager, the tales of a husband and children whom I'd never met. I didn't know what she wanted or needed from me, except to talk, most often when her children were spending the weekend with their father. I could hardly wait to see her on my next trip to California.

2. "SpiritHouse is a multigenerational Black women-led cultural organizing tribe with a rich legacy of using art, culture and media to support the empowerment and transformation of communities most impacted by racism, poverty, gender inequity, criminalization and incarceration." See https://www.spirithouse-nc.org/#intro.

. . .

Weekly, I wrote with other women at Alexis's apartment, all or most of us with histories of abuse. Alexis's apartment comprised small rooms strung together by a corridor that ended in a kitchen that might have once been a porch. On the kitchen table, we put our offerings for the group meal: homemade pitas and hummus, a portion or two of leftovers, a plastic container of blueberries, some celery and carrot sticks, a bit of macaroni and cheese. We wrote. We ate. We danced. We met in the in-between times—at other meetings and at vigils and hearings. I imagined I could write poetry.

Nia Wilson describes SpiritHouseNC's intergenerational work: "SpiritHouse began using poetry, art and performance to talk about the ways violence, prison and policing had seeped into our homes, work, and schools. We dreamed about what a community founded in love would look like, with the understanding that no one gets thrown away. Sharing food, political education and healing methodologies in our living rooms came easily. As survivors of domestic violence, sexual assault, gang aggression, displaced/fractured families, and drug dependence, using art to help ground our visions came naturally."

SpiritHouse combines being grounded in community, fostering young leaders, seeing a broad political context that is Black-centered, and daring to dream. This drew me to SpiritHouse. The first time I saw their performance piece about the school-to-prison pipeline, *Collective Sun*, Sabra Shanell Pacheco—daughter of Amina Rachman, sister-friend of my Harlem activist youth—came to Durham to see it with us. It was complex and heartfelt and Black-community-based and women-centered. I was alive.

HFZ is no rigidly focused group. At one meeting, Nia said she could not continue the meeting without speaking of Haiti and the earthquake that had devastated the country. Her green eyes follow a moral compass. Haiti! Where so much had happened to me. Haiti! Right here in Durham. Months later, Nia said in a meeting, "That toddler that her mother sold and who died, I cannot go on without speaking of that baby girl." There had been TV footage of a man carrying the little one into a motel room. Nia said, "As a member of the HFZ,

I should feel compassion for that man, but I do not. Someone else will have to do that."

At the first Durham *Hands* reading and launch, Nia Wilson and Mya Hunter of SpiritHouse were speakers. Mya was nineteen years old, the age I had been in Georgia. Erin, a daughter of mine and Vicki's, came down from Maryland and took photos. Erin had been a child of eight when I met her. With us, fifteen years of work by *Hands* editors and writers, the legacy finally in print.

A lawyer phoned to say Carmela had relinquished her children to her husband and hospitalized herself. She had been transported to a hospital in San Francisco, strapped to the gurney. I didn't know enough to know what to ask. I had one phone call from Carmela, who said, while in the hospital, that she was doing her ballet barre work for the first time in more than a decade. Vicki and I were on an adventure, exploring pottery studios south of Durham, working our way into our new landscape. Vicki had activated her turn signal for a country road that promised what I was craving—trees, trails, drop-offs into a distant valley—when my phone rang. Carmela. She had just been released from the hospital and was waiting for a cab to take her to the room she had rented, using her small savings. Savings! Everything about Carmela, whom I had not yet seen, was so new and strange and, every time, wonderful. I do not know what the diagnosis was.

There weren't cliffs as I'd expected. There was a wide, slow river but no cliffs. Vicki and I left the park, driving back to an area with better cell phone reception. My life as the mother of an absent daughter had ended. With the exception of our first year or two together, Vicki and I had never shared Carmela's presence, only the enormity of her absence.

She was released to St. Francis Hospital's outpatient program designed for patients with dual diagnoses (bipolar disorder/substance use disorder), although as far as I knew, she was not a substance user. She was given several prescriptions. For the first month, Carmela stayed in SROs, or single-room-occupancy hotels (what my parents' generation called *welfare hotels*).

· · ·

With about 1,500 pages of raw material for *Hands*, coexisting and contradictory narratives had appeared. After much back and forth (you *cannot* imagine the back and forth), we agreed that when two accounts contradicted one another, unless there was an outside consequential verification of one view or the other, we included both accounts, trusting both the writers and the readers to make sense of the layers. We felt an obligation to get things right, a long and complicated process with six women on the verge of elderhood, each with deeply held beliefs and values. How to pick and choose and do what was best for the manuscript, this work we were creating to embody our life in SNCC? Big things mattered. Little things mattered. We felt a sense of obligation to ourselves, to our sisters in SNCC, to SNCC as a whole, to the communities where we had worked, and to history. One of us reviewed all 1,500 pages and found the only pieces that contained the word *ain't* were the manuscripts of Black southern women. Some editors thought we should let this stand as *local color*; some of us, not. We checked with each writer and asked what she wanted and all wanted the *ain't* changed. When we came to proofreading, one writer whose name bears national and international weight (one of two MacArthur Genius Grant awardees in the book), objected to the publishing company's stylebook, which would not have capitalized "Civil Rights Movement." The writer said she would pull her piece, rather than change "Civil Rights Movement" to lowercase. Still fighting after all these years. The press modified their customary practice.

I wrote my piece for *Hands* at the same time I was projecting an imagined present day for Carmela from her barely known past; in writing for *Hands*, I was pulling from an abundant body of knowns as I had experienced them. There were questions for me of accuracy as there were with *Hands* as a whole; there was the trickiness of strata of memory. In my piece, only one woman's voice—mine—would be present, without the congregational upwelling of fifty voices raised with and against one another. Only when the book was complete would what I wrote work within the context of the whole.

· · ·

I am riding Amtrak from Durham to New York City. I think of my sister and me, elementary schoolgirls in the 1950s, being put on a train in Manhattan by our mother and riding north by ourselves to be picked up by our aunt, our father's redheaded sister, in Boston. I think of Black children riding the train south to live with family over the summer. Emmett Till. And how the Brotherhood of Sleeping Car Porters offered care to Black travelers, particularly children as they rode trains into the segregated South. And A. Philip Randolph and the Brotherhood of Sleeping Car Porters, a primary organizer of the 1963 March on Washington. The train today pulls into Selma, North Carolina, evoking the Edmund Pettus Bridge in Alabama. The train I ride in 2019 glides past an abandoned former train station. It announces in stark contemporary letters: *Selma, NC, station built 1855*. I am passing into slavery time embodied in an abandoned wood building with a brand-new sign lettered in white. *1855*.

Stories, freewheeling concentric tree rings. As a high school art student, I preferred oil paints for their warmth and for the layers upon layers I could create, conceal, and reveal with a palette knife; however, some oil paints were toxic—Van Gogh—so people began to use acrylics. I found acrylics inert and without heat. I did a poor job of depicting reality (inner or outer) with watercolors. I couldn't *master* the elusive perfect, first and only line. The inescapably flat plane couldn't support what I saw and felt. But. Sometimes you need the simple line. I knew in writing my piece for *Hands* I needed to be brief and clear. My two mothers. Haiti. Emmett Till. The vicious Algerian War. What I was reading. My sisters Amina and Candy. How impossible to tell a single story without telling dozens of others.

SpiritHouseNC. A dozen black- and brown-skinned people hold jo sticks aloft. They wear jeans and T-shirts, long skirts, sweaters, hoodies, as they face the pipeline from school to prison. *SpiritHouse uses art, culture, and media to support.* The length of the jo stick is approximately from the ground to the human armpit. It is not a hunting knife, which is illegal. *SpiritHouse supports the visions and voices of underrepresented communities.* The practitioner thrusts the stick forward, can run it between the fingers like a pool stick or move it behind as if sculling. This can happen on the cracked sidewalk in front of your house. It can happen in front of the courthouse. It can happen in the jailhouse. *SpiritHouseNC reclaims their role as historical actors.* The people on the city grass circle their sticks overhead, changing the stick from one hand to the other. They wear black, white, red, gray, pink, dark blue, light blue. *SpiritHouse uncovers stories of resistance, hope, healing, and transformation* right here on our sidewalks. The practitioners could be working the ground as they step forward and back, step forward and crouch. They are carrying jo sticks, narrow as the ankle of a ten-year-old. *SpiritHouse: truths are distorted or erased from history, including our own.* In the body of the group is Nia, at its core as the group advances, falls back, digs deep, circles the sticks overhead, in harmony and yet each practitioner moving differently.

Nevertheless, We Mothered, 2009–2014

St. Francis Hospital, San Francisco. A corridor with power drills, whining saws, and masked workers leaving tracks in white dust: too much force and veiling for this pass-through corridor. This is where I caught my first sight of her. A social worker watched. Would she want me to hug her? What was *natural* for us, mother and daughter so long separated by the daughter's choice? Me, the mother from whom this daughter had protected herself, my trepidation as much a barrier as the sound and dust. But then she stepped into me and I put my arms around her so-thin body. She might have died, that fact in my arms. We were allotted twenty minutes to meet with Carmela's psychotherapist, a door between us and the mayhem. With a few minutes left on the clock, the therapist asked, "Your daughter has been subjected to horrific experiences. What do you have to say?" I felt how the seven or whatever minutes left to us were not sufficient. Felt how to not answer could be held against me. My future with her in the balance. I took in my daughter with my eyes. The sealed holes in her unmistakable ears. Her thin hands. The pale splash of a café au lait mark above her eyes, the same splash visible when she was swaddled in flannel after birth. Her thin, always thin, hair. I couldn't say to the therapist, *You have put me in an untenable position.* I feared the words hanging like Sheetrock dust: *bad mother.*

Carmela and I began to piece together how to be with one another. She and I moved her to the SRO of the week. I was dumbfounded to be admitted to this mundane layer of her life. She and I went out to get dinner before I took BART back to Berkeley. We stood on the sidewalk in front of a plate-glass window that both reflected and distorted our image, the two of us, an image I had thought I might never see again. Carmela said she was protected but could not explain. Protected, but she was on her own. I felt how slippery this was, sliding like our distorted images on the plate glass. I felt how I had thought she and I would never be in touch again, yet there we were skating on the glass surface, recognizably mother and daughter. "If you're protected, why . . . ?" and I waved down the block to the SRO. I noted that she did not have a jacket for the San Francisco wind. That she seemed pretty damn unprotected.

Carmela's life is subject to forces that intrude upon her in her home or purposefully run into her body in the street. Hers is a life without privacy. Even her words, the outward expression of her inner self, can be stolen and used against her. Sometimes the forces are helpful and keep the terror and loneliness at bay. They came into her life decades ago, a preschool child's bulwark against terror. To stave off annihilation, she taught herself to reinvent her one self into many selves.

She claims the identity multiple personality. She turns on the TV in the afternoon to quiet her alters, many of whom are preverbal babies. The voices create chaos. She holds meetings with all alters present. She has named over 150 alters (she who taught herself to read before she went to school). Some of the alters are malicious and some supportive, creative, resilient. She is integrating—the alters not consolidating into a single identity but sharing a coconsciousness. Sometimes her internal forces are not helpful, but they are inextricable from who Carmela is. And yet not. To her mother, these forces appear malign; she has used the word *torture*. Once or twice, she has said in anger that if I, her mother, wanted, I could go to the authorities and have it stopped and even that I am a participant in her pain. She has said, *Why aren't you down at the police department picketing, demanding answers? You're so good at that.* And when I ask, *What specifically would I tell the authorities?* she falls silent.

That word, "consent"; its two syllables weigh heavy.

• • •

When we reunited, I bought Carmela a notebook, one of the spiral-bound, college-ruled notebooks she has used since her teens. In more than three decades, she has filled page after page. I imagine that some earlier pages contained adolescent circles for dots over the I's, that some pages are covered in pink or purple ink. I think, depending upon who was writing, one page may have looked different than the others. All these pages written in all the places she has lived. All gone. The words disappeared and dispossessed, but deeply possessed, and possessing her, too.

Carmela moved into a one-bedroom apartment that her brother and I rented. I moved to San Francisco to be with her. I thought after a few months of emotional and financial support she would be back on her feet.

I spent my first California night in Berkeley with Jonah and Beth. The next morning, when I boarded BART with Jonah, I had my waist-high suitcase because all I knew was that I was going to live with Carmela. I didn't know how long I would be gone from North Carolina. I was sure this was the beginning, that with care and love, Carmela would find her way back. From BART in Berkeley, I phoned Carmela to say when I should arrive at Civic Center BART. I would come upstairs and meet her at the exit.

"Mom, where? What street?" How far between this panicky voice and the twenty-one-year-old decades ago, setting out across the United States to make her way, confident she could make a place for herself on the far coast and grounded enough to make it happen. That is the person I was thinking of when I thought of her coming *back*. I didn't know there were multiple entrances to BART at the Civic Center. I didn't know her seeming panic was based on an unclarity of my own. "Mom, what street?" *Mom. Don't hang up.*

The rush hour train was crowded and I felt beached with the outsize suitcase. I made my way upstairs, juggling the bag on the escalator. Carmela hadn't arrived. I watched pigeons land on the edge of the fountain. I watched people who'd spent the night on the street start their day, getting coffee, lighting cigarettes. In the years of Carmela's absence, I'd walked through this plaza, both hoping and dreading seeing her pretty face among those staring up at me from the sidewalk. Back then, what would I have done if the long-skirted woman fighting with a man, who veered to ask me for money, had turned out to be

Carmela? But. Now. *Carmela lost* was no longer the worry, though it was the haunting. When would she come *back*. At last, Carmela walked up Market toward me, waving her thin arm. The pigeons seemed less crowded and hungry; the fanning of their wings in the morning light had turned celebratory. Jonah had warned me how thin she was, and she was. Thin.

That first day in San Francisco, Carmela and I went into a grocery store to buy chewing gum for her. I didn't know she chewed gum. Discombobulated, walking around in a life in which I didn't know what would come, there, laid out and waiting for me was a tray of Vietnamese summer rolls, the green basil and pink shrimp gleaming through rice paper. I could eat these, walking in the street, as I had eaten pastries and winter chestnuts in the streets of my childhood. I had to have one. In the street, conscious of Carmela, rail thin and not eating. It was eleven in the morning. I was ashamed of the waste but wrapped up the remaining second roll and looked around for a trash can.

A woman in dark layers spoke to me, but I didn't understand her. Great, I was not just a glutton but a slow-witted one.

"She wants your leftovers," Carmela said from a place far from anywhere she and I had ever shared but speaking from that place with authority. I passed the leftover food to the woman, who took it from my hand. This, the moment I began to enter Carmela's world, to use her knowledge, to think differently than I had before.

Who was this thirty-eight-year-old person: Where had she been? What did she know?

In a coffee shop, she placed her flip phone in my hand. "Can we go see my kids? I haven't seen them since I was hospitalized." She dialed and I spoke to her husband. We would go after naps. His parents were living with him and taking care of the children. No, he didn't think there was a bus or train that came to Brisbane.

• • •

At Walgreens, Carmela chose shampoo and bubble bath as a gift. "It's the kind I always used with them. They'll know the scent. They'll associate it with *us*." The scent of them, her and the two children. They would know.

When our cab pulled up at the top of Mono Street in Brisbane, I recognized the house with its picture windows because I had googled her address back when I thought I might never see her, back when I hadn't heard her voice, knew only a boy with riveting hazel eyes and a baby girl with pink cheeks and dark, discerning eyes. The drapes rippled and Carmela giggled. "Bear," she said, hurrying across the front yard. The curtain was pulled back to reveal an enormous orange cat. "Stanford," she said, laughing.

And a boy, between window and the back of the couch, screaming open-mouthed. "Mama!"

Carmela was in the door and on the floor, holding him, holding him against her as she rose to stand. She whispered into his ear and he laughed.

The grandparents in the room.

"My mom, Faith," Carmela said, the geography of seventeen years inside the three words, the life she had turned from, showing up in the living room of the people who'd thought they'd known my daughter. That she was theirs and that she was solitary.

The grandfather sat in an armchair against the wall.

"We'll have to wake Cami," said the grandmother. She returned with the dark-haired girl, who slept in her arms.

"Cami," Carmela said.

The grandmother settled in a chair, looking down at the child. "She wouldn't go down for her nap. Now she's paying for it."

"Cami," Carmela said. Michael was still in her arms, her thin body bending like a sapling under his long weight, his feet dangling to her knees. Cami opened her eyes.

Perhaps I haven't mentioned that the dog had been rushing about, barking, sweeping things off surfaces with his tail, barking, barking, barking. And Michael had been laughing loudly, saying, "Mama." And the orange cat had strolled out.

"Mama," Cami said, raising her arms to be picked up.

"Cami, Cami." Carmela stooped to hug both children and held them to her, rising to her feet, a child on each hip.

Without preamble, the mother-in-law said to me, "She said you were dead."

I wanted to scream, *I haven't seen Carmela* (Carmela! in the room with me!) *for seventeen years. What if you didn't know whether your son was living or dead?* Wanted to say, *Look at my beautiful girl*. Child of my own childhood of learned silence, I knew that to say those things could be dangerous, so I went for the mundane. "What do the children call you?" I asked. Like I would be *grandma Faith*.

"They call me Grandma." Perhaps to emphasize her singular authority, she said, "Cami, come here and let me brush your hair," but Cami stayed with her arms around Carmela's neck.

"This is your grandma Faith," Carmela said. She was on the floor. They were chasing one another on all fours. They hadn't seen one another in three months. Not since she had signed herself into the hospital.

I was on the floor, too, but not scrambling around.

"Say hello," Grandma said from above.

Cami buried her face in the carpet. "Come here, little ostrich," Carmela said, pulling the girl into her lap. "In the shelter, that's what Cami would do when things got too much for her. Bury her face, with her butt sticking up in the air." She playfully patted the girl's bottom and Cami giggled. I thought of the three of them, Carmela, Cami, Michael, the days Carmela pushed the double stroller through the streets of San Francisco, up and down hills, rain or shine, hot or cold. Spending a bit of money to buy hot chocolate for her kids, so young in the double stroller.

Grandma put the gifts we had brought on the mantle, which was already a jumble of stuff. Carmela's eyes tracked the gesture, the putting aside of her gift, the animal gift of scent.

Outside, there was a bug in the dirt. Carmela, Cami, and Michael placed leaves in its path, sliding it from a sheet of paper into their palms. The remaining three of us sat on the wall. The yard was bare, except for an olive tree and a few smaller trees.

"Their dad and I bought the trees," Carmela said. "We had both kids in the car and the double stroller. And Bear."

I had a life with these children and this dog and that big old orange cat and his timid sister. I was here before these trees, which are sturdy and tall. I stared at her, the way I had stared at each of my children when they were born. A universe. *I might never have seen her again.*

"So, how are you finding her?" Grandma asked.

"You can't imagine." I started to cry, though it wasn't safe to do so.

The three bug watchers giggled, oblivious to the grandfather, the grandma, and me. Carmela was crouched so low, her face touched the soil.

A mist blew in over the hill.

"Do you think she's mentally ill?" Grandma asked.

"I've barely . . ."

"Do you?"

"I . . ."

"The court wanted to know." The state had power over Carmela and these children. Grandma must have known she was inflicting pain, or perhaps she was just thoroughly immersed in her own storyline of this daughter-in-law who had run. She pressed, "And is she legally blind?"

Maybe she couldn't bear to see. You know why. I don't.

"The court wanted to know that too," she persisted.

"I am Carmela's mother," I said, but she carried on.

"The first week after they married, he knew it was a mistake."

She could hurt me. She could cause Carmela harm.

A man walked into the yard.

"Daddy," the kids yelled. He was medium height, affable, dressed in khakis and a shirt. When the monsoon mist and wind ramped up, we moved inside. Carmela's husband and his mother put out salmon and salad and bread and some fruit. A Jesus-saturated grace. It was almost too much, the reality of the modest dining room, the grandparents, the husband, and the children. The children I'd known only in photos, a world behind the screen of my correspondence with Carmela.

Back in the living room, Carmela and the kids wrestled and played hide-and-seek and once lapsed into stillness, the two children in her lap, their arms around her torso, her head bent over the dark head of Cami, the honey head of Michael.

A cab was called and it blew its horn out front.
"Cami. Michael," she said, holding them. "Michael, Cami. Cami, Michael."
"Mama," Cami sang.
The horn honked again.
Somehow, we got out the door.
Behind us, Michael screamed, "I want to go live in the shelter with Mama."

That summer, the husband, that pleasant man in the yard, had their marriage annulled. Carmela was too fragile to fight. Legally, she has no rights to her children or to the house she helped select and furnish with him, the olive tree.

Carmela was moving from the apartment in the Tenderloin to a women's shelter. On an earlier visit, I had given her what we called my Little Red Riding Hood rain jacket. It suited both and each of us—silky and carmine. On another visit, I'd brought Carmela the patchwork quilt my mother had made for her birth. Before the shelter, Carmela handed me the red rain jacket and the quilt. I stored them in a dry shed at Jonah and Beth's.

Nevertheless, for more than a year she is walking the two or more miles from the Seneca Hotel for people with mental health conditions to Bernal Heights, where her children are in preschool. Nevertheless, she and I spend days there, on the floor with the children. Nevertheless, Cami is toilet trained. And we go down the flight of wooden steps to the preschool backyard and play in the sandbox under the trees. Nevertheless, the kids are in public school in Brisbane. Nevertheless, she takes a weekend cab to Brisbane, skipping food if she must to make the fare, and the former husband drives her home, with the two little kids all the way in the back of the van that she helped select when they were married, amid middens of Legos and snack packs and discarded clothing. And Cami wraps up in my daughter's sweatshirt because it's there in the car and my daughter may wrap up in the former husband's sweatshirt because it is there. Nevertheless, I visit and there is the black lab Bear (now graying and broad as a barrel). A cat has died, but Stanford the orange cat is still alive and on a diet, and there is a new young cat, Ty Ty, and two pet snakes and a few pet rats that a snake rejected for dinner and then what do you do in the suburbs with a rat rejected by your snake? Nevertheless, on Saturday and Sunday, Carmela makes pasta for Cami when that is pretty much all Cami will eat. Nevertheless, she still romps on the floor and is noisy-noisy with them, even when Michael's head cracks into hers and it is very loud and she starts to cry and that is part of his being mothered by her, that she cries inconsolably when her head is painfully cracked into. Nevertheless, she does homework with her children and helps them ready their work packets for the next week. Nevertheless, in the early morning she must catch the cab in San Francisco when it is still foggy in the neighborhood where Mark Zuckerberg has bought and refurbished a *home*; nevertheless, she will be driven home through the night, up the lit bay, down a hill, past the ODC studio where she once danced and worked, and will be dropped off at the corner store and walk home through Saturday night tourists to the Sunrise Hotel. Nevertheless, she goes through the Brisbane refrigerator, discarding spoiled food, placing fruit and vegetables and cheese where her children can help themselves after school, and sometimes she makes guacamole and she cleans the bathrooms because she wants her children to live in a home that is ordered and clean, and Michael will still, at age eleven, when he is angry and frustrated, protest, *I want to live in the shelter with Mama*. Nevertheless, Cami frustrated and angry, may take her fists to her older brother, may defy her father, she standing screaming on the couch, and what she does during this is growl. Nevertheless, sometimes I am so tired by my trips to California; nevertheless, I wouldn't miss them for anything. Nevertheless, my daughter begins again to attend the church in Brisbane. When my daughter returns to her eight-by-ten room at the Sunrise, she will worry about Cami and Michael, their absences from school, their sports injuries. She will talk and text with them every day. And, on the phone with me, her gentle laugh will come through. *Yeah*, she says. She loves them so.

Find a Home Place

Once upon a time, my children and I lived up Middle White Oak Holler in coal country, West Virginia. Driving my VW squareback south from the

Racine Post Office, gas station, and IGA, I followed US Route 119 above the Coal River, houses reached by steep dirt drives perched high above the road, houses looking like they might pitch forward over the road; opposite, a few houses down drives below the road in the bottom. The road my children and I drove every day: a place of aboveness and belowness, treacherous when the surface was ice, threatened when the river rose. Just past Peytona Elementary but before Drawdy Falls (where miners gathered for rallies during strikes), a tight right onto Middle White Oak, a dirt road passing the tipple before launching itself up waterfall hill. At the top, opening into a small valley or holler, we passed a few houses before reaching our drive. Perched on a point of land above the dirt road, the house was small, hand-built by working people, sided in gray, green, and red asphalt "brick." The interior walls were rough-cut oak, possibly taken off the land on which the house sat, the boards a deep coffee brown and hardened so by age that when a friend tried to cut a hole in my bedroom wall to put in a window, he burned up the motor of his power saw. We sheltered in this house, with its tar-paper roof, the wild hill of woods behind us. Up in the woods was a poorly concealed and abandoned mine pit. The changing colors and moods of the seasons made their way across the hill we faced, where the Hagers lived. We lived with change; we lived with barely concealed pits that everybody knew about; we lived with neighbors.

Once upon a time, my children's bodies were secure, or I thought they were. For immunizations, checkups, the sinus infections from air infused with sweet chestnut bloom and Kanawha Valley industrial pollution, we went to the clinic at Cabin Creek built by the United Mine Workers. I watched over their sickbeds, fed them vitamins, served liver once a week for the iron. Their bodies, which had grown from my own, delighted me, as they ran in the grass with our dogs, swam in the pool at Kanawha State Forest, emerged from evening baths with their skin glowing and their damp hair slick against their compact skulls. They were at home in their bodies.

We were a unit of three, living with our dogs and cats. Me with two young, brimming people, one learning to read at school and one who would soon teach herself, reading not only words on a page but reading the world, speaking an English my parents would have recognized but broadening their sounds with playmates. I see them running in the grass in their bright hippie clothes. An early lover of mine lived with us, but she was often gone emotionally and physically, though her presence in her absence was pervasive—I was in love with her. Evenings, home from school, Jonah and Carmela played in the fallen leaves with our dogs. In a heavy summer rain, sending brown water boiling through the creek, the two might dance under the downspout protruding from the eaves, their bodies brown and their white underpants incandescent in the storm light. My daughter might sit on our high front porch, her hair wisping, and sing with Buffy Sainte-Marie, *I'm gonna be a country girl again with an old brown dog and a big front porch and rabbits in the pen.* She could be in our little house and abroad in the world with Buffy Sainte-Marie; she did absorb the mourning and anger of Buffy Sainte-Marie—you could see this in the rose flush of her face. After baths, after the children's damp bodies were wrapped in towels in front of the gas heater, they put on flannel nightclothes and went willingly to bed. We were people who drove US Route 119 below houses that might topple down upon us, drove above the Coal River, which could rise like a motherfucker.

Carmela stands maybe, five foot five. She wears Thrift Town brown and black leggings and turquoise and pink and white camisoles. Every year or two I buy her athletic shoes. She is pale but not white; her hair wisps like a child's, and when she is playing volleyball with her children, her nose is dotted with sweat and her thin hair slicks against her scalp. Her woman's arms and legs are muscled. There are masses on her legs, resting upon the shin like Silly Putty eggs. Her shoulders slope and her bosom is ample. She may be rail thin or her camisole size may be large. Her hands are boney, as my mother's were, but thin and small, like my sister's. When the little ones, the alters inside her, get up to mischief, they have her paint her nails bright colors. Her eyes are dark and sometimes veiled. *Near homeless*: the bureaucratic label for Carmela in 2014.

Housing. San Francisco. The year we reunited, Carmela lived in the one-bedroom apartment her brother and I rented, but he and I couldn't sustain the cost, so her next home had to be a homeless shelter. Jonah brought his vacuum cleaner and they cleaned and emptied the apartment. They propped her almost-new mattress against a wall in the street. They ate an early supper. Her brother kissed her goodbye and she walked off around the corner. At the shelter, sixty women slept on the floor in an open space; one, an elder with an ostomy bag. The toilet for the women was up a flight of stairs from where they slept.

Oscar Grant was murdered by BART police. This death evokes voices of adults when I was eleven. They lowered their voices, hushed speaking I grew up within. *Emmett Till.* Those grown-ups taught me to mind the deaths. Repeatedly in the manuscripts sent to us for *Hands*, women, both Black and white, named Emmett Till's death as a force that sent us South. Emmett Till had been our age, will always be our age in absentia. Who would Emmett Till have been if he'd lived to forty, to sixty-five, to his midseventies and beyond? Would he have picketed like us? Would he have become a chemist? A lawyer? A poet?

She said, "Mom, I'm slipping through the cracks." I imagined her body sliding between granite slabs, her small head with the wisping hair disappearing, her corporality: gone. I would not allow it.

We say we abhor murder, but we live with the racist murder of Black people. Daily. Monthly. From the time we are children, hearing about Emmett Till, until we are in our seventies. Still living with it. What is our line in the sand: One murder? A dozen? Hundreds?

Sangodare writes the formation of a white woman's identity is particular. Does that include an ability to live as white women with the murder of Black people?

Ruby Sales says living with the endemic violence in our culture is a form of "soul murder" and describes the painkillers that allow us to live with the inhumanity: . . . *Empire opiates that entice them to commit soul murder.* Are there other ways to secure daily security and shelter and at the same time defy the dictates of empire? Through community: big community and personal community. What calculations do we make to stay alive within empire? Necessary dependence—we think. Soul murder—staying here is a choice.

Ruby Sales: . . . *be brave enough to free themselves to live evolved lives.* What is an evolved life? Consciousness and an imperative to act. Compassion. The year 2016: in Baton Rouge, Louisiana, a very young and lone Black woman wearing eyeglasses and a summer dress, facing police in riot gear, backed by a phalanx of police in similar gear. In 1964 in Cambridge, Maryland, Gloria Richardson of SNCC, a mother of two, cooly brushing aside a National Guard bayonet thrust in her face.

Who are the soldiers of empire whom I must confront? In what small context do I meet the soldiers? Images from the Vietnam War era: monks and nuns setting themselves on fire. Self-immolation. Add it to the vocabulary of living adjacent to death. Going back to the 1890s and coming forward to the present, massive demonstrations, legislative and legal struggles against lynching—these efforts often spearheaded and drawing upon the presence of Black women. Living with and resisting—Jimmy Carter in his late nineties, saying as long as there are homeless people, he will build with Habitat for Humanity. One house at a time, he will build.

In San Francisco, affordable housing is a chimera; a city with a large stock of near-derelict old hotels, which offer housing to the destitute and the near-destitute. In 2009, the wait list for such housing was eight years. In Carmela's fragility, eight years was an investment in an unimaginable future.

After six months on the floor of the shelter, Carmela was offered space in the Seneca, a hotel for persons with mental health conditions. It was located on Sixth Street off Market, where homeless persons and tourists and school-skipping teenagers brushed shoulders. Hundreds of people lived at the Seneca. To visit her, I had to be buzzed in and relinquish my ID. Staff were overworked. Violence in the corridors, the stairwells. Shared toilets where at least once Carmela found feces in the bathtub. She was an oddity, white and relatively young, seemingly healthy. Her approach to being different was to be friendly. Walking down Market Street, she invariably greeted, and was greeted by, people who'd known her at the women's shelter and before.

Convinced it was about to be shut down, Carmela left the Seneca and moved into an SRO, or single-room-occupancy hotel, in the Mission District. She has lived at this SRO for years, in an eight-by-ten room with its own bath in a building rife with violence, sex work, drug partying, and exhaustion. A large number of cotenants are military vets, including at least one man who served in the Vietnam era and several women. The medical examiner's van has been there to pick up a body twice when I was with her. The spring of 2014, she phoned to say a woman had been found dead in the garbage chute. Incredulous, I googled *dead woman in garbage chute*, and there it was in black and white. This is where Carmela lived when for weeks she lay on her bed and didn't go out and didn't answer her phone and didn't eat.

The margin between Carmela near homeless and Carmela homeless is the money I send. She and I are on my mobile phone plan. I mail her items, especially over-the-counter drugstore items and clothes. And I pay in never-ending fear.

Home was bathing my children's bodies. Home was second gearing the VW up waterfall hill. Home was a child figuring out vowels and for the first time recognizing the words in Dr. Seuss, a child inventing reading for herself. Home was Carmela singing her heart out from the porch above our holler: *I'm gonna be a country girl again with an old brown dog and a big front porch and rabbits in the pen*. Home was taking a sick child to Cabin Creek Clinic, stopping in Marmet to fill the prescription, and hovering over their restless sleep. Home was his guitar, her dance. Home was talking about everything. At least what I thought was everything.

The term "single-room occupancy" denotes that a person's entire domestic life takes place in one room. A demarcation: SRO. Or not SRO.

Dictated by chronology, I would have built a framework with uprights and beams, taken us down corridors and up skeletal stairs from Carmela's and my reuniting in 2009 to the crisis of 2014. Except. But. What does temporal movement have to do with the blood-muddy odor of unsafe housing, the unreliable ground of the psych world, the clamor of the body's physical pain embedded in time? A structure makes inherent sense because it couldn't stand up otherwise.

What if there is no sense? Why would chronology in a chaotic and perhaps malign universe make sense?

When we reunited in that under-construction corridor, that summer when we shared a one-bedroom apartment, she spent most of her days and nights in the only bedroom, on the IKEA mattress, door closed. At night, I heard her TV through the wall. I heard her laughter over and over again. And then I realized it wasn't laughter. She was crying. Night after night. Hour after hour. Thirty-eight years old, but baby wailing. St. Francis's outpatient program did not touch the weeping. I understood, to attempt to comfort her with touch, to come too close, would be a transgression. *Trigger Mom*, who in an instant could overshadow everything loving and good between us.

The St. Francis program was for people with dual diagnoses (bipolar disorder and substance use disorder). I confided in a San Francisco friend who is a health policy professional that the program was unsatisfactory. She told me to contact the hospital's patient ombudsman. She said, "Every hospital is required to have an ombudsman." I understood, this is a fight my friend and other health policy wonks had won. I tried to find the ombudsman at St. Francis; I believed things could be made right. When I asked the affable but harried social work dude, he couldn't tell me. Going to the St. Francis website in 2016 while writing this, I search for *patient ombudsman*. Result? *No results found for patient ombudsman.* The St. Francis website now appears under the URL dignityhealth.org, which is branding bullshit and erases the past.

Carmela was discharged from the program at St. Francis. It took long-distance help from my childhood friend Kate to find a therapist with knowledge of dissociative identity disorder, once known as multiple personality disorder. Carmela and I walked from the apartment on O'Farrell in a neighborhood called Polk Gulch to the therapist's Financial District office, which also seemed to be the therapist's apartment. Private pay. Four times a week. Paid for with thirty years of accumulated dividends on my life insurance, a policy purchased when I bought the $19,000 house that had sheltered us up Middle White Oak Holler.

During the first week in which the therapist and Carmela worked together, Carmela came out of a session with the color drained from her face. Before she entered the revolving door to get out of the building, Carmela said, "She says it isn't real." She whispered this so quietly I didn't understand it the first time. In a countermove that made sense to her, Carmela bought herself an engagement ring in a pawn shop, a defiant act: *We are real. We are pledged.* Without a supervising doctor at St. Francis, Carmela's prescriptions lapsed. The therapist arranged a private-pay prescribing psychiatrist. Almost immediately after taking the new meds, Carmela complained of stomach pains and other symptoms. We went to the University of California San Francisco (UCSF) looking for help. One doctor said in the hall outside the examining room, audible to Carmela and me: "How do you expect me to treat her? She's psychotic."

The husband canceled Carmela's health insurance, although they were still married. I couldn't private pay what she needed. I had asked the therapist for a sliding scale, but she had denied me.

Carmela's physical and psych pain were overbearing. That summer in the apartment, scarcely having learned how to speak across the years of separation, we were trying to invent how to read where we were and how to get somewhere else. I believed there was a somewhere else. I thought we would find the right doctor, the right therapist, that someone who could make things right would take an interest in Carmela. All that summer, I hoped for a save. I would walk, Carmela closed in her room back at the apartment. I would scale the heights so I could look over the bay and beyond the dread that inhabited me. I found the Whole Foods where I could buy the illusion of comfort by food. I bought a French press and some coffee beans. Wanting to guess what she might like to eat, she whom I had not known for so long. Hoping that therapy would make it better, that medications would make it better, that she would no longer need to weep, that the soft tissue masses and internal obstructions would dissipate. We needed to get back to where everyone else lived.

One day after one of my dread-filled walks, I turned onto our street, O'Farrell, from Van Ness. Police cars and officers in protective gear clustered between me and our apartment. In the middle of the street between Polk and O'Farrell, an area had been cordoned off. Was it when I turned the corner onto O'Farrell that flames and smoke burst out of the ground? People said, *Pacific Gas and Electric.* A worker told me I couldn't walk down the block, but I kept walking. Past the power erupting from below the pavement. As long as I was alive, I would keep walking toward Carmela. Smoke billowed. In the apartment building, emergency doors blocked the elevators. Perhaps I walked up the echoing stairwell. That evening, I watched the glass-fronted building across from us, watched reflected smoke billowing in perfect clarity on the surface of the glass, behind which I could see people preparing dinner in their apartments.

The shelter in place lasted for days. A day or two in, I went to Berkeley for a planned visit to my son's family. When I returned, Carmela had eaten the cabinets bare.

We existed in a place of thrall and flames shooting from below the street, where there should not be an opening between walking-around air and the air below the paved crust.

That summer, Shem Walker, an unarmed Black man, was shot and killed on the other side of the continent by a New York City police officer. The *New York Times* wrote: "In the hours after Shem Walker, 49, was killed in an encounter with the police outside his mother's home in Brooklyn last week, many details made public had the durability of soap bubbles." Durability of soap bubbles? A man who had lived 49 years; a man with a mother and other family. Mr. Shem Walker. Who would be savaged in the press for something he had done earlier in his life. Is this how we learn that harm to other people is not as wrong as harm to *us*? That this murder can be soaped out because of Mr. Walker's prior drug-related conviction? Walker's son said, "This detail is to desensitize or dehumanize the situation. Like it's justification." There was no indictment of the officer who shot Mr. Walker. New York City paid $2.25 million to settle with the family. What is the cost to all of us? Can we pay off the debt? When and how have we learned to live with the fact, the unbearable fact, of racist murder?

People had ideas about how Carmela and I could do things better. Ideas they thought were *the idea*. A friend of my son's family was adamant that the clinic where she interned could turn things around. Carmela had heard about the clinic: the crowds, the waits, the overworked staff, the ineffective services; but she agreed to try. She sat in line. The staff person she spoke to was so overwhelmed by her story that he sent her home in a cab. I don't know that he offered any services. With a city as overstretched as San Francisco in 2009, many programs that looked great on paper had wait lists that rendered them inaccessible, or they were so underfunded that they were ineffective.

People said, *Carmela should be on medication*, but half the time she was, on a cocktail that might change from month to month, from doctor to doctor. Then the insurance was canceled, and we couldn't pay for meds. And the stomach cramping and pains with the meds were awful. It took me a long time and the help of a therapist of my own to learn to say to those who asked about meds as if meds were God, "You know, if she were in an ideal situation in which she was monitored, in which she saw the same doctor month after month, in which she was housing-secure and well fed, maybe they would find the right meds." Some implied Carmela should suck it up, live with the vomiting and headaches, that somehow her behavior was the failure. I learned to say, "She has given it a good-faith effort." It was a relief to learn to say this, but it also cost me in the disbelief, the impatience, the tuning out from those I loved who could not hear me. If Carmela would try hard enough. If I would make her. Recalcitrant: the two of us. Within the year, the social work intern who had urged us to try the clinic left it for a private practice, disgusted with the clinic's inadequate services.

A friend in Durham said, "To say, *If she were in an ideal situation in which she was monitored*. That's horrible. In which she was *monitored*? How about, an ideal situation in which she was *cared for*?"

Early summer, after a month or so of therapy, the therapist in the office in a private park in the Financial District insisted I move back to North Carolina, which I reluctantly did. In retrospect, I see how the therapist required Carmela's isolation. That is the sinister version. The other version: that I was negligent or overwhelming or overemotional (heard that before). *Bad Faith.*

After I had returned to North Carolina, the therapist underwent shoulder surgery. While taking pain medications, she met with Carmela and revealed info about another client. After that session, Carmela never went back. The therapist stuffed Carmela's phone inbox with messages and showed up uninvited at

Carmela's apartment building. I told the therapist to stop. I should have filed an ethics complaint, but we were facing enough that was difficult. I was afraid if Carmela applied for Social Security disability, she would need the therapist to support her claim. We slipped into therapy and medication limbo.

Always there was the little one singing on our porch overlooking Middle White Oak Holler: she who had become a dancer; she who had first turned to psychotherapy in her twenties; she who knew her body, her mind, her heart; she who had become a mother. Always, she was looking to feel better. She took Pilates and tried acupuncture. She spoke weekly with the hotline counselor she had spoken to since she left her home in Brisbane.

The gutsy child found therapy for free at a women's program. They extended her time with them at least once and helped her negotiate her move into the homeless system. Living at the Seneca, she was assigned a therapist through the public health system, but she rarely saw the same therapist twice and the therapists contradicted one another. The therapists canceled due to government furloughs dictated by the financial crisis. Carmela's weekly therapy was more like once or twice a month. The standard for dissociative identity disorder is four or five sessions a week. Carmela told them with such a sketchy schedule she couldn't establish the trust necessary for therapy. Probably in her file, she is recorded as having rejected services. Is slipping through the cracks another way to say *rejected services*?

Carmela and I went to her ob-gyn appointment at a medical center. She was ushered into the examining room but was soon brought back. Her heart rate was so high they sent her across the street for an EKG. We gathered up our things and crossed the street, went up in an elevator to a warren of corridors. They verified her heart rate was, I think, around 150. She put her clothes back on; we went down in the elevator, across the street and up in the other elevator. I wanted to scream, *Make her safe*. I wanted to beg, *Please*. Wanted a miracle save from her heart rampaging in her chest.

If your autonomy is broken.
    If you are harmed continuously.
    Is there a possibility of home?

. . .

Carmela arranged an internship at a dance studio in Washington, DC. Carmela, Vicki, Erin, and I met in the restaurant America at Union Station. Erin and Carmela hugged, Erin in her easy, sisterly way. We pulled in our chairs with metal screeches. We were handed menus as big as a three-year-old. The conceit of the restaurant was that they served the specialties of regions served by Amtrak. There we were on Planet Food Homogenized, sitting on an interpersonal powder keg that could have blown like a Pacific Gas and Electric pipeline. The walls were covered in larger-than-life cowboys astride rearing and snorting horses, enormous splashes of pinto and roan horseflesh. Ah, the West, quintessential America to some. There were ropes and neckerchiefs, dust and swirling sunset. I guess at the restaurant America, slave ships, or historic lynchings, or *No Irish need apply* were not essential America. The rough-and-tumble cowboys and horses warred with the place's heavy-napkin gentility.

The waiter brought us a basket of very white bread. I said, "It's wonderful to be here. Vicki and me, and two of our daughters." I was aiming for amiable, celebratory, embracing.

"There are many more daughters than that," Carmela said. "One hundred fifty-eight of us." I think Vicki tensed at this flamboyance, but was it flaunting on Carmela's part or devotion to who she was? Carmela: Brand Never Homogenized. That number of alters, so many articulated parts to Carmela, but I had watched some of the parts emerge and type their names on a piece of paper, handwriting for the names often distinct, one from the other. Carmela always does thoroughly whatever it is she is doing.

Finished eating, Carmela, perhaps ready to shed us, the family she hadn't had for so many years, agreed to hasty photos. I have one from that evening of Erin in a red print rayon dress, Carmela in a similar black-and-blue rayon, their dark-haired heads close, Carmela pressing into the side of Erin's head, their slim arms wrapped around one another. Sisters. And in the background the swirl of horses' haunches and whips.

. . .

For a long time, severe PTSD was her psych diagnosis, along with possible bipolar disorder and an anxiety disorder. To get a diagnosis, a name for why she hurt. The belief: diagnosis would lead to relief.

Carmela and I were walking on Mission Street past gated doors and windowless facades. My leg pain was fierce, but we had foregone a cab. Recently, she had walked less. "I've lost my safety," she said. I was more aware of my pain than I was aware of her, focused on how many blocks we had to go. She complained: I was walking too close to her; I was walking on the wrong side of her. The sunlight was bright, and wind swirled trash. She cried out and doubled over. Something had flown into her eye. She howled with pain and terror, too. I wanted to fold her into my arms, stroke her hair, but I was also afraid of triggering the woman who had said I was walking too close to her, was doing everything wrong. *Bad Faith*. She kept howling and the city people who went by gave us hardly a glance. She was in lockdown. A long time later, the pain and fear subsided, but she still shuddered as we walked home.

Her bed has been shaken violently. She is stabbed. She has blockages in her digestive system. She has had palpable soft swellings on her limbs and in her vaginal canal. She is nearly blind and her hearing is fading—she is losing touch with the world. She had remained active, using an exercise bike in her room, doing floor exercises, joining a fitness club on Market Street, swimming at a gym, and walking the almost four miles from the Mission District to the Ferry building, but since 2013 or so she has spent more and more time in her room. Not out in the streets where the woman in the newspaper kiosk speaks to her in Spanish. Not waving to the Filipino man in his ironed shirt behind the plate glass of his SRO. Not waving to the owner of Al Hamra, Ethiopian food, as she walks past.

In 2011, she said, "Ehlers-Danlos syndrome. Look it up." The tissues become so elastic that the resulting hypermobility is life-threatening. The body cannot support itself and the organs may not support their functions. Ehlers-Danlos causes daily pain. "I've always been double-jointed," she said and bent her elbow backward in a way that turned my stomach.

San Francisco General was uphill from the Seneca. We started out passing a few smoking Seneca residents out front. Down Sixth, we passed the mobile police van, the Bayanihan House, up to Potrero, where the hospital's building five looms in my memory as dark and ancient, a Jane Eyre sorrow in its facade, though the 2016 pictures I pull up on Google are of new buildings, gleaming glass and metal. The hospital has a new name: Zuckerberg San Francisco General Hospital. This money could one day push Carmela out of her neighborhood. It muddies her medical waters and renames my memories. The corridors were dark. There were very sick people, very old people, waiting in line to reach the reception windows that looked like racetrack betting windows. Waiting for appointments. Waiting for the pharmacy to open. People betting medical care could ease their pain, others so deeply entrenched, they couldn't get out.

The first-floor interior of SF General, a dim and dull light. An unconscious person is wheeled past on a gurney. We huddle down, small as we'd like our troubles to be, huddle down inside, resisting the force that has engulfed us, that has reached to control us. We need control inside this catchment of the destitute. We need to be not business as usual. We need to know. We need to know why. What is the name for this? Does it have a name? Are we the only ones who have it? We are on an island whose name we haven't been told. Have the doctors seen this? Can the doctors speak to us—do they know how? Will the nurses remember to call our name? Will we miss our turn? What if they do not allow us a name—what then?

Sit in the plastic chair and remember: *I'm gonna be a country girl again*. Middle White Oak Holler. Daylight saving time. Light spills over the quilt. The windows open. "It's still light out," my son protests.

He had her lie on the table in her lime jockey shorts. Her no-color brassiere banded her meager back. Her legs nothing but long bones. He pressed lubricated disks onto the skin of her leg, her thigh, the bottom of her foot. Leads fed into the machine. She blurted she was wearing a pad. She had found recently that she was leaking. He turned on the juice. She gasped. He increased the jolt. She jerked. Her pain inscribed a roller coaster on the screen, unfolding like a fan. She said: *What if? And next week? And tomorrow?* She said, *Wheelchair?*

He said, "Don't jump the gun."

He placed each needle in her skin, embroidery. She said, "It will be good to know." He tapped her leg—the one with the swelling. "Move your leg." She could not. With his hand, he moved the leg. On the screen's glass, the pain scattered and darted. "We will hear your muscles," he said. A metaphor, I thought. A sound surfaced, the creak of a mast or the shift of bedrock. Not a metaphor. He exposed her spine, her shoulder blades thin as knives. When she was born, I would touch the buttons of spine below the downy hair. Her hands fluttered and she chattered.

He said, "I want to see you next week."

She said, "They will give me an appointment months from now. If you call. . . ."

He interrupted, "I want to see you next week. You can get dressed."

After more appointments, Carmela told me the doctor said he was quite sure Carmela had Ehlers-Danlos syndrome, but public health would never pay for treatment.

Ehlers-Danlos explains Carmela to herself in the context of gravity and the failure of connective tissue.

Carmela was taking classes in Feldenkrais, a somatic system that communicates with the unconscious through movement. She was taking ballet and was to perform with her class. We went downtown to buy dance clothes; on the same morning, we had bought her an emergency preparedness kit—she always felt in peril even now as she had turned to her dancer's body. Walking downtown, pedestrians' sweatshirts blasted messages at her and people blew smoke in her face. Inside the store, we fingered soft skirts, leotards, finding ourselves back to when she had been a high school dancer. The fabrics were so new, so soft under our fingertips, so expensive. The clerk measured Carmela's feet, those bunioned feet in my first photos of baby Michael. The clerk brought a bulging plastic bag of pristine pink toe shoes made by a company whose individual shoes are never identical. Carmela tried them on, finding one for the left foot and then the right. The clerk instructed Carmela to stand *en pointe*. "Careful," she warned, "Don't arch enough to break the shank." Carmela, despite the sweatshirts with hostile messages and bedeviling cigarette smoke, Carmela in her early forties, Carmela who had slept on the floor with sixty women, Carmela who had two children, Carmela rose like a miracle onto her toes.

Carmela was hospitalized for not eating. She cleaned out her room and one night checked out. Another *rejected services* probably. She checked herself into the psych ward, convinced she was a psychopath. Her physical condition had deteriorated and she told me she was dying. She said, "My children will understand." She was moved to a community-based facility. Friends, including my elementary school friend Kate, said the program looked good on paper. Much if not all of the therapy consisted of daily AA and Narcotics Anonymous meetings. Residents cooked their meals in a grease-spattered, filthy kitchen. Community and staff space were on the second floor. On the floor below, the cubicle bedrooms were unlocked to facilitate suicide prevention. At least once, Carmela, a survivor of sexual violence, was the only woman in the facility both downstairs (in an unlocked bedroom) and upstairs.

The diagnosis "somatic symptoms disorder" (SSD) was suggested. When I looked up the term on the website of the American Psychiatric Association, the definition was: Somatic symptom disorder is diagnosed when a person has a significant focus on physical symptoms, such as pain, weakness or shortness of breath, to a level that results in major distress and/or problems functioning. The individual has excessive thoughts, feelings and behaviors relating to the physical symptoms. The physical symptoms may or may not be associated with a diagnosed medical condition, but the person is experiencing symptoms and believes they are sick (that is, not faking the illness).

Experientially, Carmela fits this definition but has never received treatment or therapy for the disorder.

At the facility, a worker, another one of those affable but distracted social work dudes, told us SSD was associated with methamphetamine use. I found his attitude accusatory, as though he was challenging Carmela: *So what do you say to that?* Carmela was spitting mad, is what she said to that. Half an hour later, she had signed out of the facility. They gave Carmela her meds in a plastic bag and we caught a cab. Working Google on her phone, she had already scoped out an SRO in the Mission.

Once she had been shown her room at the new SRO, she threw her meds down the garbage chute and only used over-the-counter products for several years. And undoubtedly was again recorded as *rejecting services.*

Diagnoses that have appeared in and sometimes disappeared from Carmela's chart or have been reported by her: severe PTSD, bipolar disorder, dissociative identity disorder, an anxiety disorder, Ehlers-Danlos syndrome, a pituitary tumor, fibromyalgia, somatic symptom disorder. Can a person be a disorder? As in, *She is bipolar?*

In Durham, I had made dinner, though I don't remember what it was. Some nights, it is bread pudding with lemon zest and dried cherries, or chicken with couscous and dates, or fish with local yams and broccoli. Which is to say we have a good life. We are tired at the end of the day, especially on dark winter evenings, and pull blankets over ourselves and watch reruns of *Scandal* or *Luther* or *Person of Interest.* The anticipation of our *show* each evening is visceral. Our evening routine is so established that when Vicki and I rise from the table, the cats mill around in the TV room, waiting for us to settle and provide them with blanketed laps. We had not yet turned on the TV when the phone rang. *Carmela* the screen said.

"Hello." A long body of sound curling, breaking, disappearing down tunnels. Crying. I was thinking: *How fast can I get a plane ticket, get to the airport, and to her? What could make her cry like this?* I had been carrying my red comforter in from the living room. She was crying so hard. "Carmela, slow down, sweetheart. I can't understand." Crying as if her little dog had been hit by a car. Crying as if one of her children. . . . *What? What could make her. . . .*

"Carmela, where is your little dog?" My voice rising in panic. I imagined Joy darting between parked cars and into Valencia Street traffic. "Carmela, is your dog OK?" I put a special ed teacher's force into my voice. I wanted her to snap out of this jag. The anticipated TV show, Vicki waiting on the couch in the TV room, the tortoiseshell cat in her lap. Two-thousand-plus miles between us. *Expedia. Travelocity.*

"My little dog is OK," she sobbed. "She's right here under the covers." Her words folded into one another.

"Carmela, I can't understand."

She cried out, "The noise."

They had been renovating Hotel Sunrise, improving an area for tourists as opposed to the regulars like Carmela. The noise, of the saw cutting granite countertops (pocked and stained Formica in Carmela's room), had been hair-raising.

"The little dog is OK. Joy is OK." Twenty minutes had gone by. I went to the TV-room door and mouthed to Vicki: *It's bad.* She should go ahead without me.

"My little dog is OK. I hurt in my body." Her voice upended on that word, *bah dee*, slow-mo. She trailed into weeping.

"Where?"

"In my bah-dee. I hurt." Sobbed out: Yes, she had taken Tylenol. She hurt.

My brain: Could her brother cross the bay from Berkeley and help? Her crying, her helplessness. I felt the hurt and also, after these several years of being reunited, felt how *inadequate* I was. I had no idea what to do. I thought of a Bay Area therapist I'd spoken to the year before. We'd Skyped. The therapist's kindness. The therapist's calm inhabiting the other side of the mirror, the safe and normal side of the mirror, had filled me with longing to be safe like that. Vicki came and checked on me. *My bah-dee.* An hour had gone by. Carmela cried and cried. *It hurts in my bah-dee.* I scrolled through my contacts and found the name of the therapist. In California, it was still the workday. In the back of my mind, too, *Expedia, Travelocity, red-eye.* Still on the phone with Carmela, I emailed the therapist. Doing something. *My little dog is OK. She's right here under the covers.*

The therapist: "Do you think she'll hurt herself?"

"I don't know."

"Can you guess?"

"She's capable of. . . . but I don't think that's what this is about." Carmela incoherent with pain, I was the authority. *Expedia. Travelocity.* This was territory I had learned, had earned citizenship here, but who was I to act like an authority?

"You know if there's a danger that she will hurt herself, the police."
My little dog is OK. She's right here under the covers.
I hurt in my bah-dee.
"I don't want . . ."

The therapist typed out, "If you think she won't hurt herself, listen to her. Listen." Listen to the unabating wall of sound, jagged and rough, and the few ritual words. Her refrains plugged into the space occupied by what she couldn't say. So I listened. *It hurts in my bah-dee.* A message she cried out, from inside the crying jag. At 10:00 p.m., three hours after I'd answered the phone, I asked Carmela if we could take a break. That I would phone her in an hour, or she could phone me at any time if she had to. *My little dog is OK.*

I stretched out on the red couch, my phone within arm's reach, feeling all I hadn't allowed since I'd picked up the phone. Vicki had gone to bed; the heater was turned down. No cars moved on the street. Just me and memories I could barely give body to. I surprised myself and fell asleep. The alarm announced: time to call her back. She answered, crying. Her throat must have been raw. Into deep night and deeper. *It hurts in my bah-dee.* Phone call for half an hour. An hour's sleep. Another phone call. At 3:30 a.m. Carmela's time, management knocked on her door. I heard her tell him, "No. No. I was just talking to my mom. I'll be OK." When he went away, she told me, "I'll be OK now, Mom. Maybe I can sleep, before they start construction in a couple of hours." In a few minutes, Vicki came downstairs. Her workday was about to begin. I went upstairs to the bed Vicki had just left.

Aishah Shahidah Simmons has said, "I couldn't yell, so my body was screaming."[3]

If you can't always see through your eyes or hear through your ears; if there are soft masses in your intestines and your vaginal canal and up and down your legs; if for months you can't take in enough food; if yellow phlegm gathers in your chest; if you can hardly sleep and if your bed is shaken; if one day your legs

---

3. Aishah Shahidah Simmons, a daughter of SNCC who is about Carmela's age, is a survivor of childhood incest and later rape. She created the film *NO! The Rape Documentary*, available at http://notherapedocumentary.org. The quote here comes from episode 19, "Advice from a Loving Bitch."

no longer support you and you cannot make it across your eight-by-ten room to the toilet. If, all of these.

If your body, your first and most enduring home . . . how can you go home?

Carmela knows how to navigate danger falling in upon her, knows how to navigate floodwaters rising; knows what home can be—her three-colored, short-haired dog Charley, her orange cat Squeaky. Dance class. She is constructing home out of *near homeless*, out of two elementary school kids in a nearby town, each of whom calls her on a cell phone; out of the children's pets—snakes and cats and dog; out of her children's friends; out of each weekend night returning to the Sunrise Hotel; out of Monday through Friday alone on Valencia Street and ordering from Grubhub and sharing her food with Jay and Joyce and Julius and others at the Sunrise.

I never spoke to that therapist again, but her words *If you think she won't hurt herself, listen to her. Listen,* inform my mother's practice.

4
The Practice of Mothers

Showing Up, Autumn 2014

Up steep stairs, the bedroom was low-ceilinged. A window at the head of our bed: the sky a black mottle of stars we couldn't see at home. Respite. To sleep near the ocean. Given my cancer diagnosis, I had said, "I am going to Chincoteague every year from now on." The shifting ocean and its sounds, the deep sky, and time, a whole week's spontaneous time, accountable to no external forces. I could sleep during the day and in the same day: write. Even with Vicki's presence, there would be mornings I could go back to bed, sleeping into the luxuriance of sunlit, uncurtained windows, a low-ceilinged room with space for no more than the bed and us.

Driving from Durham to Chincoteague, Virginia, my newish Subaru was burning oil. I had traveled with three backup containers of super-duper Subaru oil. I was afraid of what I would find each time I checked the oil, or what if I read the dipstick incorrectly? When Vicki phoned, I pulled over and answered peevishly. Driving an hour behind me, her passenger window had imploded. Not knowing where to go, shards showered over the passenger seat, she had driven to an auto place, where they had handed her plastic to cover the gaping window and directed her to a car wash, so she could vacuum the scattered niblets of safety glass.

We arrived at that night's sleep by way of a car that was eating itself alive and another that had exploded inward, but we spent our first ocean day and were

Faith Holsaert and Vicki Smith, 2022, photo by Jade Brooks.

Jonah and Carmela, 2018.

Amina Rachman and Martha Prescod Noonan, 2010.

Faith and Carmela, 2009.

drifting off to sleep. No cats to weigh us down with their need. No sounds of home—air conditioner, plumbing—for which we were responsible. We drifted.

My phone rang. Carmela. Alarm one: Carmela was always mindful of the time difference. Alarm two: she rarely phoned without alerting me in advance. Alarm three: she had been unresponsive to phone and texts for weeks. Alarm four: it was Carmela. I imagined her alone in her room in the Mission: the tan walls, the sink crowded with necessities, the exercise bike. She might be full of cheer. Maybe she wasn't even in her room. Or not. That night her voice was a child's. My mind: *What's wrong?* My heart: *Make it OK.*

"We're having a bit of a security issue," she whispered. That room where she and I had spent afternoons on the bed with its worn tan, gray, and sage-green flannel sheet (though the colors were almost worn away), only the sheet on her mattress, to forestall bedbugs. Watching reruns of *Law and Order: Special Victims Unit*, mayhem and brutality and law enforcement. "I'm not supposed to be calling you, but," the voice conspiratorial, "if you come around the corner and down the hall, I can let you in." Vicki sat up, a rustle, a bulwark.

Could I tell Carmela I was not in her hotel? I was trying to figure out what to say at the same time that the words were coming off my tongue. "Carmela, I'm in Chincoteague." A pause. *Don't hang up. Don't go.*

"I must be confused. I have to go."

"Please call me back and let me know you're OK."

"I have to go."

"What?" Vicki asked, and I told her. We both were soon asleep, though the fin of worry circled.

Carmela called at 1:30 to say she was all right but that she couldn't talk.

Vicki said, "She remembered to call you."

I said, yes, Carmela had remembered, but the worry. . . . Below the star-filled window, I slept again.

Carmela phoned at 4:30. "I'm not supposed to do this, but if you come down the hall, I can let you in."

She rang off as soon as I said I was on the East Coast.

"She wants you to be there," Vicki said.

· · ·

I wanted to go home to Durham from Chincoteague and board a plane to San Francisco, but I had promised to visit my ninety-five-year-old aunt in New York and needed to drive the known roads through Delaware, New Jersey. Needed to remind myself: I knew more than dread. Needed to move and act through that mid-Atlantic landscape so I could face California.

The first morning in New York, I set off in the rain down the Bleecker Street diagonal, walking the neighborhood that had been mine in childhood. I sat on a barstool in the Cornelia Street Cafe, dripping. I didn't like the skinny-pants guy who had steered me to my uncomfortable perch. My phone rang. The screen said: *Jonah*. Jonah and Carmela were supposed to have lunch.

"Hi, Mom." Jonah's voice was high in his throat. He was sick. He had texted Carmela and left a phone message. *Oh, it's bad that he's sick. I need him to. . . .* She had not responded. He didn't know if she had received the message. He didn't think she would meet him. His voice wobbled, but he went on: he didn't want to not go and have her show up and he not be there.

A waiter cleared away my cup, cue for me to give up my seat and go back into the rain. I told Jonah I understood. We hung up. I was queasy with wishing he weren't sick, queasy with imagining how his not showing might make her turn against us. Again. There was that couple by the door waiting for seats. I did not want to go back into the seventeen years of her absence. I would sit for a few more minutes. I would not order ten-dollar pastry or French lentil soup. I would sit.

I put on my raincoat to leave the café and Jonah texted. He was on BART. The refrain in his head must have been *Carmela, Carmela*, though that was wrong; that was my refrain. He probably listened to music. Would Carmela show up? What if she didn't? He would push through the door at the restaurant. If she were not there, which she probably was not, but maybe, maybe she was, he would tell the staff he wanted a table for two and take up his vigil. He would order the biscuits and gravy (*like in West Virginia*, both Carmela and Jonah liked to say) and push the food around on his plate, remembering how sick he felt. Displaced in a rain-washed Greenwich Village café, I was in a space of my willing Jonah and Carmela to connect.

· · ·

She hadn't shown. What should he do? *Save her. Make everything all right*, I wanted to say. He asked: Should he go to her hotel? This would take another hour. My middle-aged son, gray threaded into his ponytail. Wearing his working-guy jacket, jeans, and Skechers shoes. He could not know what he would, or would not, find. She might be lying on her bed in room 230, inert. She might have decided it was time to disappear. Disappearing was something she knew how to do. I could hear him suck down the last of his Diet Coke. Despite my need for him to help her, I wanted to write, *I know you're alone*. Wanted to text: *Don't go. It's too hard.* I saw him, sitting in Mel's, having eaten food that hadn't gone down well. My boy. Standing out of the rain in a doorway, I texted he should do what felt comfortable. Because I could not jump in my red Subaru and drive to help my children, I texted that none of this was his fault and that I loved him. My do-or-die mother's heart started beaming: *I would go. I have gone. I know how awful it is to go alone, but do it. Please. . . . What if she is dead?* He texted he was on his way. People on disability or other below-poverty income, in single rooms, sometimes families, sometimes people with yappy dogs, sometimes people who turned on one another with physical brutality and other times clustered on the one double bed, drinking and playing cards. Microwaves, televisions, toaster ovens, minirefrigerators. All in one eight-by-ten-foot room.

Another text: *What is her room #?*

I wrote back, *230*, adding the names of a couple down the hall. The man was a veteran. They sometimes gave Carmela cookies they baked in their toaster oven, or they gave her food after they'd been shopping. Carmela had figured out how to obtain a wheelchair for the wife. During my time in California, I sometimes passed him going to the corner store for his midmorning beer. He pushed his wife down Sixteenth Street, her long hair white in the sun. And there were the times when the two of them did not get along but still had to live within their small single room.

When Carmela opened her door to Jonah, she thought that Vicki and I had already been there. I asked, "Disoriented like in drugs or disoriented like in mental illness?"

He was definite: not drugs or alcohol. "She doesn't want help. She couldn't talk to me. I think she was afraid of getting in trouble. She was thinner than when we had lunch last month, but I don't think the weight loss is life-threatening. Yet. She was so out of it."

"I'm glad you went."

"I couldn't not."

He continued, "I left my number with Ray. In case. . . ." Ray, the manager, a Tibetan refugee whose family lived in a tiny apartment on the first floor, a man with a thankless job. He had neither the training nor the time to be a social worker. "Ray kept saying what a nice lady she is," Jonah said. "I feel so helpless."

"You showed up."

"But."

"Whatever happens, we'll get through it." Optimism so contrary to my frightened, dread-filled, stuck self, but a gift from my childhood, from my frightened, dread-filled and stuck mother, who raised my sister and me despite her terrors.

"Maybe that *niceness* will save her. Go home. Go to bed. I love you." Things were not good, but she would last until I arrived.

Three weeks later in San Francisco, the bedroom that Vicki and I shared was downstairs in a rehabbed *working man's cottage* in Bernal Heights. Its perch was so steep, I felt like the house could slip off its moorings and slide into the flat land below. No street led to the house, just a stair-step walk from below. The house came with a cat, a calico female so ancient that to pick her up was to pick up a little furry sack of bones, a creature hoarsely grateful when we sat in her living room with our laptops, nervously playing electronic jigsaw puzzles. In our borrowed home, we had a cat, a sense of family—Jonah across the bay and the unknown of Carmela a couple of miles away in the Mission. We had a view of the bay from on high and a living room filled with sunlight.

We didn't know if Carmela would be at the Sunrise.

We didn't know if she would open her door.

We didn't know if she had eaten, or if she was lying on her bed with no sheets, lying there and not eating.

We knew: she hadn't answered her phone.

. . .

On Carmela's street, Valencia, over one hundred trees were planted in 2010. Around the bases of the trees, metal grates depict the Day of the Dead: dancing skeletons and the like. "What's that?" Vicki asked. It was too bizarre, the expenditure for beautification on the street where Carmela, and countless others, barely survived. Vicki and I stopped at Muddy Waters, half a block from the Sunrise. On the sidewalk, someone had written in pastel chalk a long screed, maybe against violence against women but maybe about the church. Or the end of the world. The writing in pink and lemon yellow and aquamarine had been laid down in panels as big as windows.

Muddy Waters was my spot: dark and coffee-centered. Baklava; vegan cookies; an unsavory, black-walled bathroom crawling with graffiti; the barista in her starchy button-down shirt and short hair. Muddy Waters predates gentrification, the new condos with doormen, for instance. The barista, originally from Lebanon, had worked there since Carmela had been in her early twenties. It comforted me to think that girl child, who broke all contact with me, had been here. Once, downhearted on the afternoon I was to fly home, I had shared a brief version of Carmela's situation with the barista. I had stood in line on weekend mornings while she took orders, but most of her attention was devoted to her phone. *My sister, back home.* The trip before, I had asked her name, and I think she'd answered *Najhat*, meaning fresh breath. She had liked my name, *Faith*. With her, I was on a dance floor I knew from the past, the play and coexistence of butch and femme, not as oddity or rebellion against assigned gender roles but simply as a way of being in the world and with one another.

Vicki scouted out a place in the back room. I had always sat in the front room with its windows on Valencia Street, its occasional moments of street life spilling inside: the young ones in feathers and neon leggings and purple lipstick; the parent urging on a uniformed child late for parochial school; the man writing page after page of numbers, neatly boxing in sets with heavy black lines, flipping pages of his pad.

"A soy cappuccino?" the barista asked. I said yes, and a chai for my partner, nodding toward Vicki. I ordered a cookie for Vicki and me to share, filling nervous time with food. "How is your daughter?" the barista asked, her eyes monitoring the front space. She told a man where to place a delivery. I said my daughter had been having a hard time. That I was about to go to her SRO. That I didn't know if she would let me in. These words were so awful, I could barely choke them out. The barista exploded that I must never give up hope. Never. I loved this, but had Carmela and I passed beyond hope? Giving up was inadmissible—I knew that. With the stubbornness of my mother Eunice and the practicality of my mother Charity, I must manage. I set down our drinks. Vicki and I started up our computers. This was all preamble. Soon I would walk to the Sunrise alone. We didn't know what might frighten Carmela. I would text Vicki as soon as . . . "I'm so glad you are here," I said.

In three minutes, I'd leave Muddy Waters.

Ray the manager sat in the cubicle behind glass. He is from Nepal, his skin the alabaster of albinism. He can't see well, so I said, "Ray. It's Faith. Carmela's mother." Outside, cars rushed by. An ambulance. Ray was worried about her, but he had too many other worries: the rooms with rancid carpets and mold-smeared walls; recalcitrant plumbing where feces from one room's toilet surfaced in the toilet of another tenant; sex trade, drugs, alcoholism; a building brimful with PTSD. Ray was worried about Carmela, as were her friends down the hall, but what could they do? My frightened determination. *She will not slip through the cracks.*

The Sunrise is an old wood hotel. Every time I climb the stairs and turn the maze of corners, passing the locked doors and the slatted wood walls, I think of *Gunsmoke* and hotel rooms above the saloon where Matt Dillon would track down wrongdoers. These halls: I have seen food garbage on the floors, breathed many kinds of smoke, heard people fighting and flailing against the walls, glimpsed rooms crammed with a welter of belongings, seen a young mother and her children set out in the moody fog for school.

You must never give up hope. Never.

I passed rooms 232 and 231. I took a breath and knocked on 230, which opened with a key card. I said into the door, "Carmela, it's your mom." Nothing. A long nothing in which I imagined her inert on the bed. I knocked and repeated myself. The last free fall, she had packed up her room at the Seneca after giving everything away and moved out. At the door, no sound. My heart pounded and my mind rabbited. That other time, she had left her room at eleven at night, signed out at the front desk, and taken a cab to the psych ward at San Francisco General, everything she owned in the cab with her. I knocked again. "Carmela, it's your mom." *This is it.* Whatever "it" would turn out to be. After the next knock, a faint cough inside.

My mind took off: A cough like the flu? A cough like tuberculosis? A cough like.... I knocked more forcefully. *You must never give up hope. Never.* "Carmela," I said in my special ed teacher voice, "It's your mother." There was a stir, a presence at the peephole, and a century or two went by while she opened the door.

"Come in." She stood aside, looking away from me. She was wearing black leggings, a turquoise cami over a pink cami. "Oh, I forgot," she said, and hugged me. Thin, her skin hot to my touch. She sat on her bed. I asked if I could sit and she said, *Yes*. She stared straight ahead at things I couldn't see. I was taking in: *She is alive. She is Carmela with the sealed earring holes, the skinny hands like my sister's, the thin hair of the hard life she has led, the still-powerful feet.* I saw her years of fighting. In her fighting, I saw myself. I saw that she could survive.

The room was barren. The cards and notes and photos that had been stuck in the venetian blinds were gone. Two large plastic bins with lids were stacked at the foot of her bed, one upon the other, where her exercise bike had been. The microwave was stowed under the sink. Under the sink, her phone was blinking. Head lowered, she whispered, "I have to move," and, "I need help." I said I was there to help. "Where is Vicki?" she asked, looking around as if Vicki might be in the room.

"Muddy Waters."

"Let me shower," she said and rose.

She touched the corridor wall on one side to steady herself. We walked the maze of turns with the threadbare carpet that didn't lie flat and was stippled with debris. She opened the door to the garbage room and tossed in a knotted plastic bag. Out into the sun of Valencia Street, down the block to Sixteenth, skirting dog poop, smiling at people she knew, at the newspaper kiosk speaking in quick Spanish with the older woman behind the counter, past the chalked hierarchy of plagues and cautions, and into Muddy Waters.

The barista gave me a thumbs-up. In the back room, Vicki and Carmela hugged. Carmela said, "I need to leave that place. I don't ever want to go back there." I thought of her room. The grated window, a cell—monastery or prison. On her tablet, Vicki searched for a temporary hotel. I ordered coffees. Vicki found a special at an old hotel downtown, near the mall where Carmela had once sat in the posh ladies room on the top floor and nursed Cami. Vicki asked Carmela if the hotel would work for a couple of nights. The room even had a bathtub, where she could soak with Epsom salts. A luxury for Carmela, who had been showering in a tiny cubicle where the floor and walls were pitted and discolored, unsavory despite her scrubbing. Carmela took Vicki's tablet into her hand. "I don't know. I would have to see the room to know if I felt safe."

Vicki said she was afraid of losing the online rate. The two of them. Though small, this difference was significant. I knew the size of its hugeness from my five years reunited with Carmela, during which I had tried unsuccessfully to second-guess solutions for her. I knew Vicki, her need to fix things; I knew her love of a bargain. I knew Carmela had issued her hesitance. She would say it only once, before she lapsed into silent refusal. I knew rooms that were wrong could terrorize her. I fell into an unstrategic posture of wishing. Wishing Vicki would hear Carmela. Wishing Carmela would like the room. Telling myself, chances were, she would. I hoped. Vicki did book the room. I don't know if I was wrong to let her do so. Maybe when we reached the hotel, it would be OK.

Since 2009, I had stayed in many accommodations, including one Carmela had insisted I leave because of bedbugs. I could place the Mosser Hotel on a spectrum. It was a nice place that had seen better days. It was like my godparents' 1940s apartment on Central Park West in Manhattan: stiff bed covered in a shiny coverlet, a ribbed radiator, a *ladies'* desk, a tiled bathroom with tub and substantial towel racks. Carmela set down her coat, her small bag of belongings. Vicki and I took off our coats and hung them over a chair.

"What do you think?"

She looked in the bathroom. She sat on the bed. "I don't know."

Vicki and I left to give Carmela time in the room by herself. We walked to Westfield Mall. We were jet-lagged. We were nervous. We ate frozen yogurt in multiflavored swirls topped with nuts and candies. The yogurt shop was too bright. Out in the mall, we found low armchairs. Chandeliers shone above us, and the stone floors and stairs glistened. The women in the mall were skinny, their children prettily dressed, everybody glossy except for occasional clusters of kids with piercings and spiked hair. Time to go back to the Mosser. We rode up in the phone booth–sized elevator. At Carmela's door, I knocked. No answer.

"Maybe she dropped off to sleep," I said, giddily wishing her so at ease in the room that she drifted off. I knocked again. "Carmela, it's your mom."

Nothing.

"Maybe she's in the bathroom," Vicki said.

Or. . . .

I used my key card and let us into the room. "Carmela," I called.

Bed. Desk. Chair. Empty.

Vicki opened the bathroom door.

"Her things are gone," Vicki said.

I fell into the armchair. The years of her earlier absence rose up in my gorge. I touched my clavicle. "I can't do this again," I said. I sat and sat. "She knows how to disappear."

We were sitting, with the long narrow windows, the filmy respectable curtains, the dark wood furniture, and the clean but old carpet, the wallpaper in broad tan-and-silver stripes, when a key card clicked in the door and Carmela appeared.

"Thank God," we said.

"You walked right past me. I was on the sidewalk by the front door," she said.

While Vicki signed us out of the room and paid for the night we hadn't used, Carmela and I stood outside, in the exact spot, she said, where she had watched Vicki and me pass by. "Didn't you see me?" she asked more than once. She needed to be seen where she was and not where we thought she was. The child Carmela had left her body, had built an inner bulwark to protect herself. That fortress was still in place. That system had asserted itself during her time alone in the room. I don't know why the room was threatening, but it was. Despite the bathtub, despite the cleanliness and the quiet, despite the good deal, she couldn't. That is all I could know.

Carmela said she wanted to go back to the Sunrise. In the cab, her face was composed. It felt to me, perhaps because I wanted this to be so, that she had recognized she could not run away. This possibility brought relief and sadness. Relief because the return was manageable. Rageful sadness, because for the more than nine hundred dollars she paid a month, why couldn't my child have a clean, quiet place with a bathtub? Why couldn't she have a place where it was safe for her children to visit her? A year later, Carmela told me, that day at the Mosser while Vicki and I were gone, she had been told we had brought her to the hotel to traffic her.

In the next days, a revolving door of cell phone calls. In a coffee shop, Vicki had phoned a California colleague who stepped outside protocol to help. In the din of a coffee shop, Carmela answered intake questions: Housing was her first priority. Pain management may have been her second. I don't remember the third. I was grateful Carmela accepted Vicki's phone and spoke into it. She said to the person on the other end, no, she couldn't be reached by her own phone. Emails dogged the three of us, the list of cc's swelling as Vicki was referred from one person to the next. A mental health–centered agency offered peer support. Peers would understand. Peer support was a favored modality of the moment. The years Carmela and I had tried to invent a system of care: her finding a free three months of counseling here, another free three months there. The two years of being sent from department to department at San Francisco General: neurologists, gynecologists, pharmacologists, X-rays, manipulations, an MRI during which she was prone in a metal tube, unable to move, for an hour. When the doctor who had thought maybe the problem was a brain tumor, but then oh, it was not, had referred Carmela to another doctor, Carmela had said, "I'm done." I hoped the phone calls Vicki was making . . . that someone could hear, could recognize, could help.

It was in Dolores Park as the three of us sat on a hillside bench, the neighborhood spread below us, children sliding down slides, children swinging, dogs barking, yellow buses lined up outside a parochial school, the path snaking back and forth toward us like the phone calls, snaking up out of the bowl of the park, and we, high on the hill, the air feeling too hot and too thin: Vicki's phone rang. The mental health agency to tell us Carmela could phone for a peer support appointment. We stared down into the bowl of Dolores Park, the three of us so separate from the *normal* lives spooling there. Carmela didn't, couldn't, was not allowed by herself and forces I still do not understand, to use her phone. She had told them this. Vicki had told them.

This was our last day in San Francisco. It was a hot day. My leg and hip hurt—the hip I'd broken twenty-plus years before; my history hurt. We walked out of the park, the descent making me grit my teeth against pain. I suggested we stop at Tartine Bakery. I imagined a flakey chocolate croissant, made even more delicious by some coffee. I was imagining sitting. And flakes of croissant on my bosom. But walked right past Tartine. Carmela said nothing. I said, maybe that bookstore—wasn't there one nearby on Valencia?—and Carmela was irritable when I wasn't sure where it was and when I hesitated when she said where it was. I did buy a book and sat a few minutes in the captain's chair in the bookstore aisle before starting our last lap to the Sunrise. Carmela veered into a restaurant. She wouldn't let me pay for her burrito and a Jarritos. She was going to take them home to her room to eat after Vicki and I had left her. She really wanted a burrito. In the hot restaurant, sweat poured off our faces and down the backs of our necks into our clothes. We gulped down cold drinks. At the Sunrise, goodbye. Her thin frame under my hands. The train roared and bodies pressed all around us. I sat, holding the handle to my suitcase as if it might make a break for somewhere else. I tilted forward to accommodate my day pack. Remembering: the agency had offered her a phone call. When they knew she couldn't. Under the bay, I thought: Could there exist a story of Carmela being Carmela and living a life of her own strength and intelligence, living without being pathologized? Could there be a culture with a place for her curiosity and thoughtfulness and tender parenting and wry amusement? Not to say that Carmela has not sometimes had agency in the harm she has experienced, but to say could there be a way to build on her strengths to create a tenable life? In her midforties, and after years of insecure housing and health care, is there a way for her to emerge on the other side?

Jonah and Beth lived in a North Berkeley bungalow with a square living room with two generous windows, a fireplace, room for a couch, one big-bottomed armchair, a television, and a coffee table. The room was filled with sailing photos, the boys' artwork, and an above-the-door niche with a small plaster Buddha that was there before they moved in—a holdover Buddha, you could say—and a rug in terra-cotta, deep blue, cream, and reds. The older son's electric guitar was propped on a stand in front of the window seat with its velvet cushions in a luscious, exhausted cherry.

Off the living room was a bedroom that held Jonah and Beth's bed with a mauve quilted spread and two locally made dressers. The bathroom, with a door to both the bedroom and the dining room, was so small I could stand in the middle and almost touch all four walls. In this house with few doors, spaces spilled into or rubbed up against one another. Beyond the living room, a dining room with a table Jonah and Beth had owned since their early days, crowded with school projects, an island with a tower of onions and oranges, permission slips from the boys' schools to be signed, the ongoing grocery list, a refrigerator covered with notes, appointment cards, photos of the boys at all ages. Beth's photographic eye is everywhere. A set of industrial shelves filled floor-to-ceiling with dried beans and Pirate's Booty, and tortilla chips, and vitamins, and dried mangos from Mexico in cellophane wrappers. This is to say, Jonah and Beth live jam-packed, among things useful or beautiful or dusty and forgotten, with little room to expand, much of their lives on open shelves, visible to all. A life so crowded with required routines, school lunch packing before first light, bathroom turns, dinner for the boys in the living room, then dinner, often steamed greens, brown rice, and tofu, after 8:00 p.m. for the grown-ups. Jam-packed and self-sufficient.

A wood spiral staircase that Jonah and Beth had had built rose in the dining room. Upstairs, the attic space was unstructured and only partially finished, full of possibilities, space that over almost ten years the family had come to live in as if there were a structure by which they all abided. Here, there was a bathroom but no doors. Both boys had their own niche. The older son slept with a light on and a white noise machine. Each boy had a music setup. The younger son's space was draped like a circus tent. Madras bedspreads covered the skylights. Mexican paper lanterns hung on wires. Shelves in the public space held games and science kits and projects and blobby shapes in butt-pale fired clay. Each night, after ritual showers including boy singing in the deluge, dessert, and toothbrushing, Jonah walked the boys upstairs. He read with his younger son and then each boy put himself to sleep, reading and listening to music.

I slept on the futon in this free-flowing upstairs, sleeping, breathing in the boys' space.

That first evening in Berkeley. Jonah asked after Carmela, but I do not remember much of a conversation. I felt *Carmela* had been our lives for the last days, and I was having trouble putting that aside. *She can phone our office for peer support* dogged me. I couldn't say how angry I was, maybe I didn't know how angry I was, that we had told the agency she couldn't use her phone and they had *offered* her phone support. I had no desire to consider the agency's point of view. I couldn't think about the situation in its totality but caught snatches of it as I sat in the beautiful and crowded living room, chiding myself for not being more present.

I had alerted Vicki that we would sleep in the open with the two boys, that there would be lights, that there would be no doors. Light leaked from everywhere, around walls, through the cutouts high in the bathroom wall. No dark haven.

Jonah carried my suitcase upstairs. Climbing the spiral stairs was hard on my knee, which had taken a beating in San Francisco. *Dolores Park.*

Vicki put her suitcase on the open shelf where on earlier visits I had stacked my clothes. "You'll need to make some room for me," I said.

Vicki didn't like the pillows on the futon.

She said, "What about the bathroom light?"

I was irritated. "On."

"Why?"

"Because."

I wanted her to fit in. I didn't want her fixer side to improve us. I wanted her to just be with us, my son and his family. I wanted her to shut up so I could breathe and collapse on the futon, but I was ashamed of this *shut up* and at a loss to deal with the boil of anger inside me. I had learned to live with the ways of this household. It was a way I showed I loved them. Learning to live with how others, my son and his sister, lived in the world had been a way to respect them and also, to be honest, a necessity, because they weren't easily changed. No fixers need apply.

"I told you it would be like this," I said.

The boys were sleeping. I was exhausted and didn't try to read. She was restless. She read her tablet. Sleeping with the lights on is like dreaming. Carmela. Dolores Park. Phone not phone. The dream interrupted by the tilting flat light of Vicki's tablet. I turned my back. I was cold. Vicki changed her position and moved the blanket. I pulled it back. She got up.

"Where are you going?"

"Downstairs."

Nobody does that.

"I can't sleep."

I didn't want to be alone. "You can read here," I said, but she was moving toward the spiral staircase.

"You threw the covers at me," she said.

"You snatched them off me."

"You threw the covers."

"I didn't mean . . ."

"Can we at least turn off the white noise?" she asked.

"I don't usually."

"Jonah said we could."

"I don't mind if you read." I did not want her to leave me in that bed where there was nothing but our having left Carmela. The three of us had agreed: no phone calls; no texts, except for scheduling; I would send her surface mail and she might not answer. If I felt despair, Carmela must, too. Was Vicki OK with the offer of phone counseling? I was seized with anger but dropped it. I did not want to be alone. "Please come back to bed. I'm having trouble sleeping, too," I said.

"But we could turn off some of the lights."

"It's what I deal with every trip."

"Well, I don't know if I can."

I ventured, "I can't bear that we are leaving Carmela with no more than when we arrived. What kind of bullshit is it to offer phone counseling to someone who doesn't use the phone? I am so scared. I know she's strong. I know she's resourceful. What if she disappears again?"

"Me, too," she said.

· · ·

Friday, school lunches packed, the proper musical instruments gathered up, socks donned and matching shoes found, they left me and Vicki. We had things to do. Laundry. We would look for my dress for Erin's North Carolina wedding. First, this famous laundry. I made a pile of almost everything in my suitcase. To avoid a second painful trip up and down the stairs, I threw my only shoes, my favorite nonleather black walkers from Earth Shoes, into the pile and baby-stepped down. With a flourish, I threw my laundry into the machine and settled in the living room with Vicki, where we checked Facebook and did online jigsaw puzzles while we talked about where we would go, whether to borrow Jonah's hiccupy Daewoo or walk. Talk of our expedition set me to thinking about necessary preparations for our adventure, and I imagined lacing up my black walkers and said, "Oh no. I threw my shoes into the washing machine." After their spin in the washer, the shoes seemed fine, in fact spiffy, though sopping wet. Their black color, which could have turned all of my clothes the color of grape juice, had not affected anything very much, except for some susceptible underpants.

I shuffled along in a pair of Beth's espadrilles as we set out. Vicki drove the Daewoo. I was working to enjoy the Berkeley day, just Vicki and me, but . . . *Carmela.* The Berkeleyites were busy. Friday. We could have spent another weekday with Carmela but were instead here. I told myself, *Enjoy this day.* We found the original Peet's Coffee and I sucked down a mug while Vicki drank chai. A few doors down, right where I had thought it was, a shoe store. To celebrate our upcoming twenty-sixth anniversary, Vicki bought me a pair of shiny bronze sandals with a coral medallion. As accomplished as Berkeleyites, we found a dress shop and a dress, black jersey with turquoise-and-purple panels, a short, flared hem, perfect for the wedding and unlike anything I'd ever worn.

It was 11:00 a.m., the time we had met Carmela each of the previous four days.

Vicki phoned the agency. It's not her customary way to say, *You were right; I was wrong,* but it is her way to fix things that need to be fixed. By phoning the agency, she said a lot. "Carmela doesn't use her phone," Vicki reminded the agency people. They said for safety reasons they didn't send staff out to *consumers'* homes and didn't do office visits for the same reason. Vicki pressed. They conceded they could set up a walk-in appointment for Carmela. Vicki texted Carmela: Would she go to a walk-in? In less than a minute, Carmela texted: *How about Monday?* And an appointment was set for 10:00 a.m.

We had a weekend of Berkeley sunshine and noisy, satisfying meals in restaurants to which we drove a fair distance; we had evenings of talking in the living room, of listening to one or the other of the boys sing in his evening shower, maybe the thump and rim smack of a basketball. I was happy and I was physically there, but I was making notes for another time when the reality *Dolores Park*, the reality *burrito and an ice-cold Jarritos*, wasn't front and center.

Saturday at 10:00 p.m., Vicki and I boarded Amtrak; our roomette was made up. *Roomette* sounds more than the reality—a space six or so feet across. In the day, there is a bench on either side of the window so two people can sit facing one another and look out or read or doze, their feet tangling pleasantly. At night, the seats are flipped and slid together, like pieces of a puzzle. Below, there is a bunk that is tight but not uncomfortable, especially as you can look out the window and watch the night sky glide past. The upper bunk is awful, though Vicki said it *wasn't bad*. It was a suspended tray, with clearance from the ceiling of a few feet, and no window. To protect her from falling out as the train took a steep curve, Vicki was strapped into place with a webbed harness. Vicki may not be a hearts-and-flowers kind of gal, but she says *I love you* by taking the upper bunk on Amtrak. And by buying me sandals when I launder my shoes. We spent the next day out of ordinary time, out of Wi-Fi range, gazing at herds of animals, the snow, going to the dining car for undistinguished food, spending hours in the tour car with its continuous windows and domed glass roof open to an immense sky, the glass a skin between us and this world. You may cross the back forty of a ranch or glide through the intersection of Main and Elm, a signal flashing red, a pickup waiting for your train to pass. The tan-and-green landscape was brushed with snow. Our decompression chamber.

Late that night, we arrived in Seattle. Our downtown hotel was comfortably luxurious, a modern cousin to the Mosser in San Francisco. A night rain sluiced against the window of our upper-story room. What if Carmela didn't attend her appointment the next day? What if she stopped communicating? Just *stopped*. Could I stand it, even if things worked out, to only be in touch with her by surface mail as I'd agreed? I told Vicki, "I'm so worried. And I'm so glad you have seen her day-to-day life." And what my life was like during visits.

The next morning, the rain was torrential. Vicki went downstairs to her meeting. I felt the distinct moment when that morning slid into 10:00 a.m., the slot of Carmela's appointment in San Francisco, and then a minute after, and another minute, and then an hour and another hour. And another day. And another. No word from Carmela. I'd venture into the rain, searching for streets that were not quite so precipitous; I couldn't stomach the luxe stores close to our hotel, but I walked into the pain in my leg and hip, more aware than I'd ever been of my poor balance and afraid of falling right off the hill and down. Carmela did not meet her brother for lunch as planned. Unmoored, I followed my phone's directions to Pike Place Market. I passed ranks of red and silver fish on beds of ice, crimson and gold Renoir flowers, and a working harbor with freighters and beeping forklifts. I laid my eyes on open water and my spirit expanded. I looked at possible shawls for the wedding and almost bought one. Despite my fear for Carmela, so much seemed possible in that dilapidated marketplace, with its battered history of work and commerce. I scoped out a seafood restaurant to take Vicki to that evening. I ate lunch in a place I had never bothered to think I needed to imagine, an artisanal cheese factory. I sat at a rickety table with my sinfully rich melted-cheese sandwich, filling nervous time with food in the tiled space beside a plateglass window. Behind the glass, two concrete pools. One brimmed with silky white liquid that shimmered, and in the other, the liquid had begun to curdle and clot. A sign on the wall said these curds would be raked until they matured into cheese. I could just move here and watch the harbor and the freighters and the curds turning into cheese, but instead, we would fly home the next day, our plane's nose facing Durham, its tail to San Francisco.

• • •

Vicki and I sat above the harbor waiting for seafood at the Pike Place restaurant. I'd said, *No word from Carmela.* Our departure the next day and Carmela's silence were more palpable than the food before us or the view of the harbor.

We took pictures of the sun settling into the horizon over the water. *Carmela our horizon.*

Vicki said it: "You have to go back to San Francisco."

"Yes."

"I'll miss you," she said.

"Yes."

"And I'm sorry you have to go alone."

"Yes."

Before, I would have phoned when I reached Sixteenth and Valencia. She would have come downstairs, and we would have set out upon our day, but she wasn't using her phone. The climb to the second floor hurt, as it did to remember how despairing and angry Carmela had been our last afternoon together, veering into the taqueria for a burrito and a cold Jarritos for her room. *Be OK, be OK.* I knew I could deal with almost anything, because I had, yet when I knocked on her door, I didn't know if I could bear what I might find. She ushered me in and hugged me. She said she was almost ready to go. She had read my text.

While she brushed her hair and packed her wallet and a few things in the plastic bag she was using as a purse, she told me a case manager from a new agency had knocked on doors up and down the hallway, offering services for people who were *one funds transfer* away from the streets. She said nothing about Monday's missed appointment, and neither did I. This new agency was three blocks away. My eyes were checking her. Thin. Moving slowly, but there was vitality in her I hadn't seen the week before. This agency had found her and so, in a way, she had found them. They were integral to where she lived. She was tired. We agreed we'd eat and call it a day. The agency offered case management. She had liked this man. She had meant to go to the center first thing that morning, but she hadn't. Would I go with her tomorrow?

Our routine: Fritz's our first meal together, Big Lantern Chinese our last. At Fritz's, Carmela had two fried eggs and an English muffin. I had a sandwich called Basquiat with pesto, turkey, and avocado. She talked about her children, whom she had seen the past weekend while I was in Berkeley. She said, "I was so ashamed that I didn't go see the kids when I was so bad. I wanted to go. I just couldn't."

"That is one way I knew you were in trouble. You are a wonderful mother."

"I try."

I went to the bathroom, the finest mosaic bathroom in San Francisco and perhaps the United States, with plumed and oceanic creatures and a watery voice coming over the sound system. The watery voice was a recorded French language lesson. I felt intergalactic, there with the mosaic shards of mirror and the polite French inquiries and responses. Carmela's life felt intergalactic. I walked her back to the Sunrise and boarded BART for Berkeley.

At the resource center, we sat catty-corner to one another at a table for eight. Like others, we held paper mugs of coffee. Carmela set her white wallet with the incised hearts on the table, the paper with the information about the center on top of it. I recognized a few faces from the Sixteenth Street BART plaza. As rain beat against the windows, the room became more crowded, people pulling up chairs and saving seats for one another, filling the space with their shopping carts and packs. No one acknowledged Carmela and me, though one man moved his chair to make room for us. There were more men than women. I didn't know when I'd last been in a place with such a preponderance of adult men. There were more Black people than I had seen on Sixteenth Street or Valencia, plus people who seemed Latino or Asian, a few white people, a handful of whom clustered at one table at the back of the room. We sat at a table of Black men, and then a woman with a shopping cart joined us, sitting with her hands folded in front of her, her wet shawl covering her head and shoulders; she fell asleep, unguarded in the crowd. People who knew one another called back and forth. They spoke in English and Spanish and Asian languages that I didn't know. Carmela took our empty cups and made her way through the crowd to throw them away.

At our table was a man whose cheeks were red from the outdoors. He hung his wet wool coat over the back of his chair. He opened his backpack and pulled out lidded containers and utensils. He went to wash these, then wiped each dry and replaced them in his pack. I imagined he acquired food during the day, storing it in his containers. Carmela and I didn't speak, but it wasn't uncomfortable. She patted her wallet or craned her head to watch the door of the case manager's office. She had been five or six down on the list. A Black man with a trimmed mustache took the last empty chair at our table. He had two paper mugs of steaming coffee. He pulled a thermos from his bag, washed it, then poured as much of his new coffee into the thermos as he could, screwing the cap back on and stowing the thermos. So much in this room growing out of what had come before—the street—and so much aimed toward what was to come: the street. The man with the thermos flattened a newspaper in front of him, saying "Excuse me," as he spread a few inches into Carmela's space. He fell into reading. A white woman jumped up and shouted she wasn't going to sit "next to no crack whore." She walked halfway down the room, her eyes swiveling back and forth, looking for a fight. When she returned to the table of white people where she'd been sitting, a Black woman had taken her seat. The white woman shouted. The Black woman pulled out a newspaper and began to read.

Carmela's name was called and she went off to the room with an opaque pane in the door.

The white woman tried to wrestle the Black woman out of the chair. Staff intervened.

People came to their lockers. They pulled out rain gear, or they got clean clothes before their turn to shower, and they worked on arranging that allotment of space that was theirs. A young Latino man sat at the foot of our table. He said that he had never been on the street before. That he had a job. That he had a phone. Of course, everyone had a phone. One man, young, pulled brand-new sweaters and stiff new jeans from a plastic bag; said he had found them in the trash and people rolled their eyes. A teenage man, his shaggy hair tangerine-tipped, sat in the chair Carmela had vacated. He pulled over another chair. "You can't move chairs, man," said the man reading his newspaper.

The teenager looked around the table. "My man," he said, "is coming." There was a fight, just words, at a table toward the front. A man took an orange from his locker. The shawled woman across from me slept. She must have stayed outdoors last night. She was tired, like Carmela was always tired, like many people in that room must be tired. All the time.

A man in his fifties arrived and the teenager jumped up, saying, "Baby. I saved you a chair."

The older man was too big for the chair. His face was stubbled. The teenager fussed around him, and I thought the man was going to berate the youngster, but he looked at the younger man and said, "Doctor says I'm going to be all right."

The young man said, "Oh, Baby. I'm so glad." Reaching for his backpack, the older man let his hand brush against the hand of the younger man.

I watched the door with the glass pane. Despite having walked the worn carpets of the Sunrise Hotel, despite knowing her friends there to say hello when I saw them in the street, despite having walked with Carmela on Valencia and Mission Streets from the dollar store to Thrift Town, despite our meals in YoYo and Big Lantern and Al Hamra, despite the coffees in Cafetazo, there was a pane between me and my daughter.

So recently, she had been in mortal danger. For years, like many in this room. In Durham in 2010, terrified for Carmela's safety, I had walked in Duke Gardens with my friend Alexis. It had been a paradox, walking the manicured paths past the *native and exotic* plants, talking about Carmela, who had just entered the homeless shelter system. Alexis is forty years younger than I am, and she is wise; she was my first poetry teacher. We settled on a bench in the shade garden. I love shade gardens with their secrets and their shyness and their self-protections. There Alexis and I were, in our North Carolina summer clothes, shoulders and legs and toes bare.

"What are you afraid of?" Alexis asked.

"I'm afraid she might die," I said.

"She might," Alexis said.

I sat in the resource center, waiting, and watched the order of backpacks, the arrangement of lockers, the courtesies and not-so-courtesies. This purposeful world existed inside an unfair and cruel universe. I could not, I cannot, do not, have enough money to buy my daughter out of this, much less to end homelessness for those with me in the room, for all the people without homes in San Francisco. In this room of backpacks filled with utensils and coffee mugs and documents and dry clothes, in this room where Carmela spoke to one more bureaucrat, in this room where she was still alive and devising ways to rescue herself, enough that I was there.

Incised Lines

When every tooth in my mother's head had been pulled, she ground her dentures. She hated their bubblegum pink gums and the too-white teeth too evenly spaced. She filed the teeth with an emery board to give the canines points; she mourned her teeth's brown patina of cigarettes and coffee. After my sister and I had left New York, she had lived through nights alone with my sister's aging poodle and little glasses of ginger ale. My mother was one grim-faced anti-Hallmark card. This night on a balcony above the sea summoned the poodle, the cigarette, the measured ginger ale. She had taught me we deserved pain.

A 1970s writing mentor (male): "Control your narrative; otherwise, your stories will be random lists of contiguous entries from a phone book, an inert and uncompelling line." Our line, taken as a given that there was a line, must be taut and controlled. I was a thirty-something mother of two in Appalachia, a public schoolteacher, and an MFA student. I could see his ideal was phallocentric. Other mentors said sentimental was bad, full of unearned emotion, menstrual pads, children. Try a story about boys discovering their agency while driving cars. Ah, the male-scented Nabokov. Whose writing was *masterful* artifice.

Those who are able-bodied can find pain uncompelling.

Control your narrative. Maintain admirable tautness; appeal to *the* audience—the white and able-bodied, predominantly male audience. The 1988 film *Mississippi Burning* claimed to tell the story of the murders of voter registration workers James Chaney, Mickey Schwerner, and Andrew Goodman, but it imagined a heroic role for the white FBI, a role for white men, because who would be interested in a predictable story of white racism that was Black-centered? Create a movie about our history that was contrary to our lived experience. We knew the FBI to be *the man*.

In Durham summer heat. Pain gnaws, rat teeth sink into pelvic bone; acid spills over ankles—phosphorescent as battery fluid—a drum beat in my right hip; together, cancels my brain. In the blue-gray chair and in the kitchen assembling mushroom quesadillas: pain. Later, prone in the dark beside a sleeping Vicki, the dark interrupted by the amber of a power strip, fleeting shadows of tree limbs on our ceiling, our neighbor's porch light afloat in my oval mirror. Midnight. Then an hour later. And another.

When financial disaster closed in on my mother, as it often did, she cried, *We'll be eaten alive*.

Kifu would save me from one medical office after another, save me from X-rays, save me from the rip of sanitary paper, from the examining table. Kifu would not tell me the fix would be intrusive and expensive, would never require replacing the gristle and bone of my hip with plastic. Kifu—poet, herbalist, baker of enhanced lavender cookies. A woman of duality and many locations, Kifu lives in a People of Color collective in Oakland, California, and at the same time lives across the continent here in Durham in a house brimming with children, queer activists, and artists. We each live simultaneously on the opposite edges. Kifu once inadvertently boarded an airplane carrying a butcher knife almost as long as her forearm. Passed through security. They and their machines didn't register her power nestled in her carry-on. That late summer morning, Kifu and I walked down the dirt road. I was in my seventies, Kifu younger, but silver in the soft riot of hair on the crown of her head and in the clipped sides. We wore hippie skirts. My pain had carried the dark of my bedroom into the day. She and I walked across mowed grass and down to the muddy pond. We walked into skin-temperature water, Kifu offering a hand as I negotiated scummy stones until we were free, floating on our backs in our long skirts, below the blue-and-white September sky, that temporary blue and white between summer and autumn. Kifu knows where I am from. I haven't told her, but she knows.

I had levered myself off the couch to marinate fish, to start yams baking, to trim broccoli. After dinner, I had stretched. I had taken a bath with Epsom salts and lavender before bed, where I lay in the midst of Vicki's sleep. The slumbering cats weighed against my legs. I inched forward through the minutes, but the pain was not going away. No matter how often I shifted the cats off my legs, they pressed back in. If this were my usual pain, the earlier bath should have eased it. Another half hour. If this were my usual pain, the aspirin would have helped. But. I took a second hot shower. One minute, I could see and feel nothing but pain; the next, the pain cleared. Awake again at 3:00 a.m. for no apparent reason. Count backward from one hundred, forward from one, backward. The alarm went off. I couldn't decide what to do first: put on my slippers or my robe. The Facebook revolving door. *I will walk in half an hour. No, maybe I'll swim. Why are tears rolling down my cheeks?* It is four in the afternoon again and too late to walk. It's getting dark. It's cold. I haven't written. And there are bills to be paid, but first I have to: whatever. Tomorrow. I'm tired. Tomorrow. But: last night.

I know these bad nights, but usually they are singular. Once they've put me through the meat grinder, they let up. But. Again, that night. The ghost of the neighbor's porch light in the ceiling. Something. Something like an echo. Something on the childhood black-and-white TV. My mothers. My being afraid. My mother saying, but not out loud, saying in her dark, veering eyes: *Run, hide, no, let me hold you close. Run. Hide.* The night dark and dangerously long. How could my little sister sleep peacefully in the bed across from mine? No. Maybe it is me, to Jonah and Carmela: *Run, hide, no, let me hold you close. Run. Hide.* In Durham, where everyone else slept, even the skittish cat. My heart pounding as it had at something from my mother's eyes, even as I could see my sister's sleeping shape. I have felt this before: 1955. Twelve-year-old, hearing from her mothers how a boy the girl's age had been murdered.

• • •

February 26, 2012. Not being able to get out of bed, not knowing why I was crying, not cooking. Internally jeering at my weak character—surely I could shake off a little depression.

His name Trayvon Martin.

Another child.

Murdered by a white man.

February 26, 2012.

And another child. Tamir Rice in Cleveland. Our years—our years can be told in Black children's bodies destroyed at white hands.

Matthias and Mya swirled color onto earring blanks, incised arabesques and paisley eyes. They lettered: *Seize the Day*. Or *School-to-Prison Pipeline*. Or *Freedom!* Or *Speak... Let It Play... I Am the Change*. The earrings were long enough to brush the shoulder, not like the natty stud in Matthias's own ear. On Nia, below her head, smooth-wrapped in sea green, an earring dangled and a tattoo slid down her neck.

Matthias said, "Secondly, I very damn well like my motherfucking black hoodie. It has a nice spinal cord that I might duly note I added myself." He twisted to display the painted column of white bones. He painted a black eye onto a green earring. He lettered, *Breathe. Reflect.* "If I want to wear my pimped-out hoodie to the freakin' corner store or to Best Buy or to church or to stand at the bus stop or to a gotdamn *gala*, guess what? I will wear it." He picked up a blank. "Who says hoodies are out? Who says it's dangerous for people of color to wear hoodies because of racial profiling looney-tunes? I would like to kindly state slash suggest: Geraldo Rivera and *all* those alike, *shut the fuck up*." He laid the earring on the table to dry. It said: *I AM TRAYVON MARTIN*.

I would never have to say: *I AM TRAYVON MARTIN*. My nine grandsons and my singular granddaughter would never have to say: *I AM TRAYVON MARTIN*. Our grandsons can walk up and down the streets and we need not fear for their lives in a Trayvon Martin manner. I could buy the earrings. I could delight in the minds and the spirits of Matthias and Mya, each of whom I love, but I would never be Trayvon Martin.

. . .

That autumn, Carmela lay in her room. She didn't answer her phone. She didn't text. She did answer her brother's knock on her door, but she couldn't talk with him. She was disoriented. She was in trouble with her probation officer, but she wasn't on probation. She didn't trust. She needed help. At night, her bed shook her. She had to get out of there. She didn't trust. Anyone. She needed to get out of there.

Since 1988, I have lived within a family with midwestern roots in Michigan who lived in West Virginia when I met them, their origins so different from Greenwich Village and Haiti and Southwest Georgia. Even the West Virginias Vicki and I had known are different. She and her girls are from the rivers and unmined hills of Central West Virginia; my children and I from the coalfields and Charleston's chemical valley. They were a family who didn't know my mother had filed her dentures into points. Didn't know the code of being the careful daughter of Eunice and Charity in the overtly racist and homophobic 1940s. My midwestern family didn't know that in the family of Eunice and Charity the bus boycott in Montgomery was not *the news* but a family event. The murder of Emmett Till was personal. The ways I had invented to be a parent. Vicki and her girls saw, but/and they didn't. This noncoastal family, with its own particularities, has become one place I am from. Only Vicki's daughter Amy still lives in West Virginia with her second husband, the three boys to whom she gave birth, and the three boys he had fathered.

Amy and family were coming to our house of grandmas for Thanksgiving 2014. I wanted them to come, but I was also mired in my fears for Carmela. Her lying in her room. Her not answering her phone. Pain made me grit my teeth as we grocery shopped, vacuumed, cleaned bathrooms, and hoisted the turkey into the oven. It's this private thing about pain: like our frightened cat; out of sight he slips around the corner and bounds upstairs to hide under the bed, coming out at night to sleep on our heads, to pad around the house and sniff the cookie crumbs in the TV room, maybe even to sniff the breath of a sleeping boy before leaping away. Five teenage boys and their little sibling dressed in grays and blues, except for Amy's second son in his red shirt, all with hair shorn. We grandmas heap turkey and stuffing and homemade bread and fiery sweet potatoes and gravy on plates and the boys eat and eat. The twins have cystic fibrosis and must consume a staggering number of calories to stay alive. They can't absorb enough to sustain their lives and cannot extract enough oxygen from the air without added enzymes and calorie loading and compression vests. And have survived. Teenagers, their bodies fill the space of our house, their knees knobby below silky athletic shorts; their boy laughs expand the house. The cat stays hidden, sneaking down after midnight to eat and flee back upstairs.

Amy, a brown-haired woman with pretty eyes, sits in the rocking chair where my mother had once held me, but none of these people could know that. Most of them have never met my sister and four of them have never met Carmela. While Vicki and Amy talk about Amy's job, her husband Bryan writes legal briefs. The boys watch television, open and slam our front door to walk up and down our street, finger their miniscreens, listen to music through earbuds that loop down onto their chests. They even rake leaves.

Pain in my hips, my ankles; I take naproxen. The frightened cat skulks in the living room doorway.

There are rumblings—boys cooped up in a grandma house. We sit on the red couch, the gray velvet chair, the rocking chair from Vicki's married life, and the rocking chair from my childhood. I show the boys the dozens of tiny naked women in my West Virginia friend Charley Hamilton's painting of a wolf dog, a turquoise-and-fuchsia panel crammed with flowers and dogs, and, well, the women, outlined in black. His picture over our mantel in North Carolina: that is West Virginia me in plain sight. Charley had bought an electric router from Kmart and began to incise black outlines like featherstitching around even the smallest elements of his paintings, a narrative strategy of its own, tacking down the elements and giving harmony to the entirety. The little nudes are a temporary distraction—in the grandma house of all places!—while Vicki searches for an adventure. She says *trampoline* and I think: flung upward and landing at a hip-socket-splitting angle; while everyone else played, I would eat pizza with meager, saltine-like crusts. I tell Vicki they should go without me. I say it with conviction. It would be nice to be alone in the house. I can write.

As the sounds of my family's voices fade and the heater quiets, I can hear the beat of our house slow. The cat comes to sit behind me on the back of the armchair. How to get comfortable—legs up? Legs down? Tipped back? Sitting up? Everywhere, like Charley's black incised lines: pain. I'd thought I was looking forward to writing, but it becomes clear: I do not like that I have been left behind. Left behind at my own insistence.

Allan the massage therapist asks me to stand. I have to push off the chair with my hands. He says that when I stand, one hip is higher than the other. I stand on one foot at a time. The "good" leg, OK. The "bad" leg, wobble city. For over twenty years, I have thought I had a good side and a bad side. Had not seen myself as a whole. I say as a joke that my legs are codependent. Allan says yes. My right leg is dependent upon the left for strength and balance and the left has become overbearing, anticipating my right leg's needs. In the weeks to come, I watch: when I come to a curb, my left foot is in position to do the heavy lifting; my left leg leads when I climb stairs. I have to interrupt this habitual pattern and use my right leg to its capacity.

Below a sheet, on my stomach, I lie on the table. It feels like Allan is bracing his hand against my thigh and not moving, his hand warm and quiet. As his hand rests there, my hip in its socket releases, the minute hand on a clock slipping forward. Muscle and bone shift. Turning face up, I see the residue of dust on the blade of the ceiling fan; that slim rind of dust becomes my anchor.

Allan says, "You can restore full functioning." His belief in perfectibility irritates the mother Eunice who resides in me. She frowns her scowl, because I am old, because I am disabled, because these treatments are *self-indulgent*. Allan says he can lower my pain levels, but I must rebuild the weaker leg. He says: *yoga, Feldenkrais, walking*. In the ether, Charity chastises my birth mother: *Oh, Eunice, let her be.* Charity, child of Providence, had a New England belief in self-improvements. Despite the racism she had faced, she moved in the world like a woman upon whom Providence had shone.

January 1, 2015. Matthew Ajibade, Black male, age twenty-two, unarmed, death in custody.

Facebook choices in response to the death of this twenty-two-year-old man: Pick a button. Like? Love? Haha? Wow? Tears running down a cheek? Angry? No rage button.

When he was twenty-two, my son was at Berkeley, being a student, undoubtedly doing some ill-advised early twenties things. When she was twenty-two, my daughter had moved to the West Coast and out of my life into her own sometimes dangerous one. Unlike Matthew Ajibade, my son would outlive his twenties, and unlike the mothers of murdered children, I would get my girl back.

Matthew Ajibade, twenty-two, had a mother. He was unarmed. Murdered.

Futile Facebook clicks. Angry. Angry. Angry. Click it. Wear the button out. At two in the morning, read Nia's posts, Mya's posts. Fitful, interruptive flicker of passing cars on the night ceiling.

#MatthewAjibade.

The Feldenkrais brochure had said I would connect my hips, my spine, and my neck. This sounded absurdly harmonious. My unbalanced body could not achieve such unity. My left side is Barnard girl, MFA certified, activist, editor of an anthology about women in the Civil Rights Movement; my right is the woman who wallows in pain, is short-tempered with her partner, the woman who would not be corrected even when she is wrong, the woman who shreds herself down to a nub with self-criticism, the woman who doesn't believe she deserves to feel better.

I enter Carrboro, North Carolina, in a split and vengeful mood. This Feldenkrais will be like yoga: *spandex*. Charity chides me, *Darling, give it a chance.* Carrboro has a reputation—hip and home to an outstanding co-op grocery store. I am half an hour early. I drive in loops through residential neighborhoods and around a school, past hundreds of lives I cannot see. At the center, the lot and walkway are treacherous with welts of ice. I lever myself out of the car and negotiate the sidewalk. The studio is up a flight of stairs carpeted in an oaty, rough texture which may personify everything I loathe about a health-promoting studio in a granola haven. Clutching the sturdy banister, I haul myself upward, my saturnine mother Eunice's girl.

In sock feet, I walk into a room of white women. One or two my age, the others mostly in their forties and fifties, one who is younger, one with elaborate props and blankets. There isn't as much spandex as I had expected. We each take a large pad, like the quilted blankets moving companies use. Some people have water bottles. Others have brought their own pillows. How can this be the same world in which six Black people have been murdered by racist police? Keep calm and improve yourself. So, there is less spandex than I'd expected, so, what? Wanting swaddling, I keep on my sweater. I lumber down to my knees and tip myself over into a seated position. How in the hell am I going to stand up at the end of class?

Three hours. *Yoga duty*. Check. The instructor opens with a self-deprecating joke that assumes a pact: I am making fun of myself, but don't mistake me for a person without an ego. Several laugh.

I do things that have titles: coordinate neck and eyes with legs and pelvis; release hips into pleasure; use abdomen to release your back; seesaw breathing; rolling into length across your stomach; regaining full use of the neck; a simple rolling lesson; and expanding, reaching, turning the middle of the body. Lying on my back; lying on my stomach; lying on my side with my knees drawn up. I enjoy rolling from my back to my belly to my back to my belly. I wish I had a huge room at home where I could roll from the wall on one side to the wall on the other. I draw my knees up and to one side, then straighten my legs like scissors blades and roll. Everything inside me, hard and soft, from my hips to my shoulders and neck, my stomach, my lungs, gives in to the floor, resists the floor, welcomes the floor. Rolling through pain. As if. As if I were young and limber, rolling down a hummocky West Virginia hill. At the end, I struggle to my feet. I do not feel better. I do not feel ecstatic and confident. But. I have been on the floor. I have done stuff. I can do it again.

Driving home, I think of the Thanksgiving trampoline adventure. Bolstered by a morning of self-improvement, I see how pain has isolated me. I have taken steps to remedy my pain, a seemingly private weakness, like shame. As clearly as I see the trees of Erwin Road, I see that I must say to Vicki: *I don't want to be separated like that*. It will make her defensive, but from my pained difference, I have to. I'm not sure she can hear me.

I've prepared chicken roasted with dates, almonds, and couscous. The butter and olive oil in the chicken fill our sealed-in winter house with fragrance. On our table, a lazy Susan made in West Virginia with a West Virginia basket filled with napkins and a rose and earthen West Virginia sugar bowl. On the table, Vicki and I each have a basket. Mine holds brown and blue bottles with the postsurgery anticancer drug tamoxifen, vitamins B6 and B12, vitamin D, a multivitamin. The cat Chevy vaults onto the table, sliding to a stop just short of knocking the Fiesta bowl of orange slices and dried cranberries down to the floor, as I say:

"I've been thinking about Thanksgiving and the trampoline." Vicki and I sit catty-corner to one another. "I thought I was fine with staying home while you went." Vicki stops eating. "If it's a family outing, that means the whole family, including me."

"But the boys . . ."

"I know. They were bored. I volunteered to stay home. I don't want to do that again. We wouldn't pick a family outing that the five-year-old couldn't attend."

"The five-year-old couldn't stay here by himself. You can."

That's not the point, I might have said. I felt how I might have said that, but Charity my New England mother says, *Don't push. She will think about it, because she loves you. Don't make her feel you think she has malignly done something that causes you pain.*

So I go for the gentle and supportive pressure, like Allan's hand helping my hip to release.

Shane came into our lives as a kitten, a tiger with white bib and black markings around his eyes and jowls. I tried to touch him through the wire caging and he broke into purring and rubbed his head against the cage. At home, when his near-feral self became apparent, Vicki and I realized his demonstrativeness at PetSmart had been driven by thirst and hunger. At home, we had a tall puppyish cat named Chevy, the sort who leaped onto the coffee table, slid to a landing, taking laptops or coffee cups with him. We had thought Shane would be a good companion for Chevy, who seemed depressed. Shane instantly fell in love with Chevy, who despised the interloper. Chevy liked to sleep in the patch of sun on the dining room floor, stretching his extraordinary length, all the way to the end of his long tail, on the warm floorboards. One morning Shane watched his sleeping idol. He kitten tiptoed to the end of Chevy's tail and lay down, his cheek pressed to the tip of Chevy's tail, and fell into love-besotted sleep.

For ten years, Shane mostly kept his feral ways, though, like pain, he could be cajoled into affability, especially when Vicki combed his short, dense fur; he would crane his neck, like an owl, to bring his ears closer to the comb, his face with the incised black tiger markings. He tolerated Cricket the tortoiseshell; he let her groom him, but mostly Shane was all about Chevy. I thought I could tame him by holding him as I had tamed Cricket. Shane never settled; in my arms, he dug in his claws, and I could feel his heart racketing like pain. Even when he wistfully hung in a doorway, he was marked by a fear we could not assuage.

Chevy the puppy cat died.

The vet people crisscrossed Chevy's body in an old towel and suggested we show his body to the surviving cats. Cricket, the little mother, came and sniffed, but Shane would not come close to the body; he walked around it in a wide circle. Shane watched in doorways for Chevy to come back. He was skittish and stayed to himself except when he came to wolf down his food and run back to hide under the bed. Waiting. The second night, Vicki and I were on the love seat watching TV. Cricket lay between us. Shane hung in the doorway; he padded closer and then closer. Gathering his spirit, he jumped onto the love seat between us, cast one frightened look at Vicki and another at me. He lay down with his head on Cricket's rib cage and closed his eyes, falling into a grieving sleep.

I do not equate my bodily pain or my daughter's with the pain of racist murder by the police and others, but to write about my life and pain during these years without mentioning their context of white supremacy is to imply that the viciousness of that context need not concern white people. Much as I use analgesics, massage, anti-inflammatories, bodywork to numb physical pain, they are numbed by choice to the violence around us. At a cost.

Pain is layered into the ordinary. Personal pain is sometimes demoted to a narrative niche of the uncompelling, the maudlin—which in our culture may be thought to be female. In this construct, pain is not a creation of *masterful*

Nabokovian artifice. It is obdurate and not amenable to being manipulated as part of a plot device. The pain inflicted by white supremacy is not an event or even a series of distinct events; it is strata endemic to our lives, all of our lives, day in and day out. It is a strata like the seams of coal woven into West Virginia mountains. To put pain caused by racism in a separate container labeled, *Important and separate and need not concern you if you are white*, is to segregate racist pain from universal and global human experience.

Full Circumference, 2015

> When you love the full circumference of yourself—light and shadow, broken and whole—liberation is possible for us all.
> —Mya Hunter, cultural activist, SpiritHouseNC

Durham is home. Despite: no mountains. Despite: no outcrops. Complex with history—the Occoneechee people who still live here though their land was stolen and their history disrespected; the enslaved African ancestors of many who still live here; the European-descended who still live here; the people of Asia and Africa and the Americas and the Middle East who live here. It is ground bloodied with exploitation and injustice and fertile ground that has fostered indignation and uprisings and joy.

I joined the Durham Chavurah, a free-flowing Shabbat gathering. Some of us had long opposed Zionist ideology, though one woman in particular was appalled by Israel's actions but resisted the designation *anti-Zionist* for herself. Some of us had been bar or bat mitzvah; at least one of us eschewed any religious aspects of Judaism. There were Jewish activists in Durham who did not attend the chavurah, which rarely gathered more people than a dozen on any given Friday evening. At one Yom Kippur, we practiced traditional fasting and prayers but also meditative discussions, time outside in the sun on a rooftop, and yoga. At least one attendee had grown up in the Jewish community of Durham, where there is a reform congregation and a conservative one. Some members studied together and had either learned or relearned Hebrew and had printed out our own songbook. We ate vegetarian meals, lit candles, sang, and talked. Talked. Talked. We met in small spaces, where many of us sat on the floor. One member's labor activist mother sometimes attended. One member was Black. Over time, the group shriveled: peoples' lives were full; tensions within the group simmered without resolution; we were tired. A few continued to meet for Shabbat on the Eno River. One member has gone on to rabbinical studies as a Jewish trans man.

People in the chavurah had been activists in Durham for a long time. I joined them in a campaign to end Durham County's $1 million contract with G4S, an Israeli firm with global reach that provided security at county buildings. It was not lost on us—the symbolism of Israel becoming a global purveyor of police-based *security*. One heady moment in November 2014, Durham became the first US municipality to cancel a contract with G4S. The people who worked on this campaign were affiliated with the national group Jewish Voice for Peace and formally became Jewish Voice for Peace Triangle NC, of which I am a member.

I was raised by a secular Jewish mother who, as a girl child, had received no religious training. I was named Faith to commemorate my parents' faith, bringing a Jewish child into the world during the Nazi Holocaust. This traditionally Christian name, picked in innocence, was one reason I have been called *not Jewish enough*. In the 1990s, writing a novel about a pair of women, one of whom was Jewish and one of whom was Black, the Jewish character said to me, "How can you write my Jewish self if you know so little about being a Jew?" In response, I attended services and study groups at the Morgantown, West Virginia, synagogue. I already knew many in the congregation. Once, talking about Israel, I said something like, *Isn't it ironic that our people, fleeing persecution, perpetrate persecution against the Palestinians*. One man whom I saw as otherwise compassionate said, *No one lived in Israel before 1947*. Both my children, under supervision by the rabbi, had included positive mention of Israel in their bar mitzvah / bat mitzvah speeches. In the Morgantown study group, a man asked: *Don't you feel safer in the world knowing Israel exists?* I didn't, but I didn't say so to him.

. . .

Carmela without services: not needy in an orthodox way.

Erin and Warren's March 7 wedding was approaching. Carmela had an expired California nondriver's photo ID and could not get on a plane. This fact was intransigent. She and her children would not be present, and family would not see all of me. My tooth-filing mother had taught me that sometimes there could be a small, clever fix. There must be a way to include Carmela in the wedding without her leaving the Mission.

I texted Carmela photos of Erin's bridal fitting. Erin, the girl I had met when she was a country eight-year-old, transformed in a column of lace, more than ten years of teaching in her self-assurance, but self-conscious, one hand curled against her lacy side holding unease in check. Carmela texted how beautiful Erin looked, texted of the curl of Erin's hand, *Like a little girl.* I texted Erin had considered a clinging slip dress. *Oh, she needs the armor of the dress she chose,* Carmela texted. Carmela: excited about Erin's wedding but not coming. She would want to give a gift. I couldn't pay in Carmela's name for an item on Erin and Warren's registry at Williams Sonoma. Carmela, resident of an SRO in the Mission, had to be present as who she was. The least expensive items on the registry came from a world in which Carmela no longer lived.

I needed Carmela incorporated into this wedding. During the years of Carmela's absence, Erin's older sister Amy had married in a country church near the Braxton County house Amy's father had built. Jonah and Beth had flown in from San Francisco. I had not known whether Carmela was alive or dead. Had no way to approach this loss, except to brush my fingers over my clavicle, spot sheathing my heart and lungs, to connect to my absent child. At Amy's wedding potluck, I had placed a plate of Oreo cookies on the table. Jonah met my eyes. *Carmela.*

Three in the morning. Surely Carmela and I could find something like that plate of Oreos, something that could exist in both Carmela's one-room world and in Erin and Warren's house. I took a hot shower and slipped into bed beside felines and Vicki. I thought of Erin and Warren watching TV, their legs draped in blankets. Storm, the husky, trying to climb into Warren's lap. Erin reaching forward to take a sip of cocoa. *Cocoa.* Carmela and I could find cocoa in the Mission. A gift within her means, a gift that had a place in both worlds.

• • •

Flying to San Francisco, I wore the scarf I had bought with my sister in Ireland. It is not gray; it is not purple; it is not green; it is all those colors, soft like the hair from which it is woven. It is sheep on purple-gray Irish hills, where Shai and I had sat on the ground, two women in their sixties, while my sweetheart worried at a distance. I wrapped the scarf around my shoulders: wrapped about me my sister who lives too far away, the tossing Irish sea, the afternoon my sister, her husband Nicola, Vicki, and I drank tea made from leaves and flowers snipped from the walled garden behind us. I wrapped myself in the scarf's animal sheen.

Carmela texted when I landed at SFO:

> Welcome! Really happy about being able to be local to each other while you're visiting with us all out here! See you Tuesday noon time. Love, Carmela.

I walked past the second-floor garbage room. I worried that Carmela's homeopathic medicines might not work. I worried that I did not know enough. Passing rooms 232, 231, coming to 230, I hoped I could ask and she would answer. I could imagine her meditative smile as she talked. We would make the changes she needed. The pillow from Vicki, wrapped in a blanket from Thrift Town. Why does she keep some things and not others? Her white leather wallet with its incised hearts. I had bought it at TJ Maxx, thinking she might reject it, but here it was. "My list," she said, folding a slip of paper into the wallet, repository which traveled out of and back into her room. This is how we talk about her desires: toilet-cleaning supplies, wipes, cold medicine, Walgreens-brand Benadryl, stomach medicine. We walked into the sunlight of Valencia Street with its pedigreed dogs, its parents pushing strollers with pockets and shelves for water bottles and snacks and toys.

Carmela asked, "Fritz?" The place offering crepes with names like Botticelli, a sandwich named Basquiat. The place with the intergalactic mosaic bathroom. "And then Walgreens. Mom. I didn't sleep at all last night. It's been months.

Years. I am seriously sleep deprived." We had crossed Sixteenth. *Only another block*, I cheered on my achy legs.

"I wish I could make it better," I said.

"It's torture," she said.

"I'm so sorry."

"*Sorry* and *I wish*, don't cut it, Mom."

A force outside herself kept her awake. I could not ask, *What if . . . ?* Was she forbidding conversations that answered *if* differently? Was I risking her safety with my timidity? Was a childhood response to terror holding Carmela hostage? We passed the chichi store with stiff clothes on mannequins with pewter and green skins. The threat: she could repeat seventeen years' absence. How to escape my mannequin stiffness? How to reach her inside who she was? Would she ever know me? *Self-indulgence*, my mother Eunice said, snorting, and I didn't know if she was snorting at me or at my child. *Eunice, Carmela's a frightened child*, Charity chided.

"Did you see that woman with the stroller? I hate when they try to hit me."

I said nothing. *Say something*, I exhorted myself. It was not *self-indulgence* but my frightened mother's sister jumping out of a window. Just as compensating with the other leg had skewed my spine, her sister's death had traced itself into who my mother was, and who I am and who both of my children are.

At Fritz, Carmela wanted eggs and steak. The goateed man turned to me. I picked a sandwich with avocado and neither blue cheese nor bacon. Carmela collected napkins and cutlery. She was still alive. We were together. I would ask if she was seeing the counselor. She would answer. But what if . . . those years of protections and hidden trails and sealed entryways—intergalactic spaces.

Once, at Chincoteague, that osprey had drawn Vicki and me in our canoe away from her nestlings (her heart). In Fritz, Carmela talked about what she could or could not eat (take in), that she was intentionally bumped into by people with yoga mats. I stripped off the top slice of bread and plowed into my sandwich. It was rich, the chèvre smearing softly onto the impeccable, frilled tentacles of arugula, the creamy avocado. Carmela ate only a portion of her meal, boxed what was left. "I'll eat it tonight. Or I'll give it to a man down the hall. Mom, I'm too tired to go to Walgreens."

"I could go for you."

"No. I need to go to my room and rest. We can meet tomorrow at eleven."

. . .

An afternoon and night before I would see her. A night on bleached sheets, under a slippery hotel duvet. I rolled my suitcase behind me. Two miles to the Opal Hotel. Easier to think about breakfast the next day than to think about Carmela in her room, without pain meds from Walgreens. Carmela with eggs congealing in Styrofoam. My suitcase no longer rolled as smoothly as it once had. I scolded myself: I was much stronger and more competent than last autumn when I had floated face up in the pond with Kifu. When I walked, I kept my eyes on the horizon, rather than the ground. But my feet hurt. Foot pain was blurring my vision. OK. I'd take BART to Westfield Mall. There I'd find takeout for dinner and walk up Van Ness to my hotel. I would put aside Carmela on her bed, in double camis and leggings, engrossed in pain.

Filling time is not coloring inside an outline. Time is long. Time is kinked, impenetrable except when it is suffused with light.

Carmela texted that she was too sick to meet. Should I have asked *how* was she too sick? Would that be intrusive? If I didn't ask, would she think I didn't care? How big should my nightmare be: one missed day or the advent of prolonged absence? In my writing that morning, I couldn't reach the depth I wanted. My stomach said I was hungry. *OK*. My skin said I was cold, so I put on long underwear and that made me think I needed to rinse out socks. Back at the laptop, I lost myself in the shallow sunshine glancing off the buildings across Van Ness and at the same time separated myself from the windowed facade. I did my exercises, cycling through coordinate neck and eyes with legs and pelvis; releasing hips into pleasure; using abdomen to release; seesawing my breathing; rolling into length across the stomach; rolling; and expanding, reaching, turning the middle of the body. The works.

To think of Al Hamra is to think of spinach and saag paneer, is to remember how much Carmela and I share, including the green saturated dish with its cubes of cheese, and for me to know that my sister who had once lived in India knew the green depths of saag paneer, too. Above the restaurant facade, a red, yellow, blue canopy promising Indian food, vegetarian and vegan, halal. Through the plate glass: an aluminum stove top on which pans steamed. The manager cooked in the window and waved to Carmela. Seated at our table, I asked about the counseling, and she said it was never more than twenty minutes a week. Naan arrived, its fragrance softening the air. Only twenty minutes a week when she was living with decades of trauma and devising duct-tape solutions to profound wounds. And then the saag paneer, the heat going straight into my blood. Carmela took most of her meal in a carryout box. Warmed and filled, we crossed Sixteenth Street to the dollar store, looking for instant cocoa for Erin and Warren. Carmela was not satisfied with the selection in the aisles, which offered items ranging from Tiger Energy Biscuits to off-brand disposable diapers. I told her the wedding's theme was black and white. She said, *Hah*, at the aptness. She insisted on an ulna-sized rawhide bone, present for Erin and Warren's husky Storm. At Walgreens, we filled two bags with cleaning supplies, cold medicine, and stomach soothers, the iron of spinach powering us on, along with the sweet, sweet memory of naan.

First, we went to Thrift Town. Carmela held up leggings in brown and black and gray. Suspended from the hanger, each limp pair's emptiness implied the legs of previous owners. Three camisoles. Short pajama bottoms to wear in her room. No item cost more than three dollars. At the other dollar store, we found Swiss Miss cocoa mix, which met with Carmela's approval, and a black-and-white gift bag for the black-and-white wedding. *Hah*. We picked out a couple of silly toys for Carmela's son and daughter.

On to YoYo, the Japanese place. At least once that week, the owner, Jessica, had spotted us from behind her plate glass and waved, but we had continued down Sixteenth Street. Today was YoYo day. "Jessica gives me a hard time about not eating, but . . ." Carmela said. I could feel the words on my tongue: *Why can't you keep food down? What don't you want to swallow?*

"But you can't just not eat."

"I think there is nothing in my stomach. It comes up clear yellow. But I had a bite of cracker this morning."

"A doctor . . ." I started.

"I don't want to talk about it."

Inside, there were booths upholstered in red, mirrored walls, a sushi bar, and a wall of bottled alcohol. On the flat screen, a train in flames. A tanker car had spilled three million gallons of oil outside Boomer, West Virginia. The spill had burned night and day. Was the burn in my gullet too much coffee or the residual slow burn between me and my daughter? Jessica hurried forward to say how worried she was about Carmela. Carmela asked about Jessica's mother and sister. YoYo had almost sold several times. This place where Carmela and I were known might cease to exist, its presence ephemeral like the smoke rising above the scrubby brush of Boomer, West Virginia. I ordered agedashi tofu and avocado sushi rolls. Carmela ordered vegetable tempura. Jessica brought us rice tea and a gift of green gyoza on a bed of slivered cabbage, the cabbage sweet as fresh corn.

Carmela said the homeopathic meds from the community clinic seemed to be working.

"What are they for?" I asked.

"For, you know, brain trauma."

I didn't know.

2/19: Hi Mom. I just want to confirm that Saturday I'll pick you up at Opal at 7:10ish AM with Catherine (from Sunrise, Ray's wife) and we're scheduled to be at the house in Brisbane by 7:40. . . . see you at 7:10 AM tomorrow. Thanks for your company, assistance and acceptance. Love, Carmela

Carmela and Catherine did not pick me up. Carmela and I caught a cab to Brisbane. It took us between hills covered with houses. In the years of Carmela's absence, in a cab speeding from the airport to Jonah and Beth, I had passed these hills and wondered: Could she be there, in plain sight? I would wish so hard it hurt that she could know I was in her city. This sadness, this longing for her to know she was wanted, was still with me, even with her sitting beside me rushing to Brisbane. "I hope you don't mind," she said, pulling the rawhide bone intended as a gift for the Maryland husky from her bag. "For Bear," she said, the dog in Brisbane. "We can buy another for Storm, can't we? I was afraid we'd be late, but no, here's the Candlestick exit. I wonder if Cami and Michael will be up." We were bearing left around the park, passing the skate park, and up the hill—three blocks of pizza place, taqueria, Midtown Market, the church she and her family had attended, Mad House Coffee.

Michael opened the door, sleep-tousled, wearing the previous day's basketball shorts, loose synthetic sheen down to his knees. The kids' dad had started coffee for his men's bible group. The toys and baskets of belongings and laundry and athletic shoes had been pushed back to make room for a circle of mismatched chairs. There was the upholstered chair designated as Michael's and the one designated as Cami's.

"Hi." Cami gave me a half-mast wave and a half smile, her hair a black cap, her eyes wary.

I walked down to get coffee for me and Carmela, negotiating the steep sidewalk, afraid of falling, privately impressed that I did so well. When I returned, Carmela took a sip and set the paper cup on a shelf above the TV. A physical marker: *Stand here. Without looking, reach up at this angle, shift to the edge of the shelf, and your cup will be waiting.*

Carmela fed the dog and the cats. The black cat raced from behind the couch to hide in the wall upstairs. In the back room, where the fish tank bubbled, a cage with Michael's corn snake, named Kernel (for a long time, I'd thought the snake was named Colonel), and a cage with Cami's boa. In another cage, three rats, ones the boa had rejected. Carmela will take out the snakes one by one and drape them over her children's shoulders. She will take out the rats one by one, letting them shimmy up and down her. The lumbering orange-and-white cat, Stanford, strolled to the front door and asked to be let out. I took out my iPad. The excess of animal life alarmed me, but Carmela's face was soft with happiness. Sometimes I wondered about the family life Carmela had been part of. I knew she had helped raise Stanford and Bear while she was having babies. I knew she had sung in the choir in the little church on the corner. I knew she had pushed a double stroller up and down the hill, Bear on a leash beside her. She had worked in Midtown Market and for a while for a chiropractor in town. Former customers from the market greeted her in the street, as did mothers from the Brisbane mothers group. Her children played with the children of those mothers, went to Girl Scouts with some of them, went to birthday parties. I knew the Brisbane building where in 2017 the owner had refused to rent to Carmela.

Late afternoon, we arrived at the restaurant Red Robin. Cyrus, the bonus kid, had shown up after soccer, making six of us. Cami wanted pasta with butter and parmesan; Michael wanted a burger; their dad wanted a burger, as did Cyrus. I ordered my second burger of the week, craving red meat after sitting in the living room and avoiding sitting in someone's designated place, after going to the skate park where Michael zoomed down one ramp and up the other on his Razor scooter and Cami climbed up one side, ran fast down, and ran back up the other side to perch beside her father, blocking her face with her hand when I started to take a picture. Red Robin, all seated, but a kid wanted to go to the bathroom with Carmela, and a fight about who sat next to Carmela and how. Carmela ordered something with eggs. The kids' dad said, *Oh, I'd like a milkshake*. And Michael wanted a milkshake; and Cyrus wanted one. We said, *Yes, but the kid size*, and Cami said she wanted one and we asked the waitress could she bring the fries immediately.

The van ride back into San Francisco, squabbles about which kid sat in the way back because I was in one of the designated kid seats in the middle row, in the way and without a designated seat, overwhelmed by snakes and rats and Bear chewing on Storm's gift and burgers and milkshakes and quarrels. In the dark, how unknown I was to these children, Grandma Faith, who appeared a few times a year, but also: I liked being in the dark van driven by the kids' dad, Grandma Faith, a member in the dark vehicle of this family.

Sunday, Carmela texted she was too tired to go to Brisbane. Yes, she'd like instead to meet for lunch in the Mission. Our last visit before I flew home. She and I bought another toy for Storm and we walked up Sixteenth Street to Big Lantern. We walked past the store that makes ice cream sandwiches with fresh-baked cookies. The store's name, Cream, conjures soft ivory richness. Cream was of the new Mission, where operating costs had squeezed out previous businesses. Cream will only last until someone buys the building, tears it down, and puts in condos with a Mission flare in the fake tile roofs.

A man slept on a bench in the vestibule at Big Lantern. "He does the deliveries," Carmela said, as she always does. Facing us was a carved wood screen with swirling dragons, the dragon's scales cut into the brown wood as delicately as decoupage. I loved how, despite the artifice, the wood showed its innate grain. My daughter, with all her difficulties, had kept her grain, from the strength in her thin hands to her nerdy-girl self-confidence about things to be learned. We slipped red cloth napkins into our laps. Carmela could talk about what she wanted to eat, selecting wonton soup and vegetarian pot stickers and crab cheese puffs—with a digression to Jonah's younger son who also loved crab cheese puffs, though he assiduously discarded from his any trace of crab. She liked this connection with a nephew she rarely saw. A dish with vegetables. This was more than she could eat; she would snack on it throughout the night or give it away. I was fueling her life for a few more hours. When I hugged her goodbye, her back under my hands was more muscular than I tended to remember.

Killed between December 31, 2014, and March 7, 2015, the day of Erin and Warren's wedding:

> *Matthew Ajibade, Black male, age 22, unarmed death in custody, county sheriff of Savannah, Georgia*
>
> *Frank Smart, Black male, age 39, unarmed death in custody, police department of Pittsburgh, Pennsylvania*
>
> *Brian Pickett, Black male, age 26, unarmed taser, police department of Los Angeles, California*
>
> *Andre Murphy Sr., Black male, age 42, unarmed death in custody, police department of Norfolk, Nebraska*
>
> *Artago Howard, Black male, age 36, unarmed gunshot, police department of Strong, Arkansas*[1]

In that time span, thirteen unarmed Black people in the United States, including one woman, had been killed by the police. This does not count the Latinx people killed by the police. It does not count the Pacific Islanders. I did not count the people listed as being armed with that bizarre entry for a weapon:

1. Details on deaths of Black people at the hands of police come from The Counted, published by the *Guardian*: https://www.theguardian.com/us-news/ng-interactive/2015/jun/01/the-counted-police-killings-us-database.

vehicle. I did not count those counted as armed with a knife or a firearm, even though in some cases the so-called weapon was described as being *found at the scene*, which does not mean that the person killed by the police had been in possession of it.

Death was the context of that first week of March 2015, when our beloved daughter married Warren, her best friend and lover, but it would have been frowned upon to name these weekly if not daily deaths in the same breath as the wedding. Deaths had happened at all the moments of all the sections in this memoir. What effort goes into not feeling how each of the people killed had kin, a neighborhood, a place to be. What work do we do, to get up, eat breakfast, take our walks, do our jobs, speak civilly to one another, even to speak at all, to turn this backdrop of death into business as usual?

I wanted to look nice for Erin and Warren's rehearsal dinner. For Erin. For Warren. For Vicki. For myself. My hair had been cut. My black shoes polished. My clothes laid out on the bed, as my mother had taught me. Showered, I pulled on my black-and-cream ikat-print pants, slipped on the silk camisole. Over that, the cream silk blouse, the fabric translucent and soft on my arms. Invisibly, I wore over this the mantel of everything I had ever been. Stood on feet and legs that, despite Feldenkrais and Allan, hurt even before we had left the house, my left foot taking a bossy lead. Vicki was also dressed in party clothes, black pants and a green-and-soft-brown Tencel jacket, her hair cut, shoes shined.

Walking into the upscale barbecue place, I entered a different zone. Not time zone different. Not weather zone different. A different being zone. People who rehearse anticipate the future and expect it will be benign. We rehearse and things become smooth and pleasing. The word comes from Latin *to harrow*, to break up clods after plowing. This was not the Mission zone of hardship and peril. Not the zone of unarmed Black citizens killed by the police. Vicki and I entered the private dining room, the round tables set family style. Amy sat ensconced among Erin's West Virginia family: their father, who had been in the military when I had been an antiwar protester, and his second wife; Amy and her second husband and five of their boys; Erin's sister Courtney and two preschoolers and Courtney's marine husband. Warren and Erin would sit at the Winston-Salem table: Warren's parents, both of whom are Baptist ministers, Warren's sister, his uncle and aunt with the four each-different-from-the-others daughters.

I was handed packets of index cards and pens to place on the tables so people could write their wishes for the couple. The niceness surrounding me irritated me, yet why was I feeling surly about the assumption of shared realities and desires? As I allotted cards to each table, I answered: my mother Eunice's disdain for Hallmark. If I was the anti-Hallmark in the room, I needed to stop wanting to be welcomed in my party silk shirt and polished black shoes, but I wanted so much to be welcomed and known: child of my mothers, who would have loved this Black/white wedding; schoolgirl, some of whose classmates' families had been red-baited; child of a world where parents made their livings as book editors and film editors, writers, teachers, dancers, and musicians, not a military or business person among them. My ikat-patterned pants, though understated, had marked my difference: respectability imposter.

Pull in your horns, Darling, Charity cautioned. *It's like your strong leg and your so-called weak leg. Your mother Eunice and I, your sister, the Movement, West Virginia, your beloved Jonah and Carmela, we are your foundation, but this family, here, can carry a lot of weight. It has supported you, ikat-weird as you may be. Use both sides and your spine will unsnarl itself.*

Across the room, Erin conferred with Warren and his mother, Yvonne. Erin with her long, dark hair, her brown eyes with their dark lashes, her curvy figure in its green—always green!—dress. She looked at Warren and smiled. He was handsome in his suit jacket and khakis, his elegant head shaved and glistening, his eyes on Erin.

Erin is from beside Little Buffalo Creek, from a house her father built; she is from my ridgetop house in Charleston, and a house with ferns in Takoma Park, and her own place in Alexandria, where she planted calla lilies. She is from pancakes and sour candies and ranch dressing. She is from cats named Ginger, Krazi, and Samein. She is from years of teaching. She is from sisters and sister friends. She is from three mothers and one father. She is from herself.

Warren is from Winston-Salem, North Carolina. He is from church and athletics. He is from seafood and pancakes. He is from family games of Risk and singing on Christmas Eve. He is from the University of North Carolina Chapel Hill. He is from logistics. He is from the US Marines. He is from overseas duty. He is from Yvonne and Victor. He is from his sister and brother. He is from himself.

Warren's mother's head bent toward Erin, and Erin laughed. Warren touched Erin's waist. Erin had dreamed herself the woman who would rise the next morning after sleeping apart from Warren, put on her waist-pinching garment and over that her friend Danae's white sweatshirt with the word *Bride* printed on the bosom; sitting beside the hotel window, her hair would be *done* by a professional; she would step into the yards of lace, and Danae or Elise would fasten the tiny buttons that walked up Erin's spine and pin in place the cloud of veil; Erin would walk down the aisle with both her mother and her father at her side and into the arms of Warren.

This was a day to put aside how I dreamed myself different.

I took Warren's sister to meet Erin's mustached father; Lauren, his second wife; Erin's sister Amy and her husband and the five boys. West Virginians made their way to the Winston-Salem table. Warren's father leaned forward to touch Erin's West Virginia marine brother-in-law on the shoulder. "Where have you served?"

Erin had been planning this for years. There they were, children of this room, preparing to marry, a marriage that decades before would have been dangerous and that on the *wrong* street confronting the *wrong* strangers could be dangerous still. My mother Charity said into my ear, *Hush, Darling. Just enjoy the day.* At my other shoulder, my mother Eunice ground her teeth with joy. A "We Shall Overcome" moment. *Aren't they beautiful?* my mother Eunice said, and she and my mother Charity left me to it.

I rose in my silk blouse and my slightly out-of-place black-and-cream pants to offer a toast and began to weep, not a pretty little gesture, but messy weeping. I gasped out that I loved Erin and Warren, engulfed by tears—*this* was happening—the clash of dreams in the room, and the racist mayhem outside, which I didn't mention but could not ignore.

Dissociations

A universe of eggs, mine since birth. With each child, for nine months we lived as one—the accretion of every cell constructed of myself. They were nourished by my blood and by the oxygen I breathed. I carried their increasing weight as my own. We were indistinguishable to the naked eye. The sundering of birth. A baby is solitary, even a baby of your soft heart will stare at you with a shadow like a whisper in her mouth, your grandmother in her tiny, pursed mouth. Her navy eyes placeholders while she is removing herself from where she came from, or maybe returning there.

On the ocean beach slope, one foot levers harder than the other. I like the image. Maybe I like it too much. What if Carmela and I are not walking a gentle slope? What if the chasm deepens and each of us is dropped into a slot, alone with no phone, with no texts, no mornings in El Cafetazo, to remind us we are mother and daughter? Neither can empathize with the other. Or does each of us stand with one foot on either side? When the shift begins, we are each ripped in two.

My sister's house in southern Italy has marble floors and white stucco walls. In room after room the walls are covered in books. The partially belowground first level has high windows that open inward on dark hinges. From the living room, above my head, I can see the dog outdoors lying under the shrubbery. My sister's sandals *slap slap* as she walks. We eat breakfast in front of sliding glass doors that open onto Nicola's garden. Rampant light and impenetrable green. The walls of books whose spines are brown and rose and gold and chestnut and black and turquoise and mahogany. We drink coffee from painted Italian mugs, always instant coffee, as my sister learned in India. We each have a cloth place mat and napkin that are stored in an antique wood chest. To eat: a piece or two of toast, butter, perhaps marmalade that my sister has made from the trees outside the glass doors. One morning, as we are putting up our napkins, my sister, a practitioner of yoga and tapping therapy and psychotherapeutic yoga, a woman terrifyingly well-read, asks using our childhood name for one another, "Cif, do you feel joy?"

. . .

I am at a loss there in the light thrown in upon us. "I feel happiness, yes." I can't say the word *joy*. I feel her wait. "Well, maybe a little," I say.

She says, "Hmm," in her seventy-year-old wisewoman way, which, I admit, can irritate me.

Carmela asked if we could go to the ASPCA to look at dogs. Hours later, we walked out with a dog dancing happy at the end of the leash, a seven-pound doe with slender legs, light brown coat with black tips on her boney head and a snowy neckerchief of white hair. Her name was Joy. Carmela said, *Best birthday present ever.* Joy snuggled in Carmela's pink-and-gray coverlet. She scampered around the room. Jonah and Carmela's lunch dates became pizza or other takeout to eat back at the Sunrise. Carmela bought Lunchables, eating the crackers and giving Joy the cheese.

My next visit, on the sidewalk, a big dog came toward us, and Joy leaped out of Carmela's shoulder tote and flung herself at the dog, spitting epithets at the top of her mini lungs and choking on her own leash. The next visit, I crossed paths with a man who lived down the corridor from Carmela. He said Carmela was hardly leaving her room at all. "But the dog?" I asked, and he looked down the street.

"I trained her to use puppy pads," Carmela said. "People are spreading broken glass in the alley. All the other dogs have disappeared." Then in midsummer, Carmela's legs were paralyzed. She couldn't get across her room to the toilet. I couldn't come from North Carolina. Carmela stranded on her bed. She said on the phone, "Tonight, I'm calling an ambulance." She called the ASPCA to relinquish Joy. Carmela was taken to the hospital by ambulance, carried down the twenty-one steep steps to the street, and a few days later she was carried back up the stairs. I think of Joy's small, boney head under my hand, the silken ears between my fingertips, and taste the word: *relinquish*.

Tightly woven hillside, green over blue over green. Tree limbs layer one upon the other like words. At the limbs' tips, the coordinating conjunctions: and, but, or, nor, for, yet, so. At the foot of the tree, in baby-soft debris, the subordinating conjunctions: although, because, since, unless. Christmas lights in the trees are conjunctions.

My mother said, when her parents lived on the Lower East Side and Cardinal Spellman was a parish priest, that Sears and Roebuck delivered the baby carriage intended for my uncle to the parish house. That the priest came barreling down the block to my grandparents' wheeling the carriage. My mother said, as a boy, her father—Benjamin Franklin Spellman, named after the chief rabbi of England (or was it Holland?)—took a trolley from Manhattan through the farmlands of Brooklyn to Coney Island. He saw a high-wire artist making pancakes aloft on a little stove. My grandfather yelled up that he, Ben, would eat the pancakes, to convince the crowd the act was *real*. He ate all the pancakes, and the man gave him money, too. He bought a chicken to take home to his family. My mother said she was *almost* molested by her brother. My mother said when she ran away from home, she worked in a restaurant frequented by *the mob*. Delivering a plate of hot food, she spilled it on the boss and was thankful she escaped with her life. My mother said when a man sat next to her in an almost empty movie theater and put his hand on her thigh, she stubbed out her cigarette on that hand. My mother said when she lived in Paris, she met a sex worker who had *the clap*. I, the listening child, had no idea what this signified. My mother invited this woman to share her room, until penicillin had taken effect. When I was in my thirties and my mother was dying, my uncle, the almost-molester/molester, told me that the high-wire pancakes was not their father's story but the story of . . . and he named a Jewish Broadway figure. In that lunchtime restaurant, he told me about going down on another boy in college and smiled at me. I said nothing, smiled in return, couldn't wait for the meal to be over. Which of these are the stories of my mother as she lived and which are those of the life she wished she had lived, plucky and independent, defender and protector?

His hand. I saw the lemon tree. I saw the silky concrete of the verandah floor. I saw the wood grain of the table where a few hours later my family would eat dinner. My skull froze. I kept my eyes on the book I was learning to read. I smelled dust. Rather than a belt, he held his pants up with a rope, which he untied. I see Fifine, I see Marie Denise, and I see Jean Marie so far away it makes me go cold. Gone. I lie my head on the table and dissolve. The avocado trees above the road. I didn't know if the avocados fell to earth, or did someone climb the long, long trunks growing into the sky to pick the fruit? His hand rubbing. I felt the dirt. I felt the cutting blade of grass. I saw the whirling sky. The dirt smelled of hot. The sun was far away. My feet were far away. His hand pinning me to the earth. His hand.

During my twenties, after the man I'd married and I had had words, I would go into the bathroom. I would stare and stare into the mirror. Into my own eyes with the circles, the hair awry, my nipples discernible beneath the batiste gown. I would stare until I could climb out of my eyes.

My daughter says, *When I was little, I had to clean house all day.* Like Cinderella. I'd find her at age five in the lower bunk. *Shhh*, she'd say, *I'm Cinderella. These are the ashes.* Carmela's mother found the child Cinderella's life acceptable. My daughter says someone phoned her the day of 9/11 and said her brother and I had been killed. *I wore mourning for a year.* Women in the street intentionally bump into her with their yoga mats. *You saw it*, she says. Or, *That man is playing that song on his radio to intimidate me.*

As I remember, the four of us cleaned house together. Half a Saturday of cleaning and we were done for the week.

There is a Bad Mom/Bad Faith in my daughter's heart, in the system that structures her world. That Faith is capable of doing her harm; that Faith is capable of closing her eyes when harm is done to Carmela; that Faith rises between my daughter and me. Therapists suggested to me that I had not perpetrated the abuse of which Carmela once accused me, but . . . *Believe the child.* This possibility of myself: perpetrator of harm beyond the usual admonitions and insistences of mothering. To stay in her world after she disclosed, I tried on the idea of lying: *Yes, I remember*, but couldn't, because the problem was the nature of truth.

. . .

Carmela and me. Driving back across the continental United States after delivering Jonah from West Virginia to his freshman year at UC Berkeley. The sun beats mallets on metal. Her nostrils sandpaper. No need for a map—it's just one road from one side of the desert to the other. The car windows down because the Dodge Colt has no air-conditioning. My/her teenage daughter, in shorts and a cami, her thin hair on her sweaty neck, shifts with discomfort in the passenger seat. There is, finally, a gas station on the horizon, and that's wonderful because she doesn't want to steer anymore. And she has to pee so badly she can barely see. She pulls in beside the derelict building. Her daughter says no, she doesn't want to come in, and if the mother weren't in such a rush, she might have worried what the refusal signified, but she is all sand and heat and need. The floor is wood, the shelves mostly empty, a glass counter on which sits a toddler with sunburned cheeks. Ah, in the corner, two battered doors—is this a movie or what?—with the words: LADIES. GENTS. Though she hadn't noticed before, a man in a Stetson—the man looking old but probably her own age—smacks the cash register. "No bathroom until you make this ring."

She grabs a candy bar and practically throws the money at him. In the bathroom, the walls are gray boards with cracks running vertically, and there are occasional sections where a board may not quite meet the board next to it. Toilet bowl full of rusty water. Her face in the dirty mirror red. Another hundred miles of desert to go. She bangs out the front door. The heat comes at her. The car door squawks open.

"Would you like this?" she offers the candy bar to her daughter.

"You know I can't eat that," her daughter yells, sweat running like disgust down the skin of her neck into her cami. That morning, the cami and boy shorts had been pale and clean as baby clothes. Maybe on the other side of this day, there will be a cheap motel on a gentle rise and it will have a pool and her daughter will settle into the turquoise. And her daughter will smile. And if it is a good evening, her daughter will cling to the side of the pool with water in her eyelashes and her daughter will giggle, restored.

The mother pulls away from the gas station where she has not bought gas—she will regret this in an hour, watching the needle hover closer and closer to "empty." In her rearview, on a pole against the sky, the name of the place: The Bad Faith Cafe.

Is our language seventeen missing years? What is the shape and smell of that? I clung to the dust in the air after a car went down the dirt road. Instead of knowledge, I took who she had been when she left at twenty-one and projected it year by year, imagining but not living her present. She gave birth without me, as I had given birth without my mother. A photo with a sliver of her bunioned foot beside a baby with hazel eyes embodied silence until she came into my arms in a hospital corridor.

Mothering: Who could have thought it would include a text from my grown child saying she thought she was having a seizure? And I went on, preparing that night's dinner while she was in her room in San Francisco, our lives separate geographically and by this text interlaced. I went on with dinner, not because I didn't care but because we had weathered other disasters. Other times, rising in alarm to her call and rallying and then hearing nothing from her for weeks. Or she said, *The cough is worse; I'm spitting up this yellow phlegmy stuff like my friend down the hall*. I knew her body was being wracked, but the hospitals and the EMTs and the neighborhood clinic did not reach it. I had to pray, and by pray I mean go into a blank state where nothing could disrupt my concentration: *Keep her safe*. The next text arrived: *Yup, that's what it was. A seizure.* Who would have thought I wouldn't call an ambulance to that room three thousand miles away? I could tell her *I'm worried* and *I love you* by text. It had not been a phone call kind of month with her.

That space between who I think I am and the woman I am who can hear my daughter say, *I'm having a seizure* or, *When I cough this yellow stuff comes up*, and I don't get on the next plane. Or I don't weep, except inside, my salt-washed organs. She doesn't need me crazy. She doesn't need me weeping. She needs me in this space we occupy in our love, occupy together in our differing realities.

We live a continent apart. That is how big the separation, whether we are standing side by side on Valencia Street or each on her home coast: between us a continent of years and misaligned perceptions. We are who each of us is, in a relationship that began in our shared body four-plus decades ago.

Carmela went into the hospital by ambulance, paralyzed from the waist down. Although unable to walk, she was discharged, carried by EMTs up the twenty-one steps to her room, where she was left with a bedside commode. The home health aide said she needed to help Carmela wash. Carmela said she could wash herself. The woman said she was required to at least touch Carmela with the washcloth. Carmela said, *No*. I think this is what happened.

I went with Carmela to cardiology. She was optimistic. She was going to get some answers. There would be a plan. The cardiology nurse practitioner met us in a claustrophobic room. She did not say hello. She did not ask, *How are you feeling?* Did not ask, *What difficulties have you faced?* Did not ask, *How can I help? What do you need?* The cardiology nurse practitioner jabbed Carmela's leg and said, "You are not swollen." The nurse practitioner spent half an hour facing away from Carmela looking at the computer screen, going over medications. She recommended that Carmela stop taking one of the many on her chart and said because Carmela's Medi-Cal status was pending, we should fill that prescription at the hospital pharmacy.

Separately she told us to have a Zio Patch put in place to monitor Carmela's heart rate and told us where in the hospital complex to have that done. Across a windy courtyard, we entered another building to stand in line at the pharmacy, just weeks after she'd been carried up twenty-one steps because her legs were unable to support her. In the pharmacy's records, the only medicine that the nurse practitioner had ordered was the one she had told Carmela not to take. Back across the windy courtyard. The nurse practitioner had gone to lunch but was paged. Carmela noted reception did not seem surprised at the nurse practitioner's error. The nurse practitioner came back through the waiting room in such a rage I thought she might slap Carmela in the face. We waited. We were to return to the in-hospital pharmacy in the other building. There, the pharmacy said yes, the correct prescription had now been ordered; however, they could not dispense the meds as the nurse practitioner had suggested because Carmela's Medi-Cal status was pending. We went to the other building to have the Zio Patch applied. It was to stay in place for two weeks. We cabbed back to the Mission, stood in line at Walgreens. They could not fill the prescription; Carmela would have to go to an office downtown to have her status certified. Four hours since we had set out for the hospital. Just weeks after she'd been carried upstairs by the EMTs. Carmela could have bolted after the initial visit with the nurse practitioner who didn't say, *How are you*; she could have left after the pharmacy told her the wrong prescription had been ordered; she could have left after the stormy nurse practitioner incident, but we returned to the pharmacy; we went to Walgreens; then we went to eat and returned home to the Sunrise. Carmela tore the Zio Patch off her chest and vowed never to return to San Francisco General Hospital. Oops. It has a new name: Zuckerberg San Francisco General Hospital. Money talks.

Words related to schizophrenia: dementia praecox, psychosis, disorder, catatonic, borderline, latent, paranoid, hebephrenic, reactive, paraphrenic, acute.

The words are separate from ordinary human experience. The words are off-putting. Except for the word *borderline*, no sense that this existence is contiguous with others' lives.

For years, instead of a conventional diagnosis or label, I used words like *ephemeral reality* to describe the difference between what my daughter lived and what I lived. The separation between us felt dangerous—walking down the street together, she saw people purposefully running into her and I might not. The things she reported had been said to her. She disavows the term *schizophrenia*. Some of what happens with Carmela around the question of reality seems to fit words associated with schizophrenia, but if I used the term *schizophrenia*, it would be out of laziness and it would feel wrong. The term is inadequate. Because Carmela disavows the term, it is not useful in figuring out what might help. When she has gone on meds, she has felt demeaned by the bureaucratic safeguards at pharmacies. With her sensitive physiology, they make her sick. The term *schizophrenia* pathologizes and is narrow.

The medical model, in which Carmela is sick and needs to be fixed, has not been helpful in the context of the state, even a liberal one like California, and not in the context of for-profit medicine. There are promising treatment approaches: both peer support and trauma-informed care have been touted as the answer in the last few years; maybe no matter how good the theory, if the patient is destitute, or not easily labeled, or ornery, or the treatment plan is being driven by external professionals and experts concerned with the bottom line, any innovative approach will be ineffective. If professionals miss that moment of the patient's disenchantment, that moment of the patient's withdrawal, the patient may seem to have *rejected services* when maybe she's saying by her absence: *This isn't working.*

There is a difference between thinking that a person with multiple personalities can integrate and thinking that such a person might become coconscious, with all aspects of the personality present and active. One approach demands the survival of the fittest alter; the other embraces the full circumference of the person, including the challenging aspects and even the rogue spirits. Using her inner resources and cleverness, Carmela has constructed a system that works for stretches of time. She modifies it when her situation changes. It is not perfect. The system sometimes turns on her in dangerous ways, but she seems over the years to have devised ways to cope with and respond to her system's vagaries. If I could, I would prescribe for Carmela a small, secure home where she could cook, where her children could visit and spend the night. Ideally, she would have a bathtub in which she could soak in Epsom salts. As an accommodation, in place of pills and Zio Patches and MRIs, I would prescribe the smallish allowance she would need to spend time with her children: cab fares, the pint of strawberries they might ask for, lunch for them from the deli.

Ideally, perhaps no one would *prescribe.*

What would a system look like if providers responded to what Carmela says she needs and to what she is already good at? Small peer and therapeutic groups may seem to outsiders like a good fit, but what if they trigger her? If she built her own program; if one plan didn't work, she could evaluate and either fine-tune or replace it. Who knows? Maybe this would be cheaper than the cyclical hospitalizations, perhaps cheaper than her improvised regimen of homeopathic and over-the-counter remedies, more effective than her days of being sequestered in her room, listening to construction workers power saw through granite.

"When did you first think your daughter might have schizophrenia?"

The asker, with whom I have swum at Falls Lake, just the two of us, the water, and the sky. She is about half my age. She is a singer and dancer, a keeper of stones and crystals, a burner of sage. She is a survivor of child sexual abuse. She is the mother of an elementary school child who, like the mother, is brown-skinned, whose wide, deep eyes can smoke with ancestral anger, whose eyes see more than literal reality—who can close those eyes to me: *Not now.* We are surrounded by morning's urgent laptops. The mother is either unafraid of being overheard or so afraid that she plunges on. Everything falls away. I tell her some say my daughter is what the medical establishment calls schizophrenic. She was gone for almost twenty years: What does that hole speak of? Since, I've learned of malign internal forces that separate her from me, forces that have defined what is happening to her. Once during her twenties, she was told on a phone call that her brother and I were dead. *I wore mourning for a year.*

I say to my friend, "Sometimes Carmela's reality seems irreconcilably different from mine."

The mother says, "But we all see things through our individual lens. Despite our closeness, you and I perceive reality differently."

"I am talking about chasmic differences." I say, "When I was six or seven, I often thought of myself in the third person." *The girl*, or *she* is jumping rope with her sister and Jean Marie and Marie Denise and Fifine. *She* is on the verandah doing her lessons. "And my mother's older sister—who could sing an entire musical score after attending the show's debut—was described by my mother as a *nymphomaniac.*" My mouth screws into the ugly word. "I do not remember a time when I did not know that my mother's sister, my aunt, had leaped from a window and killed herself."

· · ·

Schizophrenia. Nymphomania. These words are that medical practitioner staring at her screen rather than conversing with the pained woman who sat two feet from her, so close the practitioner could have reached out and touched her.

I want deeper words. I do not have better ones. Not for my aunt. Not for my daughter.

Nia is a mother. She can wear a green head wrap and her eyes are apple green; she can wear a fedora and hold a fat cigar and her eyes are darker. Nia can divide right from wrong but does not carry a hunting knife, which is illegal. Omisade is a mother. Omisade embodies audacity—pewter locks and purple lipstick. Audacity as in another name for bravery. Omi can place the tip of her purple fingernail precisely upon the crack in the moral order; Omi wears a white onion dress like it is a fall of water. At Elmo's Diner, Nia and Omi sit near a window. Their plates are full of eggs and salmon, toast, fruit. SpiritHouseNC has just been shafted by a group of local organizations. Nia's ready to move out of Durham. She's had it with gentrification. Now this, from within the community. Parking problems where they work. Zealous security guards not wanting them to dance on the sidewalk. Done. There is a house for rent in the country.

I say, *Yesterday I spoke with*—and name the mother who asked about schizophrenia. It comes back to me, the mother's fear in the morning coffee shop, her seeming to speak out of terror regardless of those around us. The mother, her head covered in gauzy white, the white draping in sanctuary from the crown of her head to below her waist. Me with my flat white woman hair and awkward way of rising from a chair. I say I know we weren't just talking about our daughters.

Nia and Omi and I eat our food. Ask for more coffee and tea. Digress to Nia's son not feeling safe working at night in a hip coffee shop just blocks from where they live: young Black man behind the counter, visible through the plate-glass windows. Gentrification.

Nia veers back to the mother. "You know, she's an empath. She is defenseless against rogue spirits." There with us, along with the half-empty plates, Omi's cup with its purple imprint; *rogue spirits*. It is there and we let it be there, allow the idea its weight: *rogue spirits*. Mischief and mayhem.

. . .

Sometimes when I walk barefoot on the slope beside the ocean, even when my *bad* leg can handle the difference between my strong and weak legs, the difference causes unease. How many times more, the gap between what I see and experience and what my daughter sees and experiences? Her commitment to what she sees and experiences is adamant. Otherwise, she would be giving up a piece of herself, relinquishing how she experiences the world. So like we six editors of *Hands*.

You wanted to bridge the cleft, to land on the other rim, but just like that, you cannot see, you cannot smell, you cannot touch, you cannot hear, not even the ringing of your ears, just the whistle and the electric eye. There are no hands. Sweat under your breasts, which, it suddenly occurs to you, are empty like old socks. You don't know where the escarpment is and you don't know where your feet are and someone is reading you on a computer screen.

rogue: bent crooked deceptive duplicitous fast fraudulent guileful shady shifty underhanded unscrupulous furtive insidious perfidious

I asked Carmela: Did she think the woman who had abused her was evil? It was when I lived with her in San Francisco. When I listened through the living room wall as she wept. When we hadn't seen one another for seventeen years. It was the spring she ate vegetable tempura out of white paper cartons. She held a disk of sweet potato in her thin fingers, the potato ardent orange.

"No," she said. She took her time. "Not evil." She set the sweet potato down. "Wounded."

I saw an animal, a fox, its breast savaged, bloodied heart throbbing in mucky fur. I saw my daughter's heart ardent and large.

Rogue stairsteps to *malign*, the gradients of malign from the earth-born fox who harms because she must feed herself, but she is focused on the satisfaction, not the hurt, stairstepping to evil, which desires harm. Reunited with Carmela, I was interested in this business of evil, but as the gradients of harm and harmers have revealed themselves, the question of evil. . . . Maybe evil in the sense of choosing to do harm could be explained. I have left behind the world where, if you live correctly, safety is a given. I have stopped thinking there are quick fixes. There is living with. Living with poverty; living with illness; living with inescapability.

Forty years ago, I had a pain in my abdomen. Every day I went to work at the schoolhouse. The pain ate at me while I was cooking dinner and putting my children to bed and when I tried to sleep. I saw a practitioner. One day, I hurt so much I couldn't go to work. My lover arranged for me to go to a clinic fifty miles south. I lay on the table, legs open to the eyes of the nurse practitioner, who called in a doctor. They exchanged looks. They said, *Pelvic inflammatory disease*, or *PID*. I asked what caused that; they said sometimes it was associated with gonorrhea. I said I had never had gonorrhea. Later, I learned the risk factors for PID include sex with multiple partners or sex when you are monogamous but your partner is not.

1965: when we were dating, after he met my mother, my children's father said, "I hope you don't turn out hard, like her." I had thought her many things, including self-righteous and unreasonable, but never *hard*. I held the idea *hard* in my mind and tried to make it fit my awkward mother. Tried to make my mother fit the small, unyielding word. He and I were in a department store, looking at bedspreads; I was holding purple fabric in my hands when I understood he was schooling me. He did not want me to become *hard*. Was schooling me not to be self-determined, or . . . queer. He called me *dilettante*. He twisted my name into nicknames I did not like. He called me *bourgeois pig*. He called me *twitch*. I did not rise up. He called homosexuals *fruits*. When things disturbed him, he could go an entire evening through to the next morning without speaking. I did not rise up.

Carmela decided to finish high school at her father's in Amherst, Massachusetts. Years later, she told me he had called her *twitch*. My friend Colleen pointed out: *Half twat, half bitch*. My friend Ancilla asked, "You didn't fight back?" And I knew, the way Ancilla asked, the way she and I loved one another, that she was asking as a partisan for that young me, that she was extending compassion to that earlier me. That she was, as she often has, teaching me there are other ways to be. If I had known he would call Carmela *twitch*, that he would tantrum against her and her brother, if I had known that it was not my fault or not entirely my fault, I would not have let her live there without my taking more care.

The deception seeps slowly through the fault. There is an anomaly, but you dismiss it and go on. It is January and then it is summer. It acts like gas. Your self is permeated and then there are moth holes in your skin and your scalp. You can no longer count upon your skin to contain you. The gas has become the light in which you see yourself.

Something knocks the breath out of you with a *squelch*. You have been dropped from not-life back into life. Underneath you is rubber and you are high off the ground. But you are in a place with a ground. A tall white woman looks down upon you. She is so tall, her head looks tiny and her eyes are pinpricks. The air is so cold the end of your nose aches. The woman is blond. When you breathe in, the cold penetrates your teeth. She is talking. You don't understand her, until she says, ". . . in recovery. . . ."

Oh. Medical. You retrieve a request and squeeze it out because you are on your back and the front of your throat is pressing upon the back of your throat. "Please hold my hand," you say, and the stranger reaches down. You hold her hand until the transit is over, you have returned, and you can let go.

My mother used to sharpen knives at the dining room table. She smiled as she drew a blade over the honing surface and tested the blade; she liked her knives sharp. She had a bone-handled carving knife that had been her father's and which an unfortunate lover of mine took when she moved out. My mother. Steak eater. Lover of roast beef. And she and my sister liked cold beef tongue sliced paper thin. She boiled the tongue in a red enamel pot I still own. I call it "Old Ma's Spaghetti Pot." When I think of how my mother used language, I think: boning knife.

What I started to say: My mother mended broken teacups and mugs. Snapped-off handles. A fragment broken out of the rim. The entire cup in several pieces. At the dining room table, on newspaper, she opened the tube of Duco Cement and squeezed out a fine bead of glue. She let it begin to dry before pressing the two matching but irregular surfaces together. The trick to success was to hold the pieces together long enough to set the glue. No trembling. No jiggling. Not even setting the pieces down so she could take a puff of her cigarette. I own at least one mug that she repaired before her death, that irreparable break in time. And I have that example of salvaging the sundered pieces and making something whole and passing that mended mug on to your daughter to carry into her separate life.

Carmela leafed through glossy magazines at her children's house. "If I had a kitchen, I could cook a feast for everyone." Around us, baskets spilling over with random shoes, piles of sports equipment, and clothing. I said that would be great, but I didn't press her. I would have said she was indifferent to kitchens and cooking. The spring of 2017, she had put out feelers about renting a room or an "in-law suite" in Brisbane, where her children and their father lived. She pulled back when threatening people showed up in the local market when she was buying strawberries for her children. She did not want to bring danger down upon her kids.

She was singing in her room at the Sunrise. Singing Cris Williamson from her Boone County childhood. She reminded me that this music had come to her by way of my ex-lover. That years later, my current lover Vicki had given her a tape of Williamson's *The Changer and the Changed*, before Carmela broke all contact, after which I played a Bonnie Raitt cassette and a Sinéad O'Connor cassette over and over again as I drove the Beltway outside DC, not so much because it was music I liked but because Carmela had liked it. I came to associate the music's spunkiness with this super-short-haired daughter I didn't know.

In 2017, in her room Carmela sometimes sang three cycles at once through the forty-three-minute Cris Williamson compilation on YouTube. She might no longer walk outdoors, but she sang, she breathed; the breath came into her and enlivened her out to the tips of her fingers.

We worked through the underbrush, hacking and throwing roots and branches aside. Sometimes we slipped; we would remember the precipice behind us and hang on. Only a few more feet to clamber up. I stopped feeling dread every single night before I went to sleep, every morning when I woke up, most days no longer walking around with the taste of dread in my mouth. In October 2016, after my visit, Carmela wrote in text after text:

Dear Mom,
    We are grateful for your time and coming back to see us and Michael and Cami, Bear, Stanford, Ty and our friends' kids too.
    Thank you for everything from the weekend Stove Top and feminine supplies, to the hospital and clinic appointments, the smart zippered bag, awesome boots, haircut and rocky rocky shoes and compression stocking, underwear and cotton socks.
    Thank you again for the Scrubbing Bubbles, Prep H, Aspercreme, disposable cups, jog bras (yay, we like 'em!!). Thank you for toothbrushes that dance and Sensodyne which does not. Thank you for understanding when we got too sick to see you Thursday and Friday and then on Halloween! Thanks for accepting my offspring! And their parents.
    Thank you for honoring how hard we 188 work at our children's [...] home. Thank you for sharing your own wife and kids with us, and letting us try to be family too.
    Thank you for cracking up over Cami's hair, Michael and soccer, Bear and Stanford Cat and Ty. Thank you for seeing why I might be houseless again as well as why I might not be able to do that, now. Thank you for rolling your own eyes, re: weird cardiologist. Thanks for letting us know it matters if our heart rate is 179. Did we forget anything? If so, sorry!
    Thank you also for fun make-up!
    Love you,—C ☺

Dear Mom,
   Thank you for my new scale and empathizing when I dropped 16 pounds too quickly and recognizing that we might be sick or otherwise not quite as okay as one might hope, given that number.
   Love, hugs—C

Christmas 2016, Carmela asked me to help her send holiday greetings with photos. She had kept track of all of our family, including our daughter Amy's second husband's three sons. Carmela had been thrilled to send the gift of cocoa for the newlyweds, Erin and Warren, and the rawhide bone for their dog. Family news was mostly filtered through me to her, but in the last year or two, she had become more adventurous and present, texting and even phoning Vicki's daughters and my sister in Italy. The list of people to whom Carmela wanted to send greetings was not long, but it was wide-ranging. There was her brother and his family; her sisters Amy and Erin; my sister in Italy; two dancers from DC whom Carmela had known since her teens; her aunt Malvina and uncle Reuel on her father's side; three families associated with her children's father's clan. Big step for a woman who spent her days sequestered in her room. She wanted to send a card and photos to her father. He has wanted no contact since she came back in 2009. I wanted to say, *Are you sure?* I checked with her uncle Reuel, who said his brother had been dismissive when Reuel tried to show him pictures of Carmela and her children. But, Reuel said, she should try. *You are my family. I am yours.*

She chose photos taken by Reuel the summer before when she had been released from the hospital with her legs paralyzed. Her aunt and uncle, her children's father, and her children, all crowded into her room for pizza. In the photos, Carmela is the pale of someone who has not been in the sun. Her uncle, who is more than six feet tall, must have filled the room to bursting. She wore a blue-green sleeveless dress I'd bought from a Tibetan store in Berkeley during one of those moments when I felt inadequate to give her what she needed—housing—so I'd bought a blue-green embroidered rayon dress. Carmela's alters wanted to include a selfie. She has always had wisping hair, so sparse her scalp showed through in patches; her skull, the helmet housing her brain exposed for all to see. That autumn, she had her hair buzz cut at a chichi place in the Mission. I can see her sitting in the barber's chair and chatting the legs off whoever was cutting her hair. In the selfie, the hair was almost yellow from minoxidil, her cheeks and forehead pink as a brand-new scar. Staring upward at the lens, she looked rosy and golden as a new chick, except for her dark brows and her penetrating eyes. I feared for her, sending this photo into the world. I admired her. *You are my family. I am yours.*

reconcile: settle one's differences, make peace, bury the hatchet, patch things up, accommodate, appease, assuage, integrate, pacify, resolve, reunite, arbitrate, win over, reestablish

Carmela injured her foot. She took selfies of her broken foot, lying on her back, leg extended over her head in a contortion. She texted the selfies to Vicki and me, Amy and Erin, Jonah, my sister Shai: *See me. I am yours.*

Carmela said, "I called"—and she named my long-ago lover. The woman had been out of my life for more than thirty years. Had been out of Carmela's. *Done.*

"How did it go?" I asked, alarms sounding.

"It was really nice. She was glad I called. We're going to speak every Wednesday, like when you guys broke up and she would take me out to Wendy's. Remember?" The roller coaster year—me weeping on the couch, messy and menopausal. Carmela sitting by the phone waiting for the expected call. *Why doesn't she call? She said she would?* "Talking to her was really nice. I'm going to put Skype on my phone because she said that way we can see one another when we talk."

"I want you to feel safe."

"Oh, I do."

Later, I asked what had changed. Carmela said, "I know those horrible things happened, Mom. I know that. But it wasn't her that did them." Integrating the disparate and once discarded aspects of her life, integrating the many alters she is. Self-invention.

. . .

Her father visited Jonah and Jonah's family. He left a box of photos with Jonah, photos from Jonah and Carmela's childhoods. Carmela's son Michael was amazed to learn of this grandfather and wanted to know him. By email, Carmela offered for her kids to meet her father; he could meet Michael and Cami even if he did not want to see her. No response. She got his phone number from her uncle. She left a message: She was sorry for the hurtful things she had said. She would like to talk with him. She told me she wanted her dad. She had been afraid of him. She had been so alone in his Amherst house. I knew she had shrunk her life while with him—I had seen the narrow convertible chair-bed on which she had slept in a narrow room. In those days, I had felt mothering a fifteen-year-old was a requirement I didn't know how to fulfill, didn't know how to mother my anxious, too-thin daughter who lived a night's drive away from me, too far to know if she was safe. I drove to be with her as she broke her Yom Kippur fast. She plucked at a bagel and said she'd eaten enough. I wanted to say *anorexia*. But I didn't want to piss her off. It wasn't the nutritional insufficiency that bothered me as much as her breaking her Yom Kippur fast on a Styrofoam plate, the plastic knife for the cream cheese. The meanness of it. And I didn't know how to say, *Carmela, you are my beloved girl*. If I had had the courage to . . .

She wanted her father. She had never had him. She phoned and left a message. Again. Would this end with her crashing or being crushed? Apprehension. Like when she'd lived in Amherst, when I hadn't known if her hostility to me was *normal* teenage antagonism, making a *normal* growing apart possible. When she was little, I had felt as loved by her as I loved her, this dancing child. Then in her late teens, every word out of my mouth seemed to sound to her like shit. She left several phone messages for him, but he did not pick up. She asked me to call him. The first time she asked, I didn't respond directly and she didn't press, but when she asked again, I agreed. I was relieved that he didn't pick up. As he talked through his message, I considered the texture of his voice. How similar. How different. The beep. I gave my first and last name. I said I hoped he and his wife were well and that his move to Santa Fe had been everything he'd hoped for. I said I was calling about our daughter, Carmela, who wished very much to reunite with him. That she had reunited with many of us. That I hoped he could find it in his heart to respond to her, that to do so would be an act of generosity on his part. Carmela's father emailed Carmela, her brother, me, and her uncle Reuel: he appreciated Carmela's apologies, but at this time he did not wish to change their status of *no contact*.

She sends photos in texts to Vicki's daughters, her brother, her uncle. People she danced with twenty years ago. She says, *He can choose to not communicate, but I can communicate with him if I want*. She finds an email address for her childhood dance teacher in West Virginia. She sends a note and a photo of her children and is thrilled to receive an answer.

In the spring of 2017, logistics in California got complicated. I was figuring out where to spend the night before my Monday flight home. Carmela said, "You could stay in my room." She said, "Amy has a home where you and Vicki can stay. Erin has a home where you and Vicki can stay. Jonah has a home where you and Vicki can stay. I want to be able to share my home with you; this one room is the home I have for now." She would sleep on the floor. She hadn't slept in a room with an outside person for years. In the past, she'd ruled out my staying at the Sunrise because of the violence and because of the bugs. Most nights, she was up half the night, dropping off to sleep at dawn. I slept early and woke earlyish. We didn't share her room that night. But we could have. We had come that far.

Sing

Carmela's children live with their father near SFO, the San Francisco airport, in Brisbane, a town clustered against a sere hill. Entering Brisbane, you drive uphill past a strip mall, a skate park, a regular park, uphill from stop sign to stop sign, passing the market and the Mexican restaurant, the pizza place and the library. At the top, before you must turn right or left, is the Evangelical church once attended by Carmela and her former husband. More than a decade ago, Carmela had lived here; she had worked in a chiropractor's office and at the Midtown Market. The black lab Bear came into their lives as a puppy and the sister-brother pair of kittens Stanford and Oreo, and her babies Michael and Cami. My daughter helped find the olive tree that is now full-limbed in the yard. She was a member of the Brisbane new mothers club and her children go to school with the cohort of babies born to those mothers. She came into her voice and sang, without being able to read sheet music, in the church choir, learning music by, as she says, following its flow. In some ways, I think this is how she moves in the world, answering a flow. Singing is a part of her life that I only know through her words. *I sang a whole Cris Williamson album in my room at Sunrise. . . . I sang in the choir at church.*

When she left Brisbane, this life, this house, these streets, Carmela was no longer welcome in the choir and was thrown out of that flow, but over the years, with her steadfastness, she eased back. She again attended special church occasions and finally regular services. The minister let her take home a hymnal. Carmela sang for hours in her room, voice and body being indistinguishable. In her body, the music cored down into the essence of who she was, and it opened that one room to encompass everything that had happened to her many selves and opened passage to her future. She sang church music, and she began to branch out to music she found online, working her phone like a full-size computer. She was singing Cris Williamson, a 1980s lesbian phenom—wild and full of longing—music of Carmela's childhood in a queer but closeted household up a holler in West Virginia. She found Charity, my mother by affection, the voice of my childhood, so in her room at the Sunrise she was singing Charity Bailey, living into my history in a way that no one else has. Voicing Charity Bailey as her own lineage. Carmela's singing was her reconciliation, between her history in Brisbane before and after her departure.

The spring and summer of 2017, Carmela was always cold. She wore a hooded gray sweatshirt, often pulling the hood over her head, which she had shorn close to the scalp. Ill, eating too little, spending the days of the weekend with her children, she decided to take in hand the cleaning and ordering of their household; she did not want her children to live in chaos. She was gray from being in her room five days a week; she was weak from a life enlivened only by weekends with her children. That summer, Cami and Michael rejected the day program their father had arranged. Several days a week, Carmela took a cab the thirty miles to Brisbane. She was deeply happy to be with her children. Communicated with me only in texts and rare phone calls.

The pastor invited her to sing at the July "Singspiration." She invited me. I would see this church that had housed much of who she had become. I would hear her sing from her inheritance of California, West Virginia, Greenwich Village. Jonah, Carmela, and I had lunch in San Francisco. While we ate various pastas, she said, "Sunday, I'm going to sing this song." In the riotous underground food court at Westfield Mall, she told us, "I'm going to sing a song my friend taught me. It is in Hebrew and I'm going to sing it in Hebrew. My friend had cancer and she died."

There was a purple tablecloth on the altar, a vase of red flowers, a US flag, and a cross on the wood-paneled wall behind her. In her gray sweatshirt with the hood folded back to expose her shorn skull, my daughter looked like a nun. Her voice rose from the time of who she had been into the time of who she was now. Her voice padding on great feet and roaring because her two cubs with their smiley-face masks were gamboling too close to the moat. A voice of alarm and power, a voice that did not suffer trifling. A voice that scared me.

The image I recorded on my phone shifted erratically up and down from Carmela to random empty pews, to body parts of congregation members. I couldn't hold the camera still. My heart was in my mouth and got in the way. Carmela, shorn and cloaked, performing as she'd performed as a child. Carmela. I settled, keeping the image of her at the screen's center. She frowned the long-ago frown of my mother, then a girl smile in one corner of her mouth, a shoulder raised to the work, her mouth open in the singer's *oh*. Her voice unfolded, feat of memory and imagination in song. My interior lens moved jaggedly from Carmela the child. Carmela once lost. Carmela recovered. Carmela who had helped build this church with her children's father, in a time when I had not seen her, an unseen time when she had chosen this Evangelical Christian world, a time when a church had been her landlord and she had attended bible study and characteristically learned all the lessons in no time.

She sang from that time when I had not been permitted to see her: *We will be known as Christians by our love.* Wobble focus. Me, the mother on the other coast, waiting those years, longing for the bat mitzvah girl in her purple heather suit, so small she could barely be seen above the pulpit at Temple Israel, beside the Kanawha River in Charleston, West Virginia. My phone teetered: bits of blue carpet, sliding grid of ceiling tiles, head-over-heels wood of the podium. Carmela back in view, occupying the screen, standing before us. With her phone she played Cris Williamson. The kindergarten girl in daylight saving dusk, windows open to summer of Middle White Oak Holler, front door wide open, girl child standing barely taller than the turntable in its place of pride in the living room. What had the lyrics meant to that child with the wispy hair? Had they meant home? Had they meant unnamed loves? Cris Williamson—ethereal and beautiful embodiment of the idea *lesbian*, years before we allowed ourselves to say the L word to our children for fear of legally losing them; Cris Williamson in the springtime of Carmela's life.

That night in Brisbane, sound from her phone was barely picked up by the church sound system; she didn't intend for us to focus on the recorded sound; the music on the phone was to guide her flow through the melody that she had practiced day after day in her room with a grated window looking across five feet into the bedroom of a man she didn't know. "I heard you singing," her friend had said in the corridor. That melody, her foot path from inner to outer. Williamson's song "One of the Light" is almost formless, or, rather, it has a shape and form, but the shifts from one point in the song to the next are surreal in their quietude. You are in one place and then you find yourself someplace else. That night, her enormous voice laid claim to every inch of the modest sanctuary. She sang from the sore spots of decades, our long-ago loss of the woman I had loved, who had owned that record player. In this outpouring, sharp or flat didn't matter. Do sharp and flat spell grief? She sang, *Watching for phantom travelers . . . So many left behind. . . .* Her voice careened in lament, wracked and sliding off the notes. *Where is the light? Have you seen the light? Finding my way in the night.* She smiled, on familiar ground. *It's only the shadows I'm sure of. . . . Where can she be? . . . So many things I cared for. So many left behind.*

The final song, the one in Hebrew, whose words Carmela had carried from her past, from the years I would never know. She had carried the cadences through her years as an arts administrator, through her years in the Brisbane mothers group, through time at the Seneca and the Sunrise. That night, as she sang, she raised her solemn and merry eyes to meet all of ours.

All the world is just a narrow bridge. Just a narrow bridge. . . . Above all is not to fear, not to fear at all.

I don't know who will be at Queer Black Sunday School Choir practice.[2] I don't know how my raspy and breathless voice will do. I am queer but not Black, but it is Black Sunday school in the tradition of the Black Southern church, our leader the daughter of a minister and herself trained in spiritual traditions. I park down the street and walk. It is such a quiet backstreet that I walk down the middle, feeling lighthearted about breaking a rule. I have never been to the LGBTQ Center and don't know what it will be like. As I approach, Nadeen unstraps her baby from his car seat and lifts him into her arms. Nadeen's little girl, Tula, stands by their car. A car rushes by. I reach for Tula's hand. She is so little, a three-year-old. Though she barely knows me, Tula takes my hand and we cross the street together. "Faith," a woman calls and says her own name, Mariel, a name from poetry workshops, Mariel from the intimate space of working on poetry. I once gave her a ride to a bus station, but I don't even know in what town she now lives. I don't know what to expect. There are maybe a dozen of us. Will I have to sing and be judged? Why did I think this was a good idea?

We are purple-, red-, and black-patterned tights. We are lavender scarf falling from shoulders to thigh. We are man with hair wrapped heavily on his head. We are maroon sweatshirt over plaid. We are shirt that proclaims: *Artist. Creator. Threat.* Another: *I met God and she is Black.* We are hands tucked into jeans pockets. We are hands clapping. We are hands held at the waist, open, waiting. We are hands clasped around the midriff, a different waiting. We are brown and brown and white and brown and brown and brown and white and white.

Julia Sangodare in white jeans and a turquoise jacket, beads at her neck and wrist, white knit cap on the back of her head, steps into the circle, consulting notes on her index cards and writing on a flip chart, as if Sangodare needs to consult notes to know. She has us make sounds, arising from inside each of us, together. The room is full of our sound—stray notes, beeps, stamping, cork-popping, zips—each of us making the needed sound. We are meeting

2. For more information, visit https://www.mobilehomecoming.org.

one another's eyes across the circle and smiling, whether we have known people before or not. Sangodare smiles, electric. Tula wanders into the middle of the circle, spinning to look at the panorama of us. Sangodare starts us on musical phrases. Half an hour has gone by. We learn another phrase. We sing the two phrases one after the other. Sangodare's hands are lifted, directing us, her fingers fitting into the air: *joy*. I feel the voices beside and across from me. Sangodare divides us into three groups. One group begins and when it reaches the end of a phrase and continues on, another group begins. Sangodare cues us in and what we are doing becomes complicated and beautiful, imagined by Sangodare and fulfilled by us. One begins, then another begins, just as the struggle, beautiful and complicated, fulfilled by us.

In October, I returned for a second Singspiration at the church in Brisbane. Carmela had planned a program of five or six songs. After three, overcome with weakness, she sat down and stopped singing. How to describe when she said she was too weak to sing, those steps down from the altar to her seat, moments I sat behind her and her children, watched her thin back cloaked in sweatshirt gray and realized: I could do nothing to lift this from her. After Carmela had taken her seat, the woman in charge of the electronics continued the slide show and recorded music for Carmela's program, although Carmela was crumpled in a pew.

Just like *that*, I was looking at an image projected onto the wall of my Charity Bailey, my chosen mother, dead almost forty years, Charity whom Carmela had carried with her from West Virginia to DC to San Francisco, from young dancer to youngish mother, to a life in a room in the Mission. My daughter Carmela, child of so long ago but never gone from who I am, Carmela, in her pew, reaching her thin hand out to Charity Bailey glimmering on the wall, Charity's mouth open, "Oh." From her pew, without a microphone, Carmela laid her ferocious voice over Charity's, my daughter's voice over the decades-old, tinny, recorded voice of Charity, my mother by affection. My childhood.

I was appalled by my child's frailty, the shorn head, the bone-thin hand outstretched, her voice filling the space between here right now in the Evangelical church and *then*.

Living With

The ICU nurse, or perhaps it was the doctor, phoned: Carmela was too incoherent to sign permission for a line directly into her chest, or maybe it was her neck. Some lead was to penetrate the circulatory system of her inner body, that singing body that could no longer sustain itself. Carmela had given my name to act on her behalf. I granted permission. Vicki booked a flight. I flew.

I spoke my daughter's name into a receiver and was buzzed into the ICU. Cloistered, she dozed on her back. There was a rotten bruise in the hollow of her throat; another bloomed below her shoulder. Was this where they had tried to insert the lines? She was hooked up to machines that read off her blood pressure and heart rate and I don't know what else. I pulled a chair close and lay my head on the bed rail. I closed my eyes. *Please, let her live.* When she opened her eyes, maybe the flicker on her face was a smile. The ICU nurse had said Carmela had told her, "My mother is probably on a plane coming here right now."

Carmela was weak; she couldn't hold her hands straight out with the wrists cocked up. She couldn't hold a four-ounce paper cup of water; when I supported her cold, bone-thin hand, she couldn't guide the rim to her lips. On her back, when she slid down in the inclined bed, she couldn't hoist herself back up. Two staff, one on each side, would take her under the shoulders and pull her upward. She was in the ICU for ten, or maybe it was eleven, days. There was an endoscopy and colonoscopies, yes, more than one. Lesions were clipped. The nurse told me Carmela had come into the hospital already bruised. Bruised with secrets. More than a month later, only after I had left California, could I say to myself, *She came this close to dying.*

When she was moved to the med/surgical floor, there was a bathroom in her room. "I can go to the bathroom by myself," she said, but the head nurse said not until physical therapy cleared her. "Please," Carmela said.

The nurse said, "You can't even stand up by yourself."

This was true, so Carmela continued with the diapers and pads, which made her wrinkle her nose. The nurse's aides donned gloves, rolled Carmela onto her side, swabbed her clean and covered her rawness with ointment, positioned the new pad, rolled her to the other side, and repeated. "Thank you," Carmela would say. Her frailty was not as present in this new room. There was the possibility of the bathroom. This room was part of the glass-sheathed Zuckerberg wing; Carmela faced a wall of windows onto possibility: Bernal Heights. She could watch the movement of the sun—its sinking and its return.

She had delayed calling the ambulance until 3:30 a.m. the day her rent was due so she could pay on her way out. She had been waiting for the EMTs, sitting on the floor in the public corridor. The EMTs started IVs, loaded her onto the gurney, and moved her down the steps to the ground floor. They wouldn't stop for her to pay her rent.

A social worker told me, of course Carmela was eligible for Medi-Cal, California's version of Medicaid, but Carmela wasn't on this woman's too-full case load; she couldn't help us apply. A social worker had come to the Sunrise and filled out a Medi-Cal application. One had been filled out her last hospital stay as well. She still was not approved.

TO DO

Pay the rent.
Get her certified for Medi-Cal.
Her room.

Step one. BART into San Francisco from Jonah's. The night before, I was haunted by an imagined expulsion: Omar the manager saying, *Carmela's room has been given away. Her things have been put in the rubbish.* The few camis and leggings she swapped out to keep them near fresh. The photos of her children. The folder with medical and other appointments. As I tried to sleep, Omar asked, *Carmela who?* All night, this footage. *Carmela who?* The room had been Carmela's safety for over six years; it had also been a nightmare of deprivation and shrinkage. The room had been hers and she would clean it herself. I walked Sixteenth Street from Mission to Valencia. All was sunny. My mouth was dry. I felt I was the only person on my side of the street. Everyone else walked on the normal side. Carmela and I would never be normal or safe. I walked into the foyer at the Sunrise. Now I would know. With no questions, Omar's wife took the money. Rent paid. Done.

Carmela had forbidden me to go to her room. There would be discarded food. How much? Was it littering the floor? Was it heaped around the counter at the sink? She had been unable to carry her trash down the hall. For how many months? She had told me she'd been passing blood when she peed. Her toilet must be dirty. She had been vomiting. In the past, she and I had bought Scrubbing Bubbles and their *wand* to clean her toilet, but we hadn't bought Scrubbing Bubbles in a long time. Nights at Jonah's, I tried to imagine the room, the place I hadn't seen, that her brother and her friend down the hall at Sunrise had not seen. I imagined the movement of maggots and rats but not in any completeness, because I couldn't. I imagined working hours with her to clean the room. In the hospital, on her back, weak, she insisted she would clean it herself, by herself, when the time came. Closed.

She couldn't walk and could barely stand up. She woke at 2:00 a.m. and began her exercising. In her bed, she pushed and pulled against elastic bands from physical therapy—black, the most challenging—straight out and diagonally across her body. She wound the bands over her insteps and worked her legs, straight out and diagonally. On Christmas Eve, when her twenty-one days of one-hundred-percent Medicare coverage was about to expire, Carmela was discharged to the Victorian, a *post-acute* facility, what used to be called a nursing home. Victorian?

• • •

My body, a mother's seventy-five-year-old body. I didn't want to eat. I almost passed out on BART. Was I having a heart attack? How would I know? I'd never had one. The doctor at urgent care said my lungs were clear and I did not have the flu. There was a particular flu that year. My blood pressure of 173 was stress, "Given what you've told me about your situation," the doctor said. Was my body speaking? If so, what was she saying? Was my body unreliable and lying?

I paid the rent a second time on January 3, a month after Carmela was hospitalized. Omar told me people had complained about the smell coming from her room and I said we would clean it. When I told Carmela we couldn't wait for her to clean the room, tears rose in her eyes. The impossibility of it: this supine woman, climbing the twenty-one steep steps to her room. The impossibility that she could walk to Walgreens and get cleaning supplies and carry them home and reclimb those steps, go down the corridor with its three right turns. That she could clean the room where the dimensions of the disorder were unknown.

Street clothes. She must wear street clothes to participate in physical therapy, or PT. At two in the morning, she changed out of her night clothes. Solitary in the sleeping facility, she worked the elastic bands. Gingerly, she began to stand with assistance. Next, stand without assistance. Wheeled by a therapist, she went to the basement. She wheeled herself down the corridor past the reception desk, saying hello to staff, rang for the elevator whose doors snapped closed so quickly the physical therapist joked there were bones of severed hands that had slipped through the gap between the elevator and the door. She wheeled herself up and down the green 1950s institutional corridor until she developed calluses on her hands. She wheeled herself around and around the first floor, starting at 6:00 a.m. Saying hello to staff at the nursing stations.

I watched her really eat for the first time in a long while. Nursing home food: sandwiches on white bread, meats with sauces that she didn't much like, occasionally fresh fruit, green vegetables. Medicine mostly reduced her pain, although there were days when she cried with hurting, rousing only to go down for PT. She told me one of the therapists did pole yoga and was going to a family wedding in Korea.

. . .

I am walking up a West Virginia creek bed, stepping from stone to stone. Just over the hill, I raised my children. With my cranky legs and my unreliable balance, this is tricky, but the sky snaps like a blue bedsheet, and the moss is the soft green of love. Moss covers the stones and my foot slips. Actually, it is Hawthorne Circle, north of New York City, in the 1940s. Inside a second, I have fallen, bruised my breasts on underwater boulders that rear up and shatter my wrists. I have been looking at the blue, blue sky too long. My mother loved that our picnic place beside a boulder-strewn river was not legal.

Vicki joined me for a week. From Walgreens, she and I walked toward the Sunrise. The plastic ties of the bags of toilet cleaner, all-surface cleaners, and garbage bags cut into my wrist, and this sensation made me light-hearted. We were doing something. I thought of the word *assuage*. I couldn't imagine Carmela, back at the Victorian, circling the corridors in her wheelchair, couldn't imagine that *that* woman could make this walk. The other day, the physical therapist had said, "How many steps to your room? If we got a second walker, could you leave one at the top and one at the bottom?"

"No. Not in an SRO."

Vicki and I entered to a welter of bulging plastic bags. Almost no floor surface visible. No sheets on the bed, just some cloths, a pale yellow and a gray with no suggestion in them of the natural world. By the door, bagged cartons of waiting garbage. Her clothes were not in evidence though we found them as we cleaned, some so torn or stained they went in the garbage bags. We kept filling bags. She'd kept ordering food hoping she could stomach it. Probably three months of food garbage (each parcel bagged and tied off, thank goodness). The bed had garbage bags on it and tied-off barf bags. Vicki and I tried to clean the mattress, but the plastic mattress cover held a moving sheen of bugs, black and barely more than microscopic. This nightmare had dimensions; it could be handled. I closed my mind, my nose, used my eyes in a strictly utilitarian fashion. I wouldn't listen to my heart: *Not now*. I imagined her thin body curled on the bare mattress, her self edged out by tied-off plastic bags, in the midst of what she had been unable to *keep down*, bags of what she could not swallow. There was no space for the person who was Carmela. For a long time, I wasn't able to think of this room except in snatched retro glimpses. And yet, when we had cleared away the trash, there was an orderly cluster of bags in one corner, including, as she had told me, a tote with all the documents we needed to complete the Medi-Cal application. Beneath the disorder, Carmela, systematic and careful, Carmela, documented.

In the basement at the Victorian, Carmela did ten popcorns, standing with her back to the chair and squatting to almost sit. And back up. The next day, she did fifteen. One day, forty-five. They started her on the stairs, a set of four in the middle of the PT room—the stairway to nowhere, she called it. At first she could only do one or two steps. At the SRO, there was only one banister, so PT taught her to manage holding on, on only one side. Always, the goal to not fall. Always, the goal to pay attention. She was going up and down all four steps in the stairway to nowhere, smiling fiercely, determined to go home to her room. Going up and down, with the walker over her shoulder. Up and down the Victorian's real-life staircase, the walker slung over her shoulder. At the same time, she was plucking tiny beads out of an inert and heavy version of Play-Doh. She was going to group exercise class, where many people were in wheelchairs and some slept, their heads canted back, their mouths open.

"Nurse! Emergency! Somebody please help me," called Carmela's roommate. Three of them were jammed into a room surely once meant for only two, back in the days when the 1950s wallpaper had not faded. "Nurse! Emergency! Somebody please help me." Morning, noon, and night until the bedtime sedatives had silenced her.

There was a day when the pain overwhelmed Carmela. Her chart named fibromyalgia. I went to the nurses' station. She screamed. From noon until after 9:00 p.m., when the moonlighting doctor arrived. Through an evening of increasing pain, I phoned Vicki, long after her East Coast bedtime. I was weeping. I hadn't eaten. The doctor upped the oxycodone. The nursing staff brought me a sandwich on white bread. Carmela calmed. I kissed her forehead. I took a cab all the way from Pacific Heights in San Francisco to my Berkeley Airbnb. Forty-five dollars plus tip.

Carmela was scheduled to leave the Victorian. Her accumulation of two months of clothes and coloring books and toiletries must be bagged. She had been outdoors with the walker twice. She was not walking without the walker. When we left, she was to take the facility's walker to the curb for the cab, which I would have called. She would hand the walker to a person from the facility, get herself into the cab; her things would be loaded into the trunk; we would ride to the Sunrise. She would get herself out of the cab. I would manage her things. I would go ahead to fetch the walker from her room. She would climb the twenty-one steps using the single handrail. We did somehow get into the cab. As we swept down from Pacific Heights, I felt giddy and I thought she must, too, as she looked out on this world from which she had been absent for two months. I looked at her, in her swirly-colored leggings, purple shirt, and peach tunic, all gifts from family. We were in the world. Riding in a cab. Together. In the sunshine. Past playgrounds with children. We were silent as the driver negotiated the turns that each of us, in her own way, could anticipate. We were there. At the Sunrise. Could she stay in the cab until I retrieved her walker from her room? She said no, she would walk without the walker into the Sunrise. *Always, the goal is to not fall. Always, the goal is to pay attention.* She insisted. She made it without the walker into the entryway. We were in.

I wanted to say, *Wow*, but instead I said, "I'll go get the walker."

"You can bring the walker to the top of the stairs. You go first, so I don't have to worry about you." On home ground, taking charge. We entered her room. The room's surfaces were clean, expectant, as Vicki and I had left them. With a lovely ripping, we removed the mattress cover and wiped the mattress entirely clean. Unable between the two of us to lift the mattress, she had us tuck the remnants of the cover underneath out of sight, a bit of the disrepair tucked away but present.

"What's in there?" The plastic bag Vicki and I had set atop her nonworking television.

"We washed your clothes."

I kept thinking, *She should rest*. Moving from bed to sink and back, she was forgetting the walker half the time. *Always, the goal is to be safe.*

She said, "First, Walgreens." At the head of the stairs: "You go down first." And we were out in the sunshine, Carmela standing and walking beside me. How fragile she looked with her walker; nevertheless, we were there. Two weeks before, she'd been in a wheelchair. Mere hours before, we'd been in the Victorian. *You're kind of a miracle*, I wanted to say.

We walked the few blocks to Walgreens. She picked out a little girl's nail polish set, for all the little ones inside her. "Food for tonight?" I asked, and she picked out something to take back to her room. We walked back to the Sunrise, up the twenty-one steps, she with the walker over her shoulder and I with our purchases.

"I'm hungry," she said. Back out, down the twenty-one steps, me in front and crossing the entryway and stepping into the sunshine, to look back and see her coming through the door, her—upright!—framed in the rectangle of the door and then stepping onto the sidewalk. We walked side by side to a pizza place, narrow with only three tables. Her diuretic was working her. She made her way through the narrow and crowded kitchen, stepping around or lifting the walker over obstacles, disappearing around the corner to the toilet, though I could hear her chatting to the cook. In a few minutes, when our pizzas came, we sat at the single Formica-topped table in the window. Three girls in school uniforms came in and ordered slices. Carmela dumped parmesan on her pizza, as my mother would have done and as I do. The walker folded and out of sight, we looked out the window as we ate, an elderly woman and her middle-aged daughter. We must have appeared as ordinary as the three laughing schoolgirls behind us paying for their slices.

Coda
White Woman Reading Audre Lorde

I.

We were a room of self-identified white feminist women, gathered to read Audre Lorde's *Sister Outsider*, at the prompting of SpiritHouseNC. I had attended a handful of earlier SpiritHouseNC book studies: *The New Jim Crow*, *Urban Alchemy*, *Parable of the Sower*, among others. For Audre Lorde, Nia Wilson issued a call to Black men to form their own study group and the following day issued a similar call to white feminists. As with all of their book study groups, SpiritHouseNC sent out a study guide, which included an order of suggested weekly readings, as well as a centering exercise for each session, a music and audio playlist.

Two women stepped forward to facilitate the white women feminists' group. Their plan did not follow the SpiritHouseNC guide. The organizers of the white women said there would be light snacks, because they wanted us to devote our energies to the discussion and not to distract ourselves with eating and chatting; at regular SpiritHouseNC meetings, food is part of the ritual of being with one another. We have had to scrounge to find enough paper plates and plastic forks. There have been nights when there were more homemade sheet cakes than protein or fruit; some brought their own specialized diets—but always group members sat in the horseshoe of desks, glancing across into one another's eyes, muttering to those next to us, a child running in to be tended to, someone fiddling with the AV equipment. There might be smudging with sage. There might be an altar. There was centering in which we acknowledged ancestors behind us, family and tribe to either side, the future before us.

The white women met in a spacious room hung with original art from around the world, including Palestine; the colored lines of the paintings on the brick wall looped and wove, suggesting they crossed from one piece of art to the next, like the featherstitching of a crazy quilt. A beautiful space filled with having been lived in and with echoes of previous meetings. Some of the comfy chairs made it hard to extract yourself if you had a problematic hip, as I do. I picked the corner of a couch, next to a friend. On my other side, another friend, a woman in her seventies: she and I the elders, along with a woman who had survived the 1979 Greensboro massacre.[1] There were younger women, some of whose names I knew, though I had never met them. We did not go around the room and introduce ourselves beyond giving our names and pronouns. Everyone in the room claimed *she*. What the evening might hold, what these women might say—even who these women would turn out to be—was unknown, and I was prepared to dislike all of it. Our leaders had reordered the readings from the sequence suggested by SpiritHouseNC. We had been trained, as white women who may have succeeded in academia, to be intellectually enterprising. We'd been rewarded for this all our lives, but in this way the white women organizers disregarded the structure suggested by the Black women of SpiritHouseNC and disregarded their Black female leadership.

We paired up to speak with the person next to us. I shared with my friend on my right. Seconds in, the two of us held private space. The winter before, my daughter had almost died. I had flown across the country and sat by my child's bed in the ICU, my forehead pressed to her bed rail, and begged the universe to be merciful. And it had. The previous winter, my friend, too, had flown to her endangered daughter. Our allotted minutes passed and we were called back to white women studying Audre Lorde. The leaders played an audio clip of Audre Lorde reading "A Litany for Survival": ". . . For those of us who live at the shoreline/standing upon the constant edges of decision/crucial and alone. . . ."[2]

---

1. Greensboro massacre: during a nonviolent 1979 demonstration by the Communist Workers Party (CWP), the Ku Klux Klan, with the complicity of city police, targeted, shot, and killed five members of the CWP.
2. "Litany for Survival" appears in *The Collected Poems of Audre Lorde*.

The two of us on the couch in the beautiful room still immersed in our stories of daughters who almost didn't. Survive.

"It's her voice, Audre Lorde's voice," my friend said. "That's so thrilling."

And it was. And it was odd to be in the group, after we two mothers had been sequestered.

The group plunged into Audre Lorde's "Letter to Mary Daly," written by Lorde, a Black feminist, to a white feminist who had written a 1978 *groundbreaking* book on feminist theology, an entire book in which Black feminists are not mentioned, the work of Black feminist writers not included with the exception of a brief paragraph on female genital mutilation, the sole representation of Black women, their feminism, their spirituality in this *groundbreaking feminist* theologian's book.[3] Our facilitators had found an audio clip of Daly responding to Lorde's letter. The Daly clip was longer than the one of Lorde reading "Litany for Survival." Daly, angry, defensive, poured into our ears for more time than Audre Lorde had. In a discussion dedicated to the thought of a Black feminist, we had spent more time listening to a white woman disputing that Black thinker. *Our group is acting like white women.* It took me a while to articulate this to myself.

With emotion, one woman said she was afraid that in effect she was Mary Daly and several in the room nodded. They, too, were afraid of saying the wrong thing, afraid of making racist mistakes, afraid in some existential sense of being chastised as Mary Daly had been. This room of self-identified antiracist people vibrated with racial fear and guilt. The women speaking were doing their best to speak honestly; implicit, that what they were feeling was of value, that group members would wait for them to find words to reflect their experience, because group members' experiences were valued and because at least some of us had attended schools where we were taught to value, as if they were currency, our individual expressions. The women were baring their vulnerability to show their desire to be accepted by our group. I felt it would be crass of me to say, *But a brief paragraph on female genital mutilation, that is the sole representation of Black women, their feminism, their spirituality, their personhood?* As if my pointing this out would have been the problem. Not knowing what she was thinking, I felt

---

3. "Letter to Mary Daly" appears in *Sister Outsider: Essays and Speeches* by Audre Lorde (Crossings Press, 2007).

separate from the mother friend at my side. I didn't want to feel more isolated. I didn't want these women to be racist. I didn't want to believe what I was hearing. I did not feel safe, and that doesn't mean I felt superior. I felt disgust at myself for not speaking up and tried to think how to respond in a way that honored what I saw, that respected the women of SpiritHouseNC, that didn't unfairly distress the women in the beautiful room. And perhaps all three could not be honored at the same time? The question of when (how late) Daly had responded to Lorde and whether Lorde and Daly had corresponded about this matter seemed important, a procedural question that according to some made Lorde look lacking, but no weighty discussion as I remember it, of the moral, spiritual, historical, and feminist implications of a brief paragraph on female genital mutilation. Group members said how devastating it must have been for Daly at this moment in her career to have received this criticism. I could have been in a group dedicated to Mary Daly. I saw that *we* were acting as we might have been predicted to, if a Black woman were doing the predicting.

I was clear about where my big-picture obligation lay, to the women of SpiritHouseNC, but what was my obligation to the women in the room? I was obligated to the truth, and in that group, that would especially be truth related to race and gender, right? But was I obligated to take on a fight that I wasn't sure I could handle? *Spineless racist*, I called myself. Acting in a racist manner to not stand up. When we went around the room at the end, I tried to find words to suggest my struggle. I said that each of us had her own context. I used the nerdy term of my undergrad sociology days, that we each had our own reference group, to whom we looked for guidance and structure. That my reference group included the women of SpiritHouseNC, that although they were not physically present, they were with me in a room when I was in a room. That, though the concept of white people accepting Black leadership had fallen out of favor, when Black women were generous enough to offer leadership as had the women of SpiritHouseNC, I would accept it. And lastly—the inadequate representation of Black women was damning. I didn't say *damning*, crouched on the couch, ready to flee home to Vicki, who in the months to come would feel the blowback from this gathering.

I had wanted to call them out and I had not risen to that task.

II.

> and when we speak we are afraid
> our words will not be heard
> nor welcomed
> but when we are silent
> we are still afraid
>
> So it is better to speak
> Remembering
> we were never meant to survive
> —Audre Lorde, Litany for Survival

A whipsaw has a handle on either end and a blade that can cut in either direction. White self-identified feminist women reading Audre Lorde, all summer long its whipsaw had me coming and going, churning up sawdust and cutting deep.

I berated myself: *You could have said something about the food, ancestors, the study guide, the audio.* Would I have looked ridiculous, calling people to slow down about food, to bring our ancestral roots into the room, to follow Black women? Would I look like a self-righteous prig? Why would I care if I looked ridiculous to that group? Was/am I not a white feminist? All summer, back and forth: white feminist women reading Audre Lorde had acted like white women could have been predicted to act. Not as *white liberals*, not as *white progressives*, but as *white feminist women*: white women. Does *white* preceding *feminist* negate the meaning of *feminist*? I'm not asking to make the identity *feminist* more inclusive, to benevolently reach out a hand to include my Black and Brown sisters in a preexisting entity. I want to free *feminist* from the confines of the white default, to restore it to its full self.

We had listened longer to Mary Daly than to Audre Lorde. Group members had empathized with how Daly must have felt to be publicly called out. One of us pointed out the generosity of Lorde's letter, but there was no discussion about what Lorde might have felt as she read a *groundbreaking* woman feminist theologian and did not find Lorde's own humanity mirrored in the text. Only female genital mutilation. Only one Black woman writer represented in the entire book. Why hadn't I spoken up? My loyalties primarily lay outside that room and the best way to show my devotion to those not in the room would have been to speak my mind. Isn't that the job I, as a white woman, should take on, so my Black sisters wouldn't have to?

Midsummer—a light bulb: the women bonding over their fears and pain was a form of white fragility, a term I had seen online. The display of their fragility had kept me from speaking. It had prevented the group's self-examination. It had forged a group identity based on fear of the outside and the outside was: not-white. What does it mean, long-term, if well-meaning white antiracist feminists, admittedly facing their own daily difficulties, are unable to perceive their own assumptions and practices around race and how those assumptions function to perpetuate the exclusion of Black sisters? What does it mean that this room could not face its own lack of racial consciousness? What might all of this mean for the possibility of bridging our nation's racial divide?

All summer, the arguments had me confronting me. If all white people, including myself, are racist, what is accomplished by calling people racist? Maybe I should address how particular remarks or specific actions accomplish racist work. One blog suggested it takes courage and patience to say someone is racist. I think of myself as having some courage and some patience. Why hadn't I more explicitly stepped up? Because I was afraid? Afraid of what?

I drive to the lake to swim. I have read a blog about white people responding to criticism from people of color: What if I think of Audre Lorde as the "accuser of color"? What if I think of our group as the white responder? What if we had followed the precept *do not explain or defend*? Some in our group had thrown themselves into the project of explaining Daly. What if their energy had gone into being with Audre Lorde, making note of her putting pieces together, taking other things apart, staying true to herself, and crafting a not-seen-before truth. What if we had been able to listen to how Lorde's response to Daly comes in the context of Lorde's life: that day, that month, that year, that decade, all the way back to her birth?

Listen. Over and over and from all sides I read: *Listen. Listen and don't interject your own idea-generating, enterprising self. Be still. Receive.* Listen to Audre Lorde. Listen to SpiritHouseNC.

Fearing white response had been a deterrent to my speaking up and a testament to the force of unspoken rules about calling out white people, particularly liberal white people, for their racism, but the stakes of not speaking are higher.

If I don't speak up, a Black person will have to, in that split second when calling out racism and white supremacy becomes a matter of life and death. Eventually, I shared this writing with the women in the group and met individually with the two leaders, in one case an abrasive experience, but I should have spoken up from the beginning. In retrospect, if I, with my life experience and relationships, was intimidated, all who are afraid should take heart. Speaking the truth is hard and sometimes costly, but it can be done.

At the end of August, an email: *Faith, good news to share.* To commemorate their decades of friendship, my Barnard classmates Denise Jackson Lewis and Adaeze Otue Ezokoye had endowed a lectureship within the Africana Studies Department at Barnard College. Ntozake Shange, herself a Barnard grad, would give the inaugural lecture on diaspora and movement. And I was invited, because we shared history and we shared love.

In 1964, between our sophomore and junior years, Denise had gone south to Mississippi Summer, where she taught in a Freedom School. Returning to Barnard, she wanted to know why Barnard students couldn't learn the Black and African history she had taught in Mississippi. She approached departments at Barnard and was referred to a professor at Columbia; she asked me to go with her to see him. My memory is that we climbed several flights of stairs to a professor, a white man, behind his desk in a tower. The many flights of stairs and the tower may not have been literally true. He listened politely. And then he told Denise, basically, *Not in our lifetimes.* He said if such a program were to be instituted, it would be situated in colonial studies (five years after Ghana's independence). Walking back to Barnard, Denise said, *Colonial. Hmmph.* That was that, many might have said. But not Denise.

On the train going north to Barnard, I went from southern heat to gray skies. In a cocoon I traveled internal distances. I would see Denise and Ada. And Gussie. And Juana. And Janie. When we were Barnard freshmen, there were four Black students in each class, two commuters and two dorm students. Black alums had dug backward in time and found that this pattern—what a coincidence!—dated back into the 1940s. We had known one another's mothers and fathers and siblings. They had known my mother, long dead; whereas no one in my current life could ever meet her. They had known my sister, who had left the United States in 1966. I had known their families: Denise's Detroit family when I went to her wedding; Juana's Brooklyn clan; Ada's ebullient mother who had been known to bargain with salesclerks at Macy's. In one moment on the train, more awake than asleep, I sternly told myself, *Faith, you know Ada's mother will not be there.* The sadness that Mrs. Otue, vibrant Mrs. Otue, must have passed.

We had sometimes fallen out of touch or lost current emails, but we had found one another, always. Word of one another traveled the web of this one talking to another one, who then told the next. Denise was from Detroit. Ada from Nigeria. Gussie from the Bronx, Juana from Brooklyn, Janie from Bridgeport, Connecticut. I was the white girl from Brooklyn. Two of us, Black women who met at Barnard, had remained steadfast friends; they had endowed a lectureship, *not* housed within colonial studies, but within Barnard's own Department of Africana Studies.

III.

September 24, 2018, was a rainy day in New York City. I wielded my umbrella and took care not to fall on the uneven sidewalk. My first visit was with a friend from elementary school. Even more unsettling than the slick sidewalk were the times this friend and I had lived through—me in the coalfields, she in an underground world and in prison. We had known each other since we were eight. She had known my two mothers. She and I are both Jewish and white. In our midseventies. She worked less than a block from where Gussie lived. She worked a fifteen-minute walk from where the evening's festivities would take place. Every part of the day was contiguous with every other part.

Sloshing along, I reverted to worrying about my clothes for the evening. My pants were black velveteen (fortuitously in style that year), my top one I liked from a boho chic but not cheap store in Durham, my jacket a rose silk I had found in a thrift store for my wedding. I had taken care, but I already knew I would look like . . . Faith: not quite coordinated, perhaps a bit charming but never able to shake my unkempt aura.

My friend and I had known one another since we were eight. Our parents had known one another, yet there was so much I didn't know about the time of violence, about her years of flight, the years in prison. I didn't know if she had been strip-searched after my prison visits from West Virginia in the eighties and nineties. So much she didn't know about my years up Middle White Oak Holler (snow day mornings with my children in our little asbestos-brick-sided house), my years on the crest of Kenwood Road. My children. The years since she and I had been eight.

I walked head down, carrying my improvised overnight bag. I signed in at the new building, putting down her office number. Visits to the prison had meant: locking every disallowed item in my car trunk before *processing*; buzzers, passing through gates and barbed-wire passageways; more buzzers and ID checks; the room with the carefully placed tables and chairs we were not to move or a loudspeaker voice would reprimand us. Buzzers. The enormity of her incarceration tangible between us. At the end of the sixties, she had believed that the revolution was at hand. It was a time when activists said if millions were dying in Vietnam, the response here in the United States should be on that scale. *Bring the war home!* My friend had believed that the revolution was tied to Black liberation. Had believed that this revolution would require violence. She had acted as best she knew how. Much of this I knew by indirection, because our conversations at the prison had been guarded. She didn't want to tell me anything that could endanger me, didn't want to tell me anything that I could by indiscretion tell someone who could use it against her or those who had acted with her. In those same years, I had taken SNCC's mandate that white people should work in the white community and had moved to the mountains of West Virginia. Had supported a vibrant welfare rights movement and the mine workers' movement for democracy. Had taught public school. Had lived up a dirt road above a waterfall. Had two kids, a couple of dogs, and a cat.

Sixty-seven years since we had met in an elementary school classroom.

In her office, I put down my recycled plastic overnight tote. Others at the event might be in four-inch heels—at our age!—and shaping undergarments. So the foreshadowed evening was present in the room with her and me and our history/histories, dripping from my starflakey quilted jacket. Even bigger in the room: the confrontation that had sent my classmate to prison. In the room with us, her hurried remarks the last time I'd seen her in a large gathering, that she had feared what I might think of what she had done. Of those arrested and tried, at least one had died in prison, and others have spent decades in prison. I mean to say her actions had been consequential. This, too, was in the room, along with my dripping umbrella and my anticipation of the evening. We sat while she answered phone calls and texts. After twenty-plus years of being underground or in prison, she is at the height of her post-prison work of extending justice and support to those who have been incarcerated. On our way to lunch, she told two people in the corridor that we had known one another since we were two years old. I didn't correct her. I liked her saying it.

Over takeout lunch, we sat with these things. We had been in one another's lives a long time. In the room with us, her words, *I was afraid you judged me.* I held her hands in mine and said, "We are part of one another's context. I love you." A white woman who had taken violence into her own hands. A white woman who had fought for racial justice her entire life. My childhood friend. My co-madre. "I love you."

Back into the rain to Tom and Gussie around the corner. Gussie has been president of the Bank Street College of Education, has held various positions at City University of New York, and was an assistant secretary of education in the US Department of Education during the Clinton administration—this is just a quick rush through her accomplishments. She and Tom still live in the apartment where they lived our senior year in college. They became a couple the summer of 1964 in Fayette County, Tennessee, in a tent city housing people who had tried to register to vote and been thrown off the land. Gussie, Denise Jackson Lewis, and I, sociology majors, often sharing class notes and studying together. Tom had been born in China, the child of German dissidents who moved there, fleeing the rise of fascism in their country. He had been raised in South America. He could not become a US citizen, under immigration laws that counted him as Chinese; he married Gussie (because of her race, a de facto second-class citizen) and boom! He could become a US citizen. We had come to one another after the upheavals of high school; we had brought ourselves to one another from the countries of our childhoods.

Tom and Gussie's living room speaks of the more than fifty years they have been together. Speaks of their daughters, now grown and living in Maryland and Oakland, California. The walls are covered with bookshelves that rise to the high old-style ceilings, shelves of ideas and inspirations and warnings and histories that have nurtured them and many of which have done the same for me. The soft neutrals of book bindings sheathe incendiary ideas.

Tom is thin, very thin. He was once a robust blond, strong featured, of strong and deeply held convictions. He was on the front lines of protest at Columbia in 1968 and made his life's work the struggle of tenants in New York City; he taught college for decades as an adjunct. This most articulate of men stumbles when speaking. A swallowing disorder has changed how he eats. But his hair still falls across his forehead as if shielding his powerful thoughts and his words are still carefully chosen. Gussie is small but so vibrant she gives the impression that there are no boundaries that cannot be crossed, no tall buildings she cannot leap. She has been steadfast in her devotion to social justice. She serves us tea, watches Tom, laughs her laugh that begins like a clearing of her throat and then explodes, the same laugh I heard in sociology classes in Lehman Hall, a building that no longer exists.

The three of us chat about children, about life, about that evening's event, about the state of the world, including the probable confirmation of Brett Kavanaugh as US Supreme Court justice. The hearings are being held as we speak. Dr. Christine Blasey Ford is scheduled to testify. When we were students, hearings into allegations of sexual misconduct by a powerful white man would have been unheard of. This hour with Tom and Gussie is filled with shared viewpoints that have lasted and reshaped themselves. We may have talked about my experience with white women reading Audre Lorde. They would have understood, and I would have felt safe talking about it, but—life—we may have run out of time. As we spoke in the room lined with the books and the pictures of children and grandchildren, as we spoke, Bill Cosby was removing his jacket and being taken into custody. When I rise to leave, back into that nasty New York City rain, Tom, or maybe it was Gussie, says, "Thank you for coming."

I had needed to be with them, like this, family, before the evening. "See you in an hour," I said, and the apartment door clicked shut behind me.

Barnard's campus is small. When new happens, something old must go. We meet in the Millstein Center, a new building that occupies the old footprint of Lehman Hall, the old library building where we had studied sociology on an upper floor, where my illegal abortion had finally completed. They arrive singly or in clusters, shedding dripping raincoats and propping umbrellas against the wall. Black women who have taken care with their appearance. Ada is unmistakable, upright in an ankle-length Nigerian dress. She is wearing a stiff head wrap that flares into a wide brim, all gold, glowing like Ada herself. Denise wears red, not a single wrinkle in slim skirt or sleek jacket, on those heels I'd anticipated. What I hadn't anticipated is her broad smile, almost an unruly grin—she still does that. A preschool girl runs to Denise, and she bends over the child with a laugh, for the moment not the worldly woman so accomplished that a windowed Barnard conference room upstairs is named for her. I hear her say "Nana," and murmur and the child laughs. Word travels among us: Janie is in hospice and will not attend.

The men arrive in suits. Young ones who are sons, older ones who are Ada's husband and Denise's companion. Juana, in a black and sparkly dress and an equally sparkly purse and shoes. I am suddenly back in Brooklyn when the four of us and perhaps Janie or Gussie, too, had spent Saturday night at Juana's family's apartment. Her parents cooking for us, humoring us, daughtering us, so that fifty years later I smile, though I am not much of a smiler these days. Juana also had ties to my organizing friends in Harlem. I tell her that Amina died a few years ago and that I am going to see Amina's daughter Sabra. I learn that Juana's husband died last year and feel how our lives have grown apart. And, yet, here we are together, chatting and smiling deep down so our cheeks crease. All the things she doesn't know: my plucky daughter who is near homeless in San Francisco, my years in West Virginia, my life in Durham. Her decades of teaching. Her children. Her West Coast. Her involvement in Puerto Rican and Caribbean poetry and writing.

When Martha comes through the door, the blue of her tailored jacket reaches every corner of the room. Martha, who took on many responsibilities as lead editor for *Hands on the Freedom Plow*; Martha, who chess-plays political arguments reaching back into the dusty attics and unfurling timeworn political banners; Martha, who is able to tell you when and how a slogan was first used and why she thinks that is important; Martha, who never lightly let an argument slip from her grip. Her ideas are organized like the pantry shelves of her youth, which had been organized to accommodate her father, who had lost his sight. Not a Barnard grad, Martha has known Denise and Denise's Detroit family for decades. At the reception, she sits beside the speaker, Ntozake Shange, who is in a wheelchair, the two of them chatting, heads leaning toward one another as they eat samosas.

Martha is the subject of a famous photo of the Civil Rights Movement—Martha and Bob Moses, who are Black, and Mike Meyer, who is not—canvassing in Mississippi the summer of 1963. She says the photo is staged, that for safety reasons no white workers were allowed to canvass in that community (a year later, also in Mississippi, James Chaney, Mickey Schwerner, and Andrew Goodman would be killed by Klan members). She believes it is important to get the story right. She can be unbending about the facts, though she leans intimately to hear what Ms. Shange has to say. Her attention to detail and facts, her reading of words on the page and her reading of people in the flesh, are her form of respect. The thing that is steadfast and a beacon about Martha: race is paramount. She will always go to the impact of something, the origin of something, the outcome of something, the effect of something, upon people who are Black.

It is still raining. In the dark, car lights shine on the wet black street, but we do not get wet going from dinner to the event. We are led through Barnard's tunnels, never going aboveground, protected and dry. Below, there are no signs to tell us which building we are passing, which turns to take. We follow Barnard staff. In the auditorium, we are seated up front. A bursting in of young Black women coming in the door, sheathing their umbrellas, pulling off raincoats, greeting one another with hugs, people who know one another, who are a community; more and more, until they have our backs in ranks, an auditorium of young Black women and a scatter of older white people. Juana and I say to one another, *This is more Black women in one place than were ever on campus*. Four per incoming class. Two commuter and two dorm. The animated faces are almost all young; as far as I know, there are no emerita Black faculty or other long-term Black academics at Barnard. Not yet.

Ntozake Shange reads her remarks on diaspora and movement. Her life as a dancer, her self as a Black female embodied, and the Black choreographers with whom she worked, naming Black choreographers who substantially contributed to dance in the United States. She brings the younger Shange into the auditorium with us, though in the moment the elder Shange is frail and her speech sometimes falters. When it is time for audience response, the young women rush to speak, to tell Shange that performing her work was a high point in their beginning theater careers, to tell her how much she means to them, one by one, a cohort who have seen themselves in Shange and who have understood their lives better through her work.

• • •

What I would have liked for the white women reading Audre Lorde to experience: Seeing themselves in Audre Lorde's work. Stepping far enough into her world. Risking.

At the Aloft Hotel in Harlem, the next morning, we gather, some of us desperate for coffee, all rousing from sleep in unfamiliar rooms, in an unfamiliar city, together as we come back to daytime consciousness in the lobby. Denise's son suggests a restaurant, small and narrow, locally owned, some white people scattered at a table here or there, but they are the exceptions. Martha and I sit next to one another. Denise's son, across from me, asks what I think will happen with the hearing into Dr. Blasey Ford, who remembers being sexually assaulted by Supreme Court nominee Brett Kavanaugh. Denise's son thinks there is a chance that Dr. Blasey Ford will be believed. Martha says to me under her breath, "So now it's OK they have sentenced an eighty-one-year-old man who is half blind . . ." I sit so close our upper arms can touch, conflicted down to my bones. Denise comes down to our end of the table to put her hand on my shoulder, to smile at Martha and chuckle. The moment passes.

Later in the day, Nia of SpiritHouseNC, which challenged white feminist women in Durham to read *Sister Outsider*, posts on Facebook. Her conflicted feelings about Cosby. I read perching on some coffee shop stool, in transit from one face-to-face to another. Nia as a child on the carpet in her family's living room, with her siblings watching and wholeheartedly loving Bill Cosby, an admirable and funny Black man. Nia loves that little Black girl, herself, who loved Cosby. But, she writes, some of the Black-hating things Cosby later said were wrong. Nia is clear: sexual predation is criminal and we must believe the women. She grieves for the innocence of that little girl on the carpet. She grieves for a lost lodestar of her childhood. Nia's words free me to acknowledge, despite my SNCC sister, that I think Cosby committed criminal acts. Nia's words also free me to hear Martha's words: *I want the white men prosecuted and sent to prison.* Though I do not believe in prisons, in the United States, we do not have restorative justice, so he must be sent to prison, and those legions of white men must be, too.

• • •

The Senate Judiciary Committee interrogates Dr. Christine Blasey Ford. Her memory of teenage sexual violence at the hands of Brett Kavanaugh. On Facebook, my friends post that Dr. Blasey Ford looks *fragile*; other posts, *OMG the forces aligned against her*; many others insist, *Believe survivors*. I can't watch this show of power and force. Will not. It's not only my own experience of sexual trauma and my stunned silence about it as a child. The devastation I feel is of my body and of my cosmos. The devastation is trauma from the sixties, when the government attacked the Albany, Georgia, Movement and SNCC, when the federal government prosecuted the Albany Movement. The forces of government had been aligned against the marchers and protesters and sit-inners, the long-legged teenagers and the grandmothers and the preachers and Miss Corinne the Avon lady, a government determined to have its way, placing a stranglehold until the Movement had drained its coffers and spent the energy of its members. When the Albany Movement had been choked to death, having had its way, the government dropped all charges. One example among dozens of the force and might (it is the force and might that are traumatic) of the US government, of our government, brought to bear against the Movement. An abuse of power. On Facebook, people advised, *Breathe*, but I wasn't in the mood for noncontextual *breathing*.

I spent most of the day writing and walking. I had dinner in Harlem with my Movement niece by affection, Sabra Shanell Pacheco. She is the daughter of my too-long and too-soon passed sister friend Amina Rachman, with whom I walked the streets of Harlem, sometimes working on housing surveys, sometimes running errands to the pork store for her godmother, sometimes just walking, walking, sometimes the Black-and-white-together, we-shall-not-be-moved of the National Conference of Christians and Jews, sometimes Greenwich Village. Talking and laughing loudly. In the midsixties, not long after returning from a trip to Africa with the Minister and his party, Amina came to my mother's Brooklyn apartment and spent the night. In the morning, Amina prayed on my mother's frayed rug in the living room and departed. It was the last time I saw her before the death of Minister Malcolm. Our connection lapsed at the end of the sixties and early seventies. Not long after my mother's 1974 death, in my little wood-frame house up Middle White Oak Holler in

West Virginia, the phone rang. "Sis," Amina said across the violence of the late 1960s, "I just heard the news of your mother's death." From then on, in the days before email, she and I wrote letters, long letters, adult women with children and work and daily exhaustions, but letters with that knowledge of one another that had begun in our public school years.

I am meeting Amina's singular daughter, Sabra. An Arabic name, a Hebrew name. The name given decades before Amina converted to Judaism, when she was still a practitioner of traditional Islam, the religious home she had turned to when Minister Malcolm left the Nation. It had been this daughter, Sabra, who phoned me, insisting I come to New York when Amina was dying. Because of Sabra, I was in the room when Amina passed. I had arrived from North Carolina at Penn Station. From the eastside hospital, Sabra texted two sets of numbers: Amina's failing blood pressure reading and the room number. At the hospital, I made my way to Amina's room. People made room for me in the circle around the bed, where Amina lay hooked up to monitors and machines, still as I had never known her to be. Sabra said, "See, Mom, I told you Faith would make it." Amina's high school son Josh was arriving. Sabra dispatched me to bring him to the bedside. He and I made it back for Amina's so-faint final breath. And after that breath, we stayed in the room, touching Amina, being there as Amina's sister arrived, and Amina's administrative assistant of decades. And the rabbi. The TV was on. Sabra looked up and said, "It should have been *The Godfather*." Because that had been Amina's movie. All of us in the room knew. The rabbi, her hand on Amina, said "What has just happened is a mystery. We do not know."

Waiting for Sabra on the corner outside the restaurant, I think of the first time I saw Amina after the sixties, a SNCC reunion in Atlanta to which she'd brought Sabra, a schoolchild. I walked into that meeting and miraculously into the circle of those of us who were still alive: Amina and my SNCC love Reggie. It was probably 1980. Amina had come, her head covered, her girl child's head covered. It was both natural to be together and earthshaking: I'd thought I'd never see her again. Distance and separation and that sweet surprise of reunion, and the bedrock of love.

Those years: me living in the unimaginable hills of West Virginia and she back in Brooklyn (all wrong: not Harlem). That Atlanta afternoon, I watched Amina violate her own dietary laws, eating a hamburger that was not halal at Paschal's, the Civil Rights meeting place around the corner from the old SNCC office, a sixties refuge when Paschal's was one of the rare places that served racially integrated groups. "Ma," Sabra protested as Amina bit into her hamburger. Later, Amina put Sabra to bed on top of coverlets in Reggie's room while he was partying. Maybe she didn't have money for a room? Or maybe she stayed there because that's what we'd always done, stayed with one another. Amina did not want her daughter to know they were sleeping in a man's room. Exhausted, Amina lay down, but whenever Sabra stirred, Amina jumped up and stood above her daughter. I see her, exactly as she told me, standing protectively over her girl child, whom she had willingly brought into the circle of SNCC, SNCC where Amina had worked, faced danger, grown into Movement adulthood. A weekend of transgressions and a weekend of affirmation.

I wait for Sabra, feeling something like dismay that as a white person I no longer stick out like a sore thumb on what was once Lenox Avenue and is now Malcolm X Boulevard. The waiter who is setting up the outdoor tables works around me. When she's still on the next block, Sabra catches sight of me. We wave exuberantly. Harlem has changed so much that no one stops to stare when we hug extravagantly. Inside the restaurant, she doesn't allow us to quickly choose an indoor or an outdoor table but takes my elbow to guide us through the French doors to check out the outdoor tables. We pick a table indoors. Because I have seen her so rarely over the almost fifty years of her life, it is amazing to me the worldly assurance with which my friend's child gets us situated.

Brilliant Sabra—her pearl earrings make her deep-brown skin glow, or maybe it's the resonance of her dark skin that brings out the luster in the pearls. And she is a person who brings out the luster in others. We discuss the apartment she has bought in Riverdale, the man she has been seeing who makes her happy, her brother in upstate New York, but mostly what is happening is that I am her auntie who lives far away and who was present in her mother's life before Sabra was, was present at her mother's death because Sabra phoned me, and she is my niece who is head of admissions for an academically elite high school, my niece who is filled with possibilities I can only guess. I am her elder. Her mother's only daughter, she loves me, bringing her brilliance to our being with one another. That is all.

• • •

When I was twenty-one, I returned to Albany, Georgia. It was the summer of 1964. In Mississippi, David Chaney, Michael Schwerner, and Andrew Goodman's bodies had been discovered buried in an earthen dam. In Albany, there was a warrant out for Don Harris, the SNCC project director who was in hiding in a building in Little Harlem, all of us knowing the authorities could seize him at any time and that that could be bad. I stayed with Movement lawyer C. B. King and his wife Carol. The year before, I had stayed with Carol when C. B. was out of town; back then, I didn't know the name for my listlessness, what would be diagnosed as hepatitis and would be for the rest of my life an embodied marker of that year in the violent segregated South. C. B. and Carol's children were preschoolers the year I worked in the South, but on the subsequent 1964 visit, Peggy was looking forward to her first day—ever!--of public school. Her mother had not told Peggy that with a few other Black children, Peggy would be integrating a formerly all-white school. I was horrified but didn't question Carol; I was barely into my twenties and Carol was an adult with a serious job, several children, and a husband for whom a federal courthouse would one day be named. On that first morning of school, I was alone in the house with Peggy, who was to be picked up by the mother driving the carpool. The five-year-old was excited and bubbly, checking the front window for her ride. I wanted to hold her tight and refuse to let her walk out the door—she was so bright, so vivacious, so beautiful, and mostly she was so little—but when the car pulled up out front, she ran to it, opened the door, and climbed in. On TV that evening—Peggy and the other Black children making their way into the school through heckling, hostile white adults. I asked Peggy—unharmed! still alive!—what school had been like. Her eyes merry, she threw her hands wide in amazement to say, "And guess what? All the children were white!"

That was a ridiculous number of decades ago. On one visit to Southwest Georgia, I learned Peggy was at the Columbia School of Architecture. We bobbed along through a decade or so, and suddenly we were two adult women and her mother Carol had crept into being, well, *older*. Those times when I was in New York City from West Virginia, Peggy and I usually met near Barnard for breakfast, as she had driven her two children across the George Washington Bridge from New Jersey to Bank Street School in that neighborhood. One of those mornings, sitting across from me in the College Inn on Broadway, Peggy, who was working for Mayor Dinkins, told me about the African burial site. During her first pregnancy, she would walk over to the site almost daily. At the site, women from Africa had set up a vigil and I think an altar. They would touch Peggy's stomach and bless the baby to come. "You have to go there," Peggy said to me. I sat there, where I had consumed countless coffees in the 1960s, an entirely different person from who I had been, a person who had moved beyond the pale to the coalfields, across from Peggy, still bright, still enthusiastic.

That afternoon, I went to the burial ground.

I can tell stories back to Peggy of her family. I have said to her I had loved her mother and I had loved her father. That her father taught me the word *phlegmatic* when I protested I didn't want to leave Albany and lobby US congress members for the three Civil Rights workers—Don Harris, Ralph Allen, John Perdew—who'd been arrested in Sumter County (home of Jimmy Carter) and charged with seditious conspiracy. He'd smiled and said, "We need you—smart and phlegmatic," and when I looked askance, he'd said, "Unflappable. We need you, twenty years old, white, and unflappable, to speak to those congresspeople." So my hepatitis and I went to work the halls of Congress and then home, planning to return to DC for the March on Washington. When it was diagnosed in New York City, the hepatitis kept me housebound. I watched the march on my mother's little TV, filled with rage at Birmingham, rage at the police who had patted me down in the Albany jail, rage at the rape and killing that summer of a Black girl child in Southwest Georgia by a white man who drove a bread truck. And filled with longing as I saw on TV the faces of SNCC, my people with whom I'd faced danger and with whom I'd sung the beautiful congregational music of Southwest Georgia, longing tinged with knowing I had left and could never entirely return.

Peggy's son and daughter have finished with children's schools. She chairs the board of the Classical Theatre of Harlem, where she has a meeting this afternoon. I am walking under scaffolding. A woman puts money in the meter and hurries ahead of me. It could be Peggy, but I see Peggy only occasionally and I remember her most vividly as that small, small girl. She is walking swiftly ahead of me. Her heels make the high-heel squawk and she glances back; our eyes meet; we instantly know one another and after embracing and laughing we hurry toward the Harlem restaurant she has chosen, talking, talking, talking.

Once again, I am sitting down to food with a woman who matters to me and to whom I matter.

This woman before me has begun to trace the routes of the slave trade and of slavery here in the States; I see history emanating from her like the veins of a river system. I also see in her an architect, creating small revealing models of history within place. She tells me about Saint Helena's Island in the Atlantic. In 2008, bones, many bones, were uncovered while building a new airport road. A history of ships that carried enslaved Africans stopping there to take on more water for the remaining trip to the Americas. The ships' captains supervised the off-loading of uncounted African bodies, those who had died in transit but had not been thrown into the sea. She says, "Just like that. *Off-loaded.*" It is close to the voice of the stunned six-year-old saying, with wide eyes, "And guess what? All the children were white!" Of the estimated eight thousand slaves buried at Saint Helena, 325 bodies have been recovered. Later, when I go to the website that chronicles Peggy's trip to Saint Helena's, I see shapes on the road's surface, shapes outlined with beach stones, not unlike the silhouettes drawn by the police when a person is killed in the street. These shapes mark where the African bodies were found and the bodies' exact positions. On the website, living people lie down in the road to fit themselves into the stone-outlined shapes. Sometimes it is a single person within an outline, but often two figures within the outline, at least once a child curled at an adult's spine. The forty-five reenactors range in age from three to seventy, each fitting her- or himself into the stone-outlined shape on the airport road, offering their living bodies in homage to buried ancestors.[4]

Later in the autumn, Gussie emails those of us in the Barnard group that Janie Allen (Jane Allen Petrick, PhD), who had been in hospice during the celebrations on September 24, 2018, had passed.

---

4. More information on Peggy King Jorde's work on the Saint Helena's Island African burial ground project can be found online: https://loebfellowship.gsd.harvard.edu/fellows-alumni/fellows-search/margaret-king-jorde/.

IV.

There is the framework within which we live and can't see beyond, but others have seen beyond. Audre Lorde saw outside and offered us what she'd seen. The women of SpiritHouseNC had seen outside and offered us sisterhood. If you have been the clever, educated one who sees and articulates, can you . . . listen?

Listen.
Adrienne Marie Brown in her groundbreaking book *Emergent Strategy*:

> In a fractal conception, I am a cell-sized unit of the human organism, and I have to use my life to leverage a shift in the system by how I am, as much as with the things I do. This means actually being in my life, and it means bringing my values into my daily decision making. Each day should be lived on purpose.
>
> If the goal was to increase the love, rather than winning or dominating a constant opponent, I think we could actually imagine liberation from constant oppression. We would suddenly be seeing everything we do, everyone we meet, not through the tactical eyes of war, but through eyes of love. We would see that there's no such thing as a blank canvas, an empty land or a new idea—but everywhere there is complex, ancient, fertile ground full of potential.
>
> I remember that I exist only in relationship to other people and systems.
>
> Move at the speed of trust. Connection is more important than mass.[5]

December 2018.
At SpiritHouseNC, Toshi Reagon sits squarely in her chair. When I look at Toshi, I see her mother, Bernice Johnson Reagon, who grew up in Albany, Georgia. The first time I heard Bernice sing was at a SNCC meeting at Fisk; she opened her mouth and the most beautiful and profound trumpet call rose from her lips: "Up above my head, I see freedom in the air." Toshi's father, Cordell

---

5. Adrienne Marie Brown, *Emergent Strategy: Shaping Change, Changing Worlds* (AK Press, 2017).

Reagon, came to Albany as a SNCC field secretary. He had a sweet, sweet tenor voice—it could make me cry, especially when he sang Oscar Brown Jr.'s "Brown Baby."[6]

We settled on chairs and cushions on the floor, and we began. Toshi sang a line and we sang it back to her. She said these were nineteenth-century songs. They might seem simple—she sang, *The sun will never go down go down. / The sun will never go down. / The flowers are blooming forever. / The sun will never go down*—but these old songs speak of a people's survival beyond slavery. Toshi sang a line and we repeated it. She told us with her eyes and her hands when to join in.

She said, *Look at my mouth and take the words/song from my mouth.*

She said there is a difference between singing as you are learning and congregational singing. After we allowed her to feed us the words, next would come congregational singing. In congregational singing, we would sing freely within the greater body of the music as the congregation created it. Because we were attentive, what we sang would be correct. She said, *I can sing with my eyes closed because I know where I'm going, but I want you to sing with your eyes open.*

After almost two hours, on our third or fourth song, she broke us into groups to sing harmony. Each group took the words from her mouth. We bent our bodies toward one another so we could catch every sound, so we could bolster one another, paying attention to our sound in our small group but also hearing the whole room singing. When we had worked on this final song for a while, Toshi Reagon leaned back in her chair and grinned her gap-toothed smile and said we sounded good.

Audre Lorde has the final say in *Sister Outsider*:

> To turn aside from the anger of Black women with excuses or the pretexts of intimidation is to award no one power—it is merely another way of preserving racial blindness, the power of unaddressed privilege, unbreached, intact. Guilt is

---

6. Of Toshi Reagon: "Since first taking to the stage at age 17, this versatile singer-songwriter-guitarist has moved audiences of all kinds with her big-hearted, hold-nothing-back approach to rock, blues, R&B, country, folk, spirituals and funk." See https://toshireagon.com.

only another form of objectification. Oppressed people are always being asked to stretch a little more, to bridge the gap between blindness and humanity. Black women are expected to use our anger only in the service of other people's salvation or learning. But that time is over. My anger has meant pain to me but it has also meant survival, and before I give it up I'm going to be sure that there is something at least as powerful to replace it on the road to clarity. (*The Uses of Anger*, p. 132)

Those of us who stand outside the circle of this society's definition of acceptable women those of us who have been forged in the crucibles of difference those of us who are poor who are lesbians who are black who are older know that survival is not an academic skill. It is learning how to stand alone unpopular and sometimes reviled and how to make common cause with those others identified as outside the structures in order to define and seek a world in which we can all flourish. It is learning how to take our differences and make them strengths. For the Master's tools will never dismantle the Master's house. They may allow us temporarily to beat him at his own game but they will never enable us to bring about genuine change. And this fact is only threatening to those women who still define the master's house as their only source of support. (*The Master's Tool Will Never Dismantle the Master's House*, p. 112)

One of the most basic Black survival skills is the ability to change, to metabolize experience, good or ill, into something that is useful, lasting, effective. Four hundred years of survival as an endangered species has taught most of us that if we intend to live, we better become fast learners. (*Learning from the 60s*, p. 135)

Listen.

About the Author

FAITH S. HOLSAERT is an activist, poet, and author. She began her life as an activist during the Civil Rights Movement of the 1960s with the Student Nonviolent Coordinating Committee (SNCC). She has since remained active in the community and has published two collections of poetry and coedited a collection of stories of women in SNCC. She and her partner, Vicki Smith, reside in Durham, North Carolina, and have twelve grandchildren.